AKHENATEN
EGYPT'S FALSE PROPHET

NICHOLAS REEVES

AKHENATEN
EGYPT'S FALSE PROPHET

WITH 141 ILLUSTRATIONS, 23 IN COLOR

Thames & Hudson

MUSAE MEAE

Frontispiece: colossal statue of Akhenaten, from Karnak

© 2001 and 2005 Thames & Hudson Ltd, London
Text © 2001 and 2005 Nicholas Reeves

First published in 2001 in hardcover in the United States of America by
Thames & Hudson Inc.,
500 Fifth Avenue, New York, New York 10110

First paperback edition, with corrections, 2005

Library of Congress Catalog Card Number: 00-108868

ISBN-13: 978-0-500-28552-7
ISBN-10: 0-500-28552-7

Printed and bound in Slovenia by MKT PRINT d.d.

CONTENTS

CHRONOLOGY

Late Predynastic	c. 3100 BC
Early Dynastic Period	
1st–3rd Dynasties	2920–2575
Old Kingdom	
4th–8th Dynasties	2575–2134
First Intermediate Period	
9th–11th Dynasties	2134–2040
Middle Kingdom	
11th–14th Dynasties	2040–1640
Second Intermediate Period	
15th–17th Dynasties	1640–1532
New Kingdom	
18th Dynasty	1550–1307
Ahmose	
Amenophis I	
Tuthmosis I	
Tuthmosis II	
Tuthmosis III	
Hatshepsut	
Amenophis II	
Tuthmosis IV	
Amenophis III	
Amenophis IV-Akhenaten	1353–1335
Smenkhkare	
Tutankhamun	
Ay	
Horemheb	
19th Dynasty	1307–1196
including:	
Ramesses I	
Sethos I	
Ramesses II	
20th Dynasty	1196–1070
Third Intermediate Period	
21st–25th Dynasties	1070–712
Late Period	
25th Dynasty–2nd Persian Period	712–332
Greco-Roman Period	
Macedonian Dynasty–Roman Emperors	332 BC–AD 395

Conventional chronology after J. Baines & J. Málek, *Atlas of Ancient Egypt*
(Oxford, 1980), pp. 36–37.

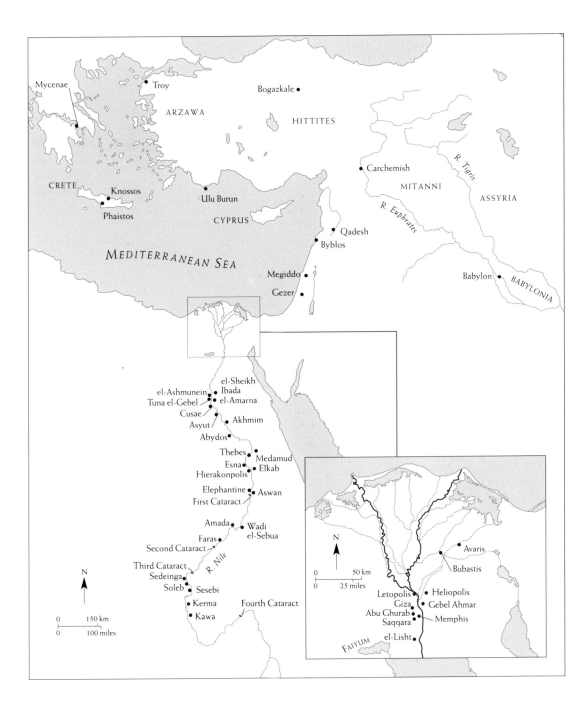

Map of Egypt and the Near East

PREFACE

'... at the name Akhnaton there emerges from the darkness a
figure more clear than that of any other Pharaoh.... For once
we may look right into the mind of a king of Egypt and may
see something of its workings ...' ARTHUR WEIGALL

The setting for this book is Egypt, and the ruins of a city founded and
abandoned more than three thousand years ago – one and a half millennia before the birth of Christ, and some twenty centuries before
the advent of the prophet Mohammed. The name given to this city in antiquity was Akhetaten, 'Horizon of the Aten'; it is a site better known today as
el-Amarna – and it is the source for almost all we yet know of Egypt's most
intriguing king.

This king was Amenophis IV, more familiar to the modern world by his
later name, Akhenaten. In the endless procession of Egypt's pharaonic
masters, Akhenaten stands alone. He looks different: his often freakish
appearance in art – elongated and effete – is totally at odds with that of the
traditional Egyptian ruler-hero. And he appears to have acted differently
also – most famously by his abandonment of Egypt's traditional pantheon in
favour of a single god, the Aten, or solar disc.

A younger son of the 18th-Dynasty pharaoh Amenophis III and his
consort Tiye, prince Amenophis became heir with the unexpected death of
an elder brother. Married early in life to the beautiful Nefertiti, the new king
fathered six children – all daughters; his only living son would be
Tutankhamun, by a secondary wife named Kiya. A mystery woman, Kiya
disappears soon after the birth, closely followed by Nefertiti herself – at
which point Akhenaten adopts an obscure co-ruler, Nefernefruaten/
Smenkhkare, to share his throne. Akhenaten's co-regent is succeeded in turn
by Tutankhamun and then by the 'god's father' Ay, with whom the greater
Amarna period draws to a final close. It was an era which, though starting off
well enough, degenerated rapidly into mayhem and widespread religious
persecution, an orgy of wanton destruction and almost total economic collapse. For the events he set in train, Akhenaten could never be forgiven: with
a ruthlessness not seen in Egypt before or since, Amarna, both as a city and a
concept, was razed and all trace of pharaoh's existence systematically
expunged.

What manner of man was Aten's 'first prophet'? Because of his religious
reforms, Akhenaten has for long struck a chord in today's predominantly
monotheistic world; and the fact that pharaoh's revolution ultimately failed

has seemed only to confirm his role as an early revealer of religious truth – a power for good. Such a spin, promoted almost a century ago by James Henry Breasted and Arthur Weigall and eagerly taken up by scholars and general public alike, is certainly wrong, and now beginning to give way to darker visions. As prophets go, it seems clear that Akhenaten was a false one, and working very much in his own political interest.

One early critic of Amarna historiography was the American anthropologist Leslie A. White: 'Only where one knows so little can one write so much', he despondently remarked in an article written in 1948; 'the absence of facts gives the imagination free reign'. It would be idle to claim that imagination plays no part in the pages which follow; inevitably it does. I trust, however, that it is an imagination checked by critical scrutiny of the available sources and balanced by considerations of historical precedent and probability. For the real problem with Amarna is not so much a shortage of good evidence as a superabundance of speculation misrepresented as fact. Readers must decide for themselves how successful I have been in separating the wheat from the chaff – and how convincing the result.

I close this preface with a quote from John Pendlebury, who wrote his own book on el-Amarna in 1935:

> 'highly theoretical … it does seem to me to fit the facts as we
> know them at present. Based as it is mainly on the results of
> excavation, [however,] where even a broken ring bezel may be a
> piece of evidence of the first order, it may easily be modified or
> even flatly contradicted by future discoveries ….'

If the picture I paint differs markedly from that of Pendlebury and others, in this respect, at least, the situation remains the same.

NICHOLAS REEVES

PROLOGUE

T he year is 1887, the place an expanse of sanded-up ruins on the east bank of the Egyptian river Nile, a short distance from the modern village of el-Till. The sky shines a clear, deep blue, dominated by a relentless sun; beneath its rays a peasant woman is occupied patiently digging *sebakh* – the decayed mud-brick, rich in phosphates, used to fertilize the land. The digger's eyes are ever vigilant. She is no stranger to the occasional find, a stray *antika* (antiquity) which might, with luck, be sold on to some itinerant dealer from Luxor or Cairo some 320 km (200 miles) south and north. The woman is startled, none the less, when her *touria* (hoe) strikes something solid. A stone? No! Investigation reveals the outline of a wooden box.

The woman's pulse quickens as she conjures up visions of buried treasure, a gift from God to supplement her pitifully meagre income. Scrabbling excitedly in the dust, her hands fall upon a curious, pillow-shaped clay tablet, its surface covered with strange markings. Puzzled, her disappointment is tangible: searching through again, she pulls out another, and yet another, her frustration mounting. Pah! Worthless! Why not gold – gold to release her from this never-ending toil? A sigh. *Maalesh* (Never mind)!

Resigned, the worker of *sebakh* gathers up a handful of the tablets and ties them in a cloth which she throws carelessly into one of the panniers of her donkey. She returns to her digging, before finally trudging homewards at the end of another, back-breaking day. The unexpected discovery grinds

The site of el-Amarna today.

itself to powder at her side; she throws it a disappointed glance. Worthless! Pah! Why not gold …?

The hopes and expectations of this 19th-century peasant woman find a curious resonance in a letter which had been read out before the king of Egypt, under this same blistering sun, some three and a half thousand years before:

> 'May my brother send me much gold…. In my brother's country
> gold is as plentiful as dirt. May my brother cause me no distress….'

The writer was Tushratta, king of Mitanni, a powerful state situated between Syria's Balikh and Khabur rivers, and Egypt's principal rival in the politics of the ancient Near East. And the vehicle for Tushratta's words, by chance, was one of the same, peculiar clay tablets first brought to light by our disappointed digger of *sebakh*.

The 300 or so 'worthless' clay lumps which the peasant and her confederates eventually exhumed were subsequently – and gratefully – sold on for a miserable 10 piastres – a few pennies. At first written off by sceptics as obvious fakes, before long the tablets stood revealed as one of Egypt's greatest archaeological treasures: a unique diplomatic archive of the 14th century BC, written in Akkadian cuneiform script ('wedge-writing'), the lingua franca of the day, addressed to and from the rulers and principal figures of the ancient world. Nothing like this archive had ever been found before; and very little comparable has turned up in Egypt since. Among historians and philologists the letters would kick up a storm; and among archaeologists they naturally inspired a new and keener interest in the site which had produced them – the ruins of el-Amarna, city of the damned pharaoh Akhenaten and his wife Nefertiti, childhood home of the boy-king Tutankhamun.

The German excavations at el-Amarna, 1914.

CHAPTER ONE

DISCOVERY

'... a trickle of fine yellow sand slipped through my fingers out of
the cracks and crevices of the rough surface beneath. Egyptian
sand. I was holding something that had scarcely been touched
since it had been found in Egypt years before, something which
might still bear the fingerprints not only of the finder, but even of
the maker.... Suddenly I was invaded by a great longing; I wanted
to know all I could about the place where the tile had come from
... Tell el Amarna; up till this moment a name meaning for me no
more than that of a heap of ruins somewhere on the eastern bank
of the Nile, where once Tutankhamun had lived, and, yes,
Nefertiti – I was clear about her – and her strange husband the
Pharaoh Amenhotep [Amenophis] IV, whose other curious name
was Akhenaten ...' MARY CHUBB

FROM SICARD TO LEPSIUS

The name el-Amarna dates back less than three hundred years, to the 18th
century and a tribe of dusty bedouin known as the Beni Amran. Here, on a
desolate Middle Egyptian plain, bordered by the great river Nile and
hemmed in by craggy cliffs to north, south and east, the bedouin settled and
established a string of four villages – el-Till, el-Hagg Qandil, el-Amiriya and
el-Hawata. The name of the first of these would combine with that of the
tribe to produce 'el-Till el-Amarna', later corrupted to 'Tell el-Amarna' and
now abbreviated to its more familiar form – el-Amarna.

Today el-Amarna is one of the most celebrated ancient sites in the world –
archaeologically, since it is one of very few large-scale Egyptian settlements
to have been preserved from dynastic times; and historically, because it
served as stage for the unfolding drama of the 'heretic' pharaoh Akhenaten
and his beautiful wife, Nefertiti. It was perhaps, too, the birthplace of a
famous prince of Egypt, Tutankhaten – better known today by the later form
of his name, Tutankhamun. Here the boy-king laughed and played during
the endless summers of an innocent childhood; here, by the shaded banks of
the Nile, he 'cut with his own hand' the simple reed which was later mounted
in gold and inscribed to accompany him in his tomb.

For years, el-Amarna's ruins lay utterly forgotten – thanks in large part to
the 'evil reputation' of the locals, whose habit of shooting first and greeting
later long deterred the curious from taking an interest in the area. One of the
earliest hints to the existence of this lost city we owe to a Jesuit traveller by

El-Amarna: a view northwest from boundary stela K in the arid, desert cliffs, the verdant cultivation and river Nile in the background. The uneven surface of the desert plain represents individual graves in the much later, Roman period cemetery.

the name of Claude Sicard. He was the first to note, in 1714, across the river at a site known as Tuna el-Gebel, one of the massive boundary stelae (that now designated A) which had been cut to demarcate el-Amarna's greater limits. The first westerners to encounter the city proper, however, were the members of Napoleon Bonaparte's expedition of 1798–99.

The French had landed in Egypt with the ultimate aim of securing a new passage to India via the Isthmus of Suez. As with all French ventures, the cultural component of the enterprise was an important one, and as part of the expedition staff Bonaparte carried with him 139 scholars whose aim was to study and record the country in both its ancient and its modern aspects. Protected from the unsolicited attentions of rowdy locals thanks to a sizeable military escort, few sites escaped the notice of the French *savants* – el-Amarna included. And the abandoned city, as something quite new and different, made a memorable impression, as Edmé Jomard, in charge of the survey, recalled:

'I was surprised to see so great a mass of ruins, … no less than two thousand two hundred metres long and a thousand wide, yet which, though situated near the Nile … does not feature on any map. I was eager to make a plan and to compile drawings of the better preserved parts. Most of the constructions are unfortunately demolished, and one can see little more than the foundations. However, one still finds a very great number of houses in brick with their principal walls; a large gateway and its enclosure; two vast edifices where the plan is distinct; [and] the great longitudinal road forty-eight metres wide....'

Two hundred years ago, the dark, pebble-strewn ruins of el-Amarna were clearly substantial, with acre upon acre of half-decayed mud-brick sparking still with fragments of coloured glaze, blue-painted potsherds or flecks of gold leaf. One building – today recognizable as the Small Aten Temple – stood in places to a height of more than 7 m (23 ft), though it had been robbed in antiquity, as almost everywhere at the site, of its limestone facings. The French, knowing nothing of the ruins' significance, nevertheless delayed their journey to map and draw what was visible, with the results eventually published in the great *Description de l'Égypte*, the official record of their scientific mission. Not surprisingly, however, among the mass of superficially more impressive monuments laid before an eager European public, el-Amarna's remains would make little immediate impression.

With the possible exception of some desultory digging in the early decades of the 19th century by the French and British representatives in Egypt, Bernardino Drovetti and Henry Salt – between them responsible for the superb Egyptological collections now in the museums of Paris, Turin and London – it was a full quarter-century after the visit of Napoleon's expedition before any serious exploration of el-Amarna was undertaken. John Gardner Wilkinson, an English Egyptologist – one of the first – who visited the ruins twice, in 1824 and again (with his compatriot James Burton) in 1826, undertook his own survey of the city. This was subsequently repro-

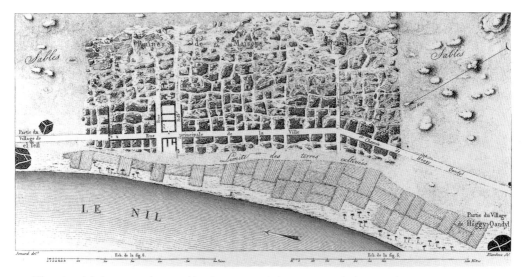

The ruins of el-Amarna, as surveyed by the engineers and savants attached to Napoleon Bonaparte's Egyptian expedition. Clearly visible in the left-centre of the plan is the Small Aten Temple and, to its west (across the Royal Road), the 'Coronation Hall'.

15

Christian graffito (note the cross above the praying figure's head) in the tomb of Huya (no. 1) at el-Amarna – one of many scrawled at the time of the Coptic habitation of the necropolis.

duced in his famous, multi-volume *Manners and Customs of the Ancient Egyptians* – the book which would earn him a knighthood and, more importantly, draw to Egyptology for the first time a wide and enthusiastic popular audience.

Influenced by the proximity of the quarries at Hatnub, ancient source of the creamy, translucent stone popularly known as alabaster, Wilkinson identified the site of el-Amarna with the 'Alabastron' of the Roman authors. But clearly it was no Classical foundation, as the same explorer realized. In the cliffs to the north of the site he located the settlement's pharaonic cemetery, and here sketched and made wet paper 'squeezes' of the relief-decorated walls in more than half a dozen tombs. Though the scenes were badly damaged (in part as a result of later habitation by Coptic-Christian monks), the results of Wilkinson's work gave scholars serious pause. The depictions were of a style and manner not previously encountered, being neither Classical nor properly pharaonic: improbably distorted images of an almost feminine king and his slender queen, accompanied, in scenes of unusual intimacy, by their equally peculiar, banana-headed brood and showered by the beams of an unusual, rayed sun. Who were these creatures?

Thanks to Jean François Champollion's decipherment of the long-impenetrable hieroglyphic script, the identity of el-Amarna's mysterious king would soon be established (in today's spelling) as 'Akhenaten', the name of his wife as 'Nefertiti', both of whom lived in the middle years of the 18th dynasty, during the second half of the 2nd millennium BC; while the solar disc proffering the *ankh*, or hieroglyphic sign for 'life', to the noses of the royal family was seen to be a god. The god was 'Aten', and an expanded version of the deity's name, presented in a kingly pair of oval frames or 'cartouches', accompanied the image at all times throughout the tombs. What was particularly odd for Egypt, however, was that Aten was the *only* divinity represented: the otherwise ubiquitous lord of the underworld, Osiris, together with his gloomy retinue, was at el-Amarna nowhere to be seen.

With Wilkinson's visit, the scholarly flood-gates were opened, and news of 'Alabastron' and the 'disc worshippers' spread among the *cognoscenti*. But it was not until the expedition sent out during the 19th century's fifth decade by the Prussian king Friedrich Wilhelm IV – 'the best-equipped [team] ... that had ever gone to Egypt with skilled draughtsmen among the members' – that any further, substantial documentation of el-Amarna and its monuments became available. The medium would be the plates of the massive *Denkmäler aus Aegypten und Aethiopien*, the official record of the Prussian expedition compiled under the direction of the project leader, Karl Richard Lepsius.

The amount of data gathered at el-Amarna over a mere 12 days in 1843 and 1845 was impressive. More impressive still, however, was the brilliance with which Lepsius, one of the period's greatest Egyptologists, disentangled from his findings the basic history of the site:

> 'Through the monuments we became acquainted with several kings of this period [the 18th Dynasty], who were not afterwards admitted in the legitimate lists, but were regarded as unauthorised co-temporary or intermediate kings. Among these Amenophis IV. is to be particularly noted, who, during a very active reign of twelve [sic] years, endeavoured to accomplish a complete reformation of all secular and spiritual institutions. He built a royal capital for himself in Central Egypt, near the present Tel-el-Amarna, introduced new offices and usages, and aimed at no less a thing than to abolish the whole religious system of the Egyptians, which had hitherto subsisted, and to place in its stead the single worship of the Sun.... Indeed, the former gods and their worship were persecuted to such an extent by this king, that he erased all the gods' names, with the single exception of the Sun-god *Ra* [Re], from every monument that was accessible throughout the country, and because his own name, Amenophis, contained the name of Ammon [Amun], he changed it into Bech-en-aten [Akhenaten], "Worshipper of the Sun's disk" ....'

What scholars found intriguing was Lepsius's subsequent observation that the names and images of the Amarna royal couple had themselves frequently been hacked out by those who came after; Akhenaten's changes, evidently, had not met with universal approbation. Nor was it the

Akhenaten, Nefertiti and their three eldest daughters (Meritaten, Meketaten and Ankhesenpaaten) bestow gifts from the 'Window of Appearance' at el-Amarna. A scene in the tomb of the god's father Ay, no. 25 in the southern nobles' cemetery, as copied by the artists of Lepsius's expedition.

Bezel of a stirrup-shaped ring cast in massive gold and chased with the hieroglyphs of Nefertiti's second name-form: 'Nefernefruaten-Nefertiti'. Found in the vicinity of the royal tomb at el-Amarna in about 1882.

memory of Akhenaten alone which had been shunned, as Lepsius recognized: his successors – Smenkhkare, Tutankhamun and Ay – were similarly ignored in the later king-lists. These rulers had one particular feature in common: each, to a greater or a lesser extent, had been associated with el-Amarna, and all that that city stood for. And they had paid dearly for it.

THE DISCOVERY OF THE ROYAL TOMB

Although Akhenaten's abandoned city clearly had an interesting story to tell – of which Lepsius had recovered a great deal more than the bare bones – no further exploration was attempted for several decades. The work of a French mission in the 1880s is memorable primarily for the title of the report on their first season: *Deux jours de fouilles à Tell el Amarna [Two Days of Excavations at Tell el Amarna]* – at a time when the typical expedition was one of several months. Only with the discovery by locals in the late 1880s of an immense sepulchre, hidden deep in the eastern desert cliffs of Gebel Abu Hasa to the east of the city, would the academic pulse again quicken.

The locals' find was kept secret for some time, to be covertly exploited by its discoverers. It proved to be the burial place of Akhenaten himself, with the robbers' loot apparently including gold jewelry (one item a ring with the name of queen Nefertiti) now divided between museums in Edinburgh and Liverpool, as well as a mysterious 'mummy' which some since have idly speculated might have been the king's own. In 1891–92, the sepulchre was 'cleared' under the notional supervision of Alessandro Barsanti, the castmaker and 'odd-jobs man' of the Egyptian Antiquities Service; sad to say, the work was badly skimped, and much important archaeological information was lost, particularly in the burial chamber where Barsanti's men seem to have concentrated their efforts.

THE FIRST EXCAVATIONS: FLINDERS PETRIE AND HOWARD CARTER

A year after Barsanti's clearance, the freshly swept Amarna royal tomb was visited by a young man in Egypt for the first time – Howard Carter, a shy and somewhat prim British artist who was to carve out for himself an enviable niche in the history of Egyptian exploration. While at el-Amarna, Carter prepared quick copies of the principal scenes which decorated the walls of Akhenaten's sepulchre, and these drawings – his first venture into print – were soon after reproduced in *The Daily Graphic* for 23 March 1892. Although little more than sketches, they accurately captured, almost for the

The young Howard Carter, who accompanied Petrie's expedition to el-Amarna in 1892 on behalf of the collector Lord Amherst. For Carter, the el-Amarna dig was to mark the beginning of a lifelong involvement with the period, culminating in his discovery of the tomb of Tutankhamun in 1922.

first time, the unique flavour of the Amarna art-style (Lepsius's copies are famously bland). Little did Carter suspect, but it was a style which would come to dominate his life when, 30 years later, he uncovered the tomb of Tutankhamun, Akhenaten's son. The burial was crammed with an unparalleled treasure of statues, sculptures and gold, made during and immediately after the 'heretic's' reign. And el-Amarna, fittingly, would be the theme to which Carter chose to return for his last scholarly contribution – an essay in Sir E. Denison Ross's *The Art of Egypt through the Ages* – in 1931, eight years before his death.

Howard Carter was of relatively modest birth with no personal wealth and few immediate prospects. He owed his presence at el-Amarna to the chance patronage of a philanthropic collector, William Amhurst Tyssen-Amherst, 1st Baron Amherst of Hackney, for whom Carter's artist father had previously undertaken a number of commissions. Detecting the boy's serious antiquarian interest, Amherst had decided to take the young Howard under his protective wing.

Keen to add to his burgeoning collection of Egyptian antiquities, Amherst sent Carter along as his personal representative on the excavations then being undertaken by the legendary but dour Flinders Petrie – soon to be appointed to Britain's first chair in Egyptology at University College London. El-Amarna was

THE DAILY GRAPHIC, WEDNESDAY, MARCH 23, 1892.

A ROYAL TOMB IN EGYPT: KHU'ENATEN WEEPING FOR HIS DAUGHTER—ONE OF THE WALL CARVINGS UNEARTHED AT TEL EL AMARNA.

Carter's rapid but sensitive sketch of one of the scenes in the Amarna royal tomb, showing the royal couple mourning the death of their second daughter, Meketaten; the princess (or a statue of her) is shown standing within a flower-bedecked shrine. From The Daily Graphic, *23 March 1892.*

19

William Matthew Flinders Petrie, the founding-father of Egyptian archaeology. His survey and excavations at el-Amarna would shed important light on the site, and the finds he collected reveal much about the history, religion, art and technology of Akhenaten's reign.

to give Carter his first taste of digging and, despite Petrie's notoriously meagre fare (the excavator's unfortunate staff famously claimed that 'You lived on sardines, and when you had eaten the sardines you ate the tin'), he found the work much to his liking.

Petrie himself had been drawn to el-Amarna not by the tombs and inscriptions which had lured his predecessors, nor even by the hope that he might discover more of the cuneiform diplomatic archive which had recently been brought to light by the local digger of *sebakh*. A pioneer in the study of Egypt's material culture, Petrie was primarily attracted by the prospect of working on a single-period site which had been but little contaminated by earlier or later occupation. A season's work at el-Amarna, he hoped, would provide a 'snapshot' of Egyptian civilization at a single, restricted moment in time, and yield dividends for the general study and classification of the pots, pans and trinkets of ancient everyday life.

Petrie set to work with his usual energy, and, by means of triangulation survey and small test excavations (*sondages*) carried out at selected parts of

Akhenaten and Nefertiti's two youngest daughters, Nefernefrure and Setepenre, seated at the feet of their parents. A fragment of exquisitely painted wall decoration recovered by Petrie from the ruins of the King's House at el-Amarna.

'...O living Aten ... Trees and grasses flourish, Birds are flown from their nests, their wings adoring your ka *....' Fragment of a painted pavement recovered from Maru-Aten in 1896 by Alessandro Barsanti; the quotation is from the Great Hymn to the Aten in the tomb of Ay.*

the site, he was able rapidly to characterize the principal areas of the city: palace and temple structures were identified, together with domestic dwellings and the waste-heaps of a variety of workshops in which had been carried out the manufacture of faience, glass, pottery and sculpture. The original opulence of the ancient city – evidenced by the remains of elaborately painted floors and exquisitely decorated walls, and by a veritable mass of fragments of local and imported, utilitarian and decorative items which everywhere littered the ground – came as a revelation. The paintings included a delightful scene of Akhenaten's daughters which the excavator delicately teased from the wall and packed up for shipment back to England, later presenting it to the Ashmolean Museum in Oxford. Almost as a matter of course, given Petrie's characteristic luck, the season was topped off by splinters of further Amarna tablets, and by the miraculous rediscovery of the original location of the initial tablet hoard – within a building close to what Petrie designated the 'King's House', pharaoh's private quarters. The building was later identified, from its stamped mud-bricks (which Petrie, uncharacteristically, had missed), as the 'House of Correspondence of Pharaoh, life! prosperity! health' – the ancient Egyptian records office.

Petrie returned to England well-satisfied with his results, having mapped out the site and provided a solid, factual framework for Akhenaten's reign; his report, *Tell el Amarna*, one of the best and most frequently cited of his several hundred publications, paved the way for all future archaeological

Limestone plaque – probably
a sculptor's model since it
is pierced for suspension
– purchased at el-
Amarna by the
American Egyptologist
Charles Edwin Wilbour
in 1881. The heads are
those of Akhenaten (left)
and Nefertiti (right), both
depicted in the later, more
subdued Amarna style.

work on the city and its period. As the excavator was himself able to boast, forty years on: 'Though so much has been written and done about that strange man [Akhenaten], scarcely anything has been added to the scanty history that was traced out in my work of 1891, which covered almost all that we yet know.'

EPIGRAPHY AND SCANDAL: FROM DAVIES TO BORCHARDT

Ten years after Petrie's brilliant archaeological success at el-Amarna (a decade marred by the destruction, at the hands of an irate farmer, of the wonderful painted pavements the excavator had gone to much trouble to preserve and protect), another Englishman was drawn to Akhenaten's abandoned city: the Lancashire-born Norman de Garis Davies, a one-time Petrie student and the best archaeological draughtsman of his generation. Davies's life would be dedicated to copying, in exquisite and accurate detail, the scenes carved on the walls of Egypt's many tombs. Having previously worked on various Old Kingdom chapels at Saqqara, Sheikh Said and Deir el-Gebrawi, and inspired by the discoveries of his former teacher, Davies decided to turn his attention to the northern and southern groups of tombs at el-Amarna. Davies's employers in the enterprise would be the Egypt Exploration Fund (EEF; later Egypt Exploration Society, EES), for whom he produced six fine volumes: *The Rock Tombs of El Amarna* (London, 1903–08), still indispensable to scholarly research. With the publication of these records, rich in inscriptions and accurately recorded iconographic detail, the intellectual analysis of the Amarna phenomenon could begin in earnest.

Further material for study would turn up a short time later, with the start of detailed, systematic excavations in 1907 under 'cocky little Ludwig Borchardt' and the Deutsche Orient-Gesellschaft (DOG), a Berlin-based equivalent of the EEF. Concentrating primarily on the South Suburb, the German excavators set to work with characteristic efficiency, imposing upon the site a letter/number grid 200 m (656 ft) square, to which features within were referenced by an additional number sequence.

In the course of their digging, the DOG uncovered much of interest; in fact, the amazing good fortune of the team is difficult to grasp, even today. The work started off well with the discovery of yet more Amarna tablets. And then, in 1912, while excavating the ruined, mud-brick villa of the king's sculptor, Thutmose, Borchardt's men brought to light a remarkable collection of royal and private portraits. This remains one of the largest and most important sculptural assemblages encountered anywhere in Egypt – a total of more than 20 prototype plaster casts (a similar, rather worn specimen had been found by Petrie years before), taken presumably from clay masters, together with a whole range of trial-pieces and finished and unfinished elements carved in a range of hard and soft stones. Here, literally at the sweeping of a brush, the excavators found themselves face to face not only with Akhenaten himself, but with his entire court.

The majority of these pieces would in due course find their way to the Berlin Museum, whose collection of Amarna art, in consequence, is today the finest anywhere in the world. The centrepiece is ancient Egypt's most

Digging at el-Amarna: excavations of the Deutsche Orient-Gesellschaft in progress in the South Suburb of the city, 1914. The outlines of well-preserved walls, buried just below the modern surface, can be clearly seen.

famous icon: the magnificent, painted limestone bust of Nefertiti, shown wearing her characteristic, flat-topped crown and an elegantly detailed broad collar. The portrait was discovered on 6 December 1912, along with a smashed bust of Akhenaten, among the remains of a built-in 'cupboard' whose shelf had collapsed with the passing of the centuries, causing the piece to fall to the ground. Fortunately, the damage sustained had been slight – the most glaring defect being the loss of Nefertiti's left, inlaid eye, which must have jolted free and dropped out.

The quality of most of the artworks in the DOG collection was superb, but the beauty of the Nefertiti bust, generally considered a work by the hand of the sculptor Thutmose himself, is beyond compare. It passed, at the formal division of spoils on 20 January 1913, to Dr James Simon, the sponsor of the DOG excavations, and in 1920 he made a formal gift of his collection to the state of Prussia; three years later, the queen was unveiled to an astonished public. Following outraged complaints from the Egyptian government that the piece had left Egypt illegally (in fact, the share-out of finds had been entrusted to a junior official of the museum – a man whose professional competence was clearly open to question), the return of the Nefertiti bust was reluctantly considered, and, in the 1930s, almost carried through. Because of the queen's flawless 'Aryan' looks, however, the plan was vetoed by the Führer: 'What the German people have', Hitler reportedly decreed, 'they keep!'

Nefertiti: exquisite portrait bust from the workshop of the sculptor Thutmose, carved life-size from a single block of limestone, with gesso overlay and painted detail. The right eye-socket still retains its curved quartz-crystal inlay, held in position by a waxy pigment employed to define the pupil; as this adhesive dried and lost its stickiness, the left eye-inlay had evidently dropped out.

THE EGYPT EXPLORATION SOCIETY: PEET, PENDLEBURY AND BEYOND

'The English staff numbers six or seven. In addition to the
Director are the architect, the epigraphist and usually three
more who have no special subject but can take on any piece of
work at need…. There are about fifteen highly trained
professional excavators from Quft [Koptos, near Luxor]. From
them the foremen are chosen. The rest of the labour is local and
the number of men may run as high as a hundred [from among
which each] actual excavator has two or sometimes three
children to carry away the sand he has removed …'
JOHN PENDLEBURY

The outbreak of the First World War in 1914 finally put paid to the work of
the DOG at el-Amarna; but, given their run of luck, the Germans could have
no complaint. Shortly after the cessation of hostilities, in 1920, while the
bust of Nefertiti was still under wraps, the Egypt Exploration Society took
over the concession to dig. The EES was to excavate extensively over all
parts of the site, including in and around the royal tomb, almost without
interruption from 1921 until 1936; after that date, enthusiasm waned with
the introduction by the Egyptian government of new rules relating to the
division of finds – a system upon which the funding of the British work very
much depended.

The British excavations were directed by a succession of well-known
scholars, including the dull but worthy Thomas Eric Peet, a philologist, the
archaeologist Leonard Woolley (who would go
on to find fame and fortune at Ur of the
Chaldees), the ill-fated Francis Newton, who died
in post of some horrible local disease, the oddly
brilliant Dutchman Henri Frankfort, and finally
the heroic J. D. S. Pendlebury; he would meet his
end on Crete, outside Herakleion, shot as a spy
('the Cretan Lawrence') by the occupying German
forces in 1941. Among Egyptologists, Pendlebury
is today celebrated as a rare, charismatic figure in a
woefully uncharismatic field, memorialized in a
striking photograph in which he models, bare-
chested, a reconstructed Egyptian faience collar
from the excavations. He is remembered also for

*British Egyptologist John Pendlebury models an Amarna collar
of colourful faience beads. 'Behind his normal façade of
conventional Public School and University man was someone
pining for a slashed doublet instead of a neat grey pin-stripe …
Amarna … for him … was … a personal chance to turn his
back … on the unromantic aspects of the present.'*

Cosmetic flask from the Egypt Exploration Society's excavations at el-Amarna, modelled in glass in the shape of a swimming fish. The technical skills – and imagination – required to produce such exquisite art-works reached new heights during the reigns of Amenophis III and Akhenaten.

his glass eye, the result of a childhood accident, an optic which – echoes of Nefertiti – had an unsettling habit of falling out on site and startling the workers.

The object-yield of the EES excavations would prove interesting rather than dramatic, though a few further scraps of cuneiform text were added to the burgeoning total, and some notable pieces of sculpture – strays from the studio of Thutmose – turned up to keep the sponsors happy. The principal achievement of these seasons was the assembling of a wide range of archaeological and inscriptional facts and clues, and much conflicting detail, partially published in three volumes entitled *The City of Akhenaten*. Upon this body of evidence scholarship, as we shall see, has since been able to build with impressive if not yet consensual result.

The British excavations at el-Amarna drew to a close 15 years after they had begun, and the site lay archaeologically abandoned for the next four decades while scholars back home played games with the material now to hand. Further grist to the Amarna historians' mill, however, would be brought to light by a German archaeological expedition digging at el-Ashmunein (Hermopolis Magna) on the opposite bank of the river in 1939. Here the Germans, to their surprise, uncovered a mass of limestone blocks, the most important neatly laid out in the foundations of a pylon, or monumental temple gateway, built by Ramesses II of the 19th Dynasty – blocks which proved once to have faced the mud-brick cores of el-Amarna's principal buildings. Shortly after the Germans had returned home, the remains of Ramesses II's second pylon were uncovered by illicit diggers; the blocks were carted off and subsequently sold, together with many of the first lot, during and immediately after the Second World War by enterprising locals who took the opportunity to pretty them up with rather frightening colours. Some 1,500 of these pre-war 'Hermopolis reliefs' are currently known, their quality and subject-matter offering a tantalizing glimpse of the former beauty and elegance of Akhenaten's city. And further examples of reused Amarna relief sculpture have been found since, though in ones and twos, both at el-Ashmunein itself and at other sites in the neighbourhood, including Asyut and el-Sheikh Ibada (Antinoopolis) and even as far south as Abydos – more crucially important additions to the el-Amarna puzzle.

The three decades following 1945 witnessed a burgeoning of book-based interest in Amarna studies, but still little attention was paid to the site itself. In 1974, however, British archaeologist Geoffrey T. Martin published, to great interest and acclaim, the first volume of his documentary and archaeological 'salvage' of the excavations which had previously been carried out by Pendlebury and others in the royal tomb at el-Amarna; for the second volume, Martin went on to copy and collate the sculptured reliefs on the tomb's walls, and then undertake (with Antiquities Organization Egyptologist Aly el-Khouly) further clearance in and around the royal wadi. Archaeological work in the city proper resumed in 1977, this time under the inspired direction of Barry J. Kemp of Cambridge University – again working on behalf of the EES. Today, after more than 20 years of detailed work, the nature and development of Akhenaten's city and its component structures and institutions are better known than ever before. These we shall return to explore in detail in a later chapter.

But first some history. What devils prompted Akhenaten to embark on his fateful journey? What was the background to the extraordinary foundation of 'Horizon of the Aten'?

The Central City from the air, 1932, showing the contrast between dark cultivation (at the bottom of the photograph) and the lighter desert to the east. The Small Aten Temple is clearly visible at right of centre, adjacent to the King's House; behind the King's House are the ruins of the Records Office – findspot of the Amarna letters – and the police barracks. The southern edge of the Great Aten Temple is just visible on the extreme left.

Queen Hatshepsut crowned by Amun-Re, king of the gods; relief on an obelisk from Karnak.

CHAPTER TWO

PRIESTLY AMBITIONS

ORIGINS: EGYPT OF THE PHARAOHS

The civilization of pharaonic Egypt was born, flourished and died over the course of three thousand years up to and beyond the birth of Christ, a span unequalled anywhere in the history of the world. It was to be a bumpy ride, far from the smooth continuum of stability the superficial changelessness of Egyptian art might suggest – a sequence of dramatic peaks and troughs, in which seemingly terminal halts in social and material progress were followed by the most dramatic of restarts. Each and every jolt in Egypt's historical course would leave its indelible mark on the character of its civilization, and more particularly on the consciousness of its people. The events documented in this book represented not so much a jolt as a virtual derailment, affecting the remaining centuries of pharaonic rule within Egypt, and the future course and intellectual development of the entire world.

The history of ancient Egypt began, by tradition, around 3000 BC with the unification of north and south by the legendary king Menes. The next 30 centuries would be dominated by three culturally brilliant high-points: the Old Kingdom, or pyramid age, which spanned the period 2575 to 2134 BC; the powerful Middle Kingdom, which flourished between 2040 and 1640 BC; and the New Kingdom, reckoned to have begun in 1550 and to have petered out around 1070 BC. What marked out this last era were its imperial pretensions, which would carry in their wake unrivalled wealth and immense international prestige; Egypt's status in the world during this time was one of which earlier kings, whatever their internal power, could only have dreamed.

The reigns of the New Kingdom, like those of the Old and the Middle as well as the final centuries of pharaonic rule, are today grouped into dynasties – the 'families' of kings into which the historian Manetho of Sebennytos, writing in the 3rd century BC (though preserved to us only in the garbled accounts of later authors), divided up Egyptian history. The dynasties making up the New Kingdom were the 18th (1550–1307 BC); the 19th (1307–1196); and the 20th – which ran from 1196 and finally ground to a halt in the face of economic collapse and external pressures just before the turn of the 1st millennium BC. Our interest lies with the first of these eras, the 18th Dynasty, in which the Amarna revolution was, in every sense, contained. A brief review of the era's origins and its subsequent development will reveal what Amenophis IV-Akhenaten, the architect of the regime, was striving to achieve, whom he was against, and why.

INVASION: THE HYKSOS

'Tutimaeus. In his reign, for what cause I know not, a blast of
God smote us; and unexpectedly, from the regions of the East,
invaders of obscure race marched in confidence of victory
against our land. By main force they easily seized it without
striking a blow....' MANETHO

The Middle Kingdom drew to an undignified close around 1640 BC under
the kings of the 13th Dynasty. Though a time of relative affluence, interfer-
ence from the inhabitants of lands to the north and east increased day by
day, producing a feeling of deep unease; the Asiatic occupation of large
tracts of Egypt's eastern Delta intensified, with an independent Asiatic
regime in the north of Egypt the inevitable result. The kings of this, the 15th
Dynasty, are today better known by their ancient Egyptian title: *heqau khasut*,
'rulers of foreign lands' – vocalized by the Greeks as 'Hyksos', the form
employed by Manetho and still current. The reputation the Asiatic kings left
behind, whether deserved or not, was one of cruelty and oppression; the
trauma of foreign occupation would prove difficult to eradicate, heightening
the innate xenophobia felt by the inhabitants of this long-secluded land.

The Hyksos kings ruled their Delta estates for almost a century, first from
the ancient capital, Memphis, later from Avaris to the northeast. Further
south, a family of lesser kings held sway. Based on Thebes, this local dynasty
(known today as the 17th) managed to maintain power over a territory
stretching from Cusae in the north as far as the first cataract of the Nile in
the south. The territory beyond this southern frontier, though formerly
under Egyptian control, was now home to an independent and pro-Hyksos
Nubian kingdom ruling from Kerma. For a time, these three separate
regimes co-existed in a state of uneasy, mutual interdependence roughly
cemented by limited intermarriage between the principal families. Smoul-
dering with resentment and wounded pride, however, the native Egyptian
kings were merely marking time.

LIBERATION: KAMOSE AND AHMOSE

The Hyksos occupation, though a severe dent to Egyptian confidence and
self-esteem, had its good points as well as its bad, particularly in the field of
innovative technology. Crucial advances in bronze-working, weaving,
pottery-making and agriculture – the introduction of the revolutionary
water-lifting device known as the *shaduf* – are generally dated to this time;
while Hyksos influence inevitably made itself felt in various ways in art,
fashion, music and dance. More significant in the shorter term, however,
were Hyksos contributions to Egyptian military science – notably the
introduction of the chariot and the composite bow, spear-thrower, sickle-
shaped sword, and scale armour. These inventions the Theban kings,
taught by recent experience that warfare was a matter of national survival,

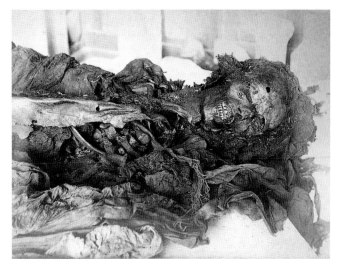

Detail of the mummy of the Theban king Seqenenre Taa, showing the wounds – inflicted by a mace, by arrows and by Asiatic axe-heads – which had ended his life. The king's body evidently lay untended on the battlefield for some time, since rigor mortis had already set in when the mummification process began.

were to adopt and turn against the occupying presence, to devastating effect, in the years to come.

An early stage in the struggle between the Hyksos 15th and the Theban 17th dynasties is celebrated in a contemporary Egyptian tale, 'The Quarrel of Apophis and Seqenenre'. For the Theban protagonist, the conflict ended badly: Seqenenre's mummy, found with a group of other kingly dead at Thebes in 1881 in the famous Deir el-Bahri 'cache', or group reburial, within tomb DB320, was riddled with spear thrusts and Asiatic axe wounds, presumably administered as the king lay stunned following a first blow. Although Seqenenre perished, the struggle nevertheless continued, with his queen, Ahhotep, for the moment taking up the reins of power. His successor, Kamose, carried on this 'war of liberation', to impressive effect, recording his successes in two stelae set up at the temple of the local Theban god Amun at Karnak. With Amun's divine support, the campaign was pursued to its ultimate conclusion by the next king, Ahmose. Within a matter of years, Egypt had been freed from the foreigners' yoke, the country reunited under native rule, and pharaoh's enemies pushed deep into their respective Palestinian and Nubian homelands. It was a new dawn.

THE DRIVE FOR EMPIRE: TUTHMOSIS I

Ahmose was recognized by later pharaohs as the founder of a new dynasty, the 18th, which opened a fresh epoch referred to by Egyptologists as the New Kingdom. The achievement of Ahmose, who ruled for 25 years, would be built on at home during the 21-year reign of his son, Amenophis I, soon to be deified (along with his influential mother, Ahmose-Nofretiri) as a patron of the Theban west bank – burial ground of the southern city. Of events beyond Egypt's frontiers, the years of Amenophis I are notably silent; perhaps the records are lost or perhaps pharaoh was happy simply to have his borders secured. Not until the accession of the dynasty's third king, Tuthmosis I – who significantly was not of the blood royal – does an interest in the outside world appear again to manifest itself.

Tuthmosis I is remembered today as Egypt's greatest warrior king, who set out 'to slake his heart's thirst throughout foreign lands'. During a series of military campaigns waged during eight short years of rule, the frontiers of Egypt were pushed relentlessly, unstoppably, to what would be their greatest ever extent: the Euphrates in the north, and deep into the Nubian south beyond the fourth cataract of the Nile. What had begun as defence developed rapidly into out-and-out aggression. Both within Egypt and beyond, this success represented a stunning turn-around in the international perception of pharaoh, whose eyes had been opened to the possibilities of foreign domination. Egypt, ever after, was seen as a force to be reckoned with.

THE QUEEN WHO WOULD BE KING: HATSHEPSUT

The seeds of the Amarna revolution would be sown but a short time later. Tuthmosis I, the architect of Egypt's empire abroad, was followed on the throne by his eldest surviving son, also called Tuthmosis. Lasting just seven years, the successor's reign was short and unremarkable; his legacy, however, would be felt for years to come. Following pharaoh's untimely death, the kingship passed to a

Indurated limestone statue of Hatshepsut as ruling pharaoh – the torso recovered from the ruins of her famous mortuary temple at Deir el-Bahri by Lepsius's team in 1845, the head found between 1926 and 1928 by the Egyptian Expedition of the Metropolitan Museum of Art. Unlike in some images of the queen, her femininity has not here been compromised by her kingly role.

mere child named Tuthmosis – III. Crucially, however, this child was not the son of Tuthmosis II's principal queen, Hatshepsut, but of a lesser wife named Isis; Hatshepsut's attachment to the boy was therefore limited.

The years which followed were a time of immense turmoil, of which, in the records, we catch only the merest of glimpses. Yet these glimpses are sufficient to signal the existence of those complex political manoeuvrings which must have been a constant feature of Egyptian court life – the less than glorious reality behind the pharaonic façade of semi-divine power. The extent to which the kingship could be, and was, manipulated by others comes as both a shock and a revelation.

What happened was this. At the death of Tuthmosis II the reins of power passed not to the designated child-heir, Tuthmosis III, but to Hatshepsut herself. Given Tuthmosis III's age, this was perfectly proper – indeed, a precedent had been set during the minority of king Ahmose himself some reigns earlier, when the affairs of state were for a time directed by his mother. Hatshepsut, however, was greedy for power: within a short time of Tuthmosis III's accession she had adopted a formal pharaonic titulary and regalia, going on to rule as senior partner in a quite irregular period of co-rule, or co-regency – a concept which has an important place in our story – occupying much of the first half of the true heir's reign.

The details of Hatshepsut's rise, and the reasons for it, are now obscure, but it is self-evident that, in order to achieve this extraordinary elevation, the queen must have had powerful support from behind the political scenes. This support came, as we now see, from within the temple of Amun of Karnak, in which Hatshepsut functioned as 'god's wife', or high priestess – an office later passed on to her daughter, Nefrure.

THE INFLUENCE OF AMUN

The great influence of the god Amun and his priests was symptomatic of the changes which had occurred within Egypt during the century following the Hyksos expulsion. These years of consolidation and growth had been accompanied by an increasing delegation of royal power, and as a direct result of this process elements within the state structure began to operate more and more independently of the king. The main priesthoods, in former times far smaller in size and operated by devout laymen for little reward beyond the spiritual and a guaranteed square meal, were now hereditary bodies grown rich, worldly and corrupt – thanks to pharaoh's generous acknowledgment, in word and deed, of Amun's support in his martial endeavours. Increasingly united in what the historian James Henry Breasted years ago described as 'a great sacerdotal organization embracing the whole land', some among the priesthood's number acquired a taste for power, and now wished to pull the strings directly.

The positions both of Tuthmosis III himself as successor and, a short time later, of Hatshepsut as the young king's co-regent were acknowledged by

The powerful executive of Amun's will – the high priest Hapuseneb, who quite exceptionally combined the office with that of vizier, or prime minister. In the inscriptions which cover this statue of the man, the name of Hatshepsut was systematically removed after her death and replaced with the prenomen of her husband, Tuthmosis II.

divine oracle of Amun; and it would not be stretching the bounds of credibility too far to recognize, behind these divine elections, the controlling hand of the god's high priest – one Hapuseneb. The rationale for this act – the superimposition of the queen over her ward – is at this remove difficult to discern; but that the Amun priesthood continued to collude in maintaining Hatshepsut in power is confirmed by the public proclamation, on the walls of the queen's magnificent temple at Deir el-Bahri, of her 'divine birth' – the

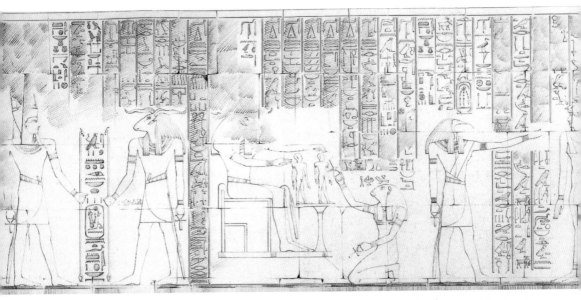

Copy by Howard Carter of a scene at Deir el-Bahri commemorating the queen's divine birth (left to right): Amun commands the ram-headed Khnum; Khnum fashions Hatshepsut and her ka, or spiritual double (both shown as male!); Thoth greets the heiress's birth-mother, Tuthmosis I's chief queen, Ahmose.

Crudely drawn sketch in a 'grotto' above Hatshepsut's mortuary temple at Deir el-Bahri, which – although there is no clear identifying text – has been interpreted as a scurrilous representation, by a disenchanted subject, of the queen and her favourite, Senenmut, in sexual congress.

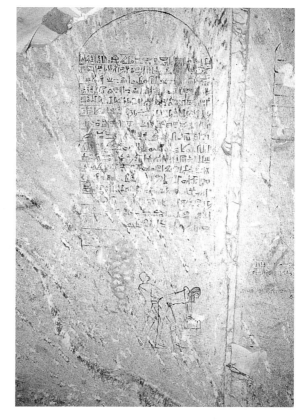

first occasion that the monarch's descent from the Theban god Amun is acknowledged in so explicit a manner. Egyptologists have perhaps been distracted from appreciating Hapuseneb's involvement in this dynastic manipulation by the support Hatshepsut received from another confederate, the influential Amun-temple administrator Senenmut. Senenmut's principal role, however, may have been less political than romantic – as the queen's lover. A rather scurrilous, but none the less intriguing sketch

Senenmut as tutor to Hatshepsut's daughter, Nefrure, found at Karnak in 1904 – one of a number of extant sculptures depicting the queen's intimate and his young royal charge.

The spectacular mortuary temple of Hatshepsut at Deir el-Bahri, a triumph of ancient architectural design rising in graceful terraces to meet the vertical cliffs behind. Beyond the cliffs lies the Valley of the Kings, and the queen's burial place, KV20 – a deep, spiralling excavation initially cut for her father, Tuthmosis I.

believed to depict the sexual union of the queen and commoner, left by a clearly disillusioned commentator on the reign, can still be seen in an unfinished tomb above Deir el-Bahri.

THE OPET FESTIVAL

Hatshepsut was to acknowledge her debt to Amun on a number of occasions, most notably on the so-called Chapelle rouge ('Red chapel') at Karnak and in another equally revealing text on the base of the northern of the two obelisks she set up at the same temple site:

> 'I did this with a loving heart for my father Amun, after I entered before his secret image of the first occasion, and after I became wise by his excellent power. I did not neglect a deed he determined. My majesty knows that he is divine. I have thus done according to his command, for he is the one who leads me. Never shall I devise projects that are not of his doing. *For he it is who gives instructions.*'

One of Amun's 'instructions' was to establish 'The beautiful feast of Opet', a festival celebrated over a period of 11 days each autumn during the second month of the annual Nile inundation. The occasion for this festival was the procession of the god Amun, his consort Mut and their offspring Khonsu from their dwelling at Karnak to nearby Luxor temple, with the gods carried out in their sacred barques on the shoulders of priests and subsequently brought back by river. After the reign of Tutankhamun, both outward and return journeys were made by boat. This popular event, together with 'The beautiful festival of the Valley' (in which Amun of Karnak visited the domain

A scene from the Opet Festival reliefs in Luxor temple, destination of Amun, Mut and Khonsu's procession from their Karnak home. Begun under Amenophis III, the carving of these scenes was not completed until the reign of Tutankhamun; this drawing, with its wealth of accurate detail, is by Howard Carter.

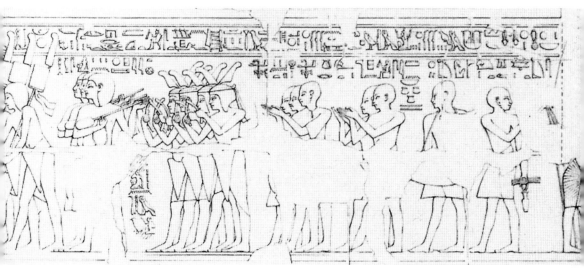

of Hathor on the west bank and the mortuary temple of the reigning king), soon became a principal focus of the Theban year. Its propaganda value – and not only for the king – was immense.

We know very little about the Opet rites themselves, though it is clear that pharaoh himself (or herself) took a particular interest in the festival. This is presumably because, perhaps as its culmination, the divine impregnation of the king's mother was at that time re-enacted and, by it, pharaoh's descent from the god reconfirmed. This formalization of the relationship at Thebes between king and god was the price Hatshepsut paid for Hapuseneb's support; and by the proclamation of this interdependence the kingship would find itself sorely compromised.

TUTHMOSIS III AND AMENOPHIS II: REASSERTING ROYAL POWER

'Every king of Upper and Lower Egypt is a god by whose guidance men live.' INSCRIPTION IN THE TOMB OF REKHMIRE, VIZIER OF TUTHMOSIS III

Not until after Hatshepsut's death, some 22 years into her step-son's long, 54-year reign, would Tuthmosis III be in a position to exercise independent power at last. As events were to show, he was a king cast in the same brilliant, militaristic mould as his grandfather; indeed, earlier historians – influenced, it has to be said, by over-modest estimates of the mummy's stature, a result of the feet having broken off prior to measurement – were tempted to compare him to Napoleon.

Pharaoh's first independent act, in emulation of the heroic Tuthmosis I, was to embark upon the long series of military campaigns – 17 in total – which, after three decades of inaction, would reaffirm Egyptian suzerainty in Palestine and Syria. The years of imperial inaction under Hatshepsut had allowed the kingdom of Mitanni to establish its own sphere of influence in these areas, and this was a threat which now had to be met – and was met, at Megiddo. Here, Tuthmosis III roundly defeated in battle a coalition of Syrian kinglets and seized a vast booty which included some 924 chariots. He did not stop there, but pushed on, in subsequent campaigns, deep into the Mitannian heartland.

But there was surely more to pharaoh's drive for foreign conquests than mere plunder – as there may previously have been in the case of Tuthmosis I also, scion of a lesser family elevated unexpectedly to the throne and anxious to make his mark. Now, it seems, after the humiliating diminution of royal influence under Hatshepsut, Tuthmosis III was determined to regain lost ground by a reassertion of pharaonic power and kingly prestige; a similar message is perhaps to be discerned in the much-vaunted athletic prowess of Amenophis II, his son and successor. With the same aim, the emphasis of the reliefs and inscriptions shifts markedly from this time on: Hatshepsut's dependence on Amun was now, under her successors, subtly reframed –

rather than Amun bestowing power on the king, it was, once again, pharaoh who would patronize Amun.

The most interesting – and significant – of Tuthmosis III's changes, however, would be the increased public emphasis placed by pharaoh on the existence and number of his male offspring, coupled with an evident reluctance on the part of the king to promote any of his consorts to the status of great royal wife – the ritual duties of the office being carried out by the trusted king's mother. These measures, clearly intended to avoid a repetition of the Hatshepsut episode, were crucial and would be continued; the queen-pharaoh's successors were evidently nervous of the way royal power, during her 'reign', had slipped so effortlessly into the hands of others.

The final dynastic precaution was taken in Tuthmosis III's 51st regnal year, close to the end of his long reign, with the appointment of Amenophis II, his son, as co-regent. Only then, with the succession secured, did the old king feel sufficiently confident at home to unleash an attack on his hated step-mother's memory, at Deir el-Bahri and elsewhere – with the erasure of her cartouches, the destruction of her images and the smashing to rubble of her sculptures.

The 'Napoleonic' pharaoh Tuthmosis III (identified by the cartouched prenomen on his belt) – a fine, greywacke statue of the warrior king commissioned early in the reign, when Tuthmosis III shared the throne with his aunt, Hatshepsut. The sculpture was recovered from the Karnak cachette in 1904.

The baptism of pharaoh: Hatshepsut receives ablutions of 'life' from ritual vessels wielded by the gods Horus and Thoth in this scene at Karnak. The queen's pharaonic image and inscriptions were erased by Tuthmosis III towards the end of his reign, by which time the succession of his son, Amenophis II, was assured.

THE FRUITS OF EMPIRE

The Egyptian empire, especially in the north, seems constantly to have ebbed and flowed; such was the nature of things, as the pharaohs, content simply to have a buffer zone between them and the greater threat of Mitanni and later the Hittites, happily recognized. This northern region was maintained at as small a military cost as possible. In the conquered cities of Syria-Palestine, the king set up vassal rulers supported by native Egyptian garrisons of between 50 and 200 men; these vassals were bound by oath and by the removal to Egypt of their children, for 'Egyptianization' – and they paid for their continuing 'protection' by an imposed annual tribute. Nubia – Kush – gateway to Africa, was regarded as an Egyptian colony. Less politically sophisticated than the northern vassals and requiring fewer concessions to local feelings, it was exploited directly for its vast gold reserves and other imported luxury goods by a brutal military administration under a native Egyptian viceroy answerable only to the king. For Egypt, the net result was a virtual monopoly of trade over much of the Near East – and the vast profits, thousands of slaves and immense prestige which accrued from it.

The martial reputation of Tuthmosis III's son and successor, Amenophis II, was scarcely less awesome than that of his father, and the benefits continued to pour across the borders into Egypt – as this list of the living plunder alone from Amenophis II's first Asiatic campaign in Year 7 of his reign illustrates:

'*maryannu* [chariot-warriors], 550; their wives, 240; Canaanites, 640; children of princes, 232; female children of princes, 323; female musicians of the princes of every land, 270, together with their instruments of silver and gold; total, 2,214. Horses, 820; chariots, 730, together with all their weapons of warfare.'

Nor was the yield from the south any less imposing, as this list of the tribute successfully levied, on a single occasion, by pharaoh's viceroy, Usersatet, reveals:

'Tally of those bearing ... tribute: those bearing silver: 200 men; those bearing gold: 150 men; those laden with carnelian: 200 men; those laden with ivory: 40 men; those laden with ebony: 1000 men; those laden with incense of southern foreign lands: 200 men; ... those bringing a live panther: 10 men; those bringing dogs: 20 men; those bringing long- and short-horned cattle: 200 men. Total of those bearing this tribute: 2,657.'

Much of this wealth, inevitably, found its way into the coffers of the Theban god. But, since Hatshepsut's *coup d'état*, Egypt's king was determined to prevent Karnak's rich and ambitious god from ever again straying into the political arena. The battle was long, and hard, equal to any pharaoh had fought abroad; and it began in earnest after Year 9 and the completion of Amenophis II's last campaign.

The differing tribute from south and north: two fragmentary wall paintings from the Theban tomb chapel of Sebekhotep (TT63), now in the British Museum. The Nubians' 'gifts' include gold rings, wood, animal skins and exotic animals, those of the Syrians elaborate vessels, a perfume horn and a child dancer(?).

Egypt's dazzling sun: red quartzite statue of Amenophis III from Luxor.

CHAPTER THREE

SOLAR KINGS

THE NEW PEACE

'Egypt had enlarged her outlook. Pharaoh was no longer god
king of an isolated realm, but must take his place among the
rest of the kings of the world…. But the spirit of conquest,
of crusade … had gone. The Egyptians were tired of war.
Henceforward they were content to keep what they had.'
JOHN PENDLEBURY

Amenophis II's successor was Tuthmosis IV, son of the lady Tiaa, a minor
wife of northern origin; the new king ascended the throne while still a
youth, and would rule for a period of eight years and possibly more. His
position within the hierarchy of royal princes is uncertain; since Amenophis II died without appointing a
co-regent, it is quite possible (and there are indeed
hints) that the actual transition of power was less
than smooth.

Whatever hiccups there may have been in the
mechanics of succession, the shift in royal
policy away from foreign affairs to matters
domestic which marked the latter years of his
father's reign was set to continue – as is indicated by the gradual phasing out of military
titles and the growth in the range and number
of administrative offices as the peace began to
take hold.

As at the start of all reigns, the first priority
of Tuthmosis IV was to secure the loyalty
of his distant dominions. Despite the
propaganda, however, the new pharaoh's
military achievements appear to have been
notional, amounting to little more than a tour
of his Syrian possessions. The days of active

*King Tuthmosis IV seated beside his mother – newly
designated 'great royal wife' – in a diorite sculpture
discovered by French Egyptologist Georges Legrain
at Karnak.*

conquest were now over; stability would henceforth be guaranteed by the occasional, limited military foray and, increasingly, by diplomatic means.

It was a strategy in which Amenophis II had again already led the way, by the securing of a negotiated peace with the Hittites; this had followed the cessation of campaigning in his ninth regnal year, in a tacit acknowledgment of Egypt's inability to colonize successfully so far from home. Tuthmosis IV was similarly wary of growing Hittite power, and to forestall the plundering of Egypt's possessions he signed a treaty of peace with Artatama I, king of Mitanni, by which the two rulers hoped, and indeed for some years managed, to contain the Hittite threat. This peace is referred to in one of the Amarna letters (EA 29), and was sealed by the gift to the Egyptian king of a Mitannian princess – the first of several foreign ladies who would, over the next few years, be sent to grace the Egyptian court and pharaoh's bed.

TROUBLESOME PRIESTS

The lengthy absences abroad of previous kings and their troops may have proved something of a mixed blessing: for, despite the propaganda of official texts promoting the king's superhuman nature, and for all pharaoh's much-vaunted prowess on the field of battle, there are hints that his authority at home was in practice circumscribed, and under continuing pressure from petty rivalries within and without the governing structure of the country. The general peace engineered by Tuthmosis IV and his advisers was not only an intelligent one, therefore, but opportune. With pharaoh's attentions focused firmly on the domestic scene, attempts to counter the damage done to kingly authority by Hatshepsut's blasphemous interregnum could continue – and with a vengeance.

Pharaoh was aided in his day-to-day running of the Egyptian state by a cabinet of ministers and other advisers. Foremost among these advisers were the two viziers, one for the north and one for the south, who were supported in turn by a range of executive officers, including various treasury administrators, officials charged with the oversight of the king's crops and cattle, and of course officers of the military; most notable of these was the king's son of Kush, whose successes had so enriched the country. Several of these individuals will have been related to the king in a minor fashion, with their sisters or daughters inducted into the royal harem, or else have been schooled with him. Their loyalty was at least hoped for, if not assumed.

The same could not be said for the priests of ancient Egypt, particularly those of Amun, 'the hidden one', god of Karnak, and his various borrowed manifestations. The god's rise to prominence had begun during the Middle Kingdom, and, as we have seen, with the resurgence of Theban power following the expulsion of the Hyksos, his star was very much in the ascendant. Victory against the Asiatic infiltrators and the subsequent expansion northwards of Egyptian power and influence had been officially credited to Amun's divine intervention and support, and, from this open acknowledg-

Head from a statuette of Amun, wearing his characteristic flat-topped crown with its tall double plumes – a rare, early image of the Theban god. The powerfully modelled facial features are those of Ammenemes III of the 12th Dynasty, during whose reign the sculpture was commissioned.

ment of the deity's power, he and his followers had reaped the benefits in full. Karnak was set to grow beyond all recognition, both physically (with the erection of extensive temple precincts, obelisks and statues) and in temporal power and prestige. Amun's temple, serviced by vast agricultural estates, administered by an immense bureaucracy and controlling numberless serfs and slaves, gradually grew in influence to take in shipping, manufacturing, mining and other worldly concerns. The Egyptian king's constant battle was to hold the influence of Amun's troublesome priests – now controlling a virtual state within a state – firmly in check. But it was very much an uphill struggle – and it would ultimately fail.

Amun, though some hundreds of years from his ultimate glory, was moving rapidly towards achieving the status of Egypt's principal god, with the cults of other deities falling one by one, and ever more swiftly, under his all-controlling sway. The byzantine political manoeuvrings of the high priest Hapuseneb and his cronies, which had resulted in the elevation of Hatshepsut to supreme power, nevertheless marked a peak in the god's 18th-Dynasty influence. Amun's support of the woman pharaoh had been a sorry miscalculation – a political meddling which the heirs of Tuthmosis III were not readily to forgive or forget.

RE AND AMUN

For all its success, the Amun priesthood seems not to have enjoyed a wholly clear run in its drive to achieve domination within the country. The god's principal rival in the religious power stakes at this time was the ancient cult of the sun god Re at Heliopolis, the influence and antiquity of which the southerners had 'acknowledged' (i.e. attempted to harness) by the adoption for their god of a composite name-form, 'Amun-Re' – the solar manifestation in which the god of Karnak was increasingly celebrated. This Theban conflation of the country's two principal divinities dated back to the heady days of the Middle Kingdom, and was perhaps inspired as much by political as by religious considerations, seeking to unite the two ancient and rival tribes of Upper and Lower Egypt under a single banner. The Heliopolitan priests, for their part, had countered with a rival theology which assimilated all other gods with Re. There is little reason to believe that either view did much to bridge the age-old north–south divide; indeed, each probably only exacerbated it.

Certainly, the royal family itself was not free from regional prejudice: composed of members from north, south and all points in between, geographical origins will inevitably have had a bearing on politico-religious sympathies. Following Amun's support of Hatshepsut and effective suppression of Tuthmosis III, the dialogue between king and Amun was severely strained; and with the accession of Tuthmosis IV, a northern king, tensions with the southern god were set to increase.

THE DREAM STELA

The son of Amenophis II by Tiaa, a northern queen, Tuthmosis IV's sympathies had been decided in the womb. The earliest evidence of these may be detected in one of Egypt's most famous historical documents – the 'Dream Stela', a monumental inscription erected by Tuthmosis IV between the paws of the Great Sphinx at Giza.

This text recounts how pharaoh, while still 'a puppy', had been chosen to succeed his father not by Amun but by the god at that time regarded as immanent within the Sphinx – Harmachis, 'Horus in the horizon'. The relevant portion of the stela reads as follows:

> 'One of these days it happened that prince Tuthmosis came
> travelling at the time of midday. He rested in the shadow of this
> great god [the Giza Sphinx]. Sleep and dream took possession of
> him at the moment the sun was at its zenith. Then he found the
> majesty of this noble god speaking from his own mouth like a
> father speaks to his son, saying: "Look at me, observe me, my son
> Tuthmosis. I am your father Harmachis-Khepri-Re-Atum. I shall
> give to you the kingship upon the land before the living. You
> shall wear its white crown and its red crown upon the throne of
> Geb, the heir. The land in its length and breadth will be yours,
> and everything which the eye of the lord-of-all illuminates.
> Good provisions will be for you from within the Two Lands, and
> the great produce of every country, and a lifetime great in years.
> My face belongs to you; my heart belongs to you, and you
> belong to me. [But] behold, my condition is like one in illness, all
> my limbs being ruined. The sand of the desert, upon which I
> used to be, faces me aggressively; and it is in order to make you
> do what is in my heart that I have waited. For I know that you are
> my son and my protector ..."'

The tone of this inscription has led many Egyptologists to conclude – and they are surely correct – that Tuthmosis IV's elevation owed less to the law of primogeniture than to political connivance; that the Dream Stela in fact represents the confirmation by oracle of a disputed succession – the same technique which had been employed to legitimize the reigns of Tuthmosis

Monumental stela of Tuthmosis IV, set up between the paws of the Great Sphinx at Giza following the god's appearance to the king in a dream: 'I am your father Harmachis-Khepri-Re-Atum. I shall give to you the kingship upon the land before the living.... For I know that you are my son and my protector'.

III and Hatshepsut years before. Certainly, Tuthmosis (IV) had not been the only candidate for the kingship – Amenophis II, as we know, had left several sons from which to choose, and in the absence of a formal chief-queen – the threat of another Hatshepsut had held back both Tuthmosis III and Amenophis II from appointing any of their wives to this office – the precise ranking of these princes may have been somewhat uncertain.

What the Dream Stela further reveals, and clearly, is the identity of the future king's sponsors. In promoting pharaoh as the offspring of Atum, creator of the universe, appointed by Harmachis (a god who, with his growing assimilation to Horakhty, was now raised to the ranks of a major solar divinity in his own right), we have an apparent acknowledgment that the guiding hand behind Tuthmosis IV's candidacy was the Heliopolitan priesthood. Nor is this emphasis simply a matter of a northern monument reflecting the influence of a northern god, as the stela dedicated on this same site by Amenophis II demonstrates. In the monument erected at the Sphinx by Tuthmosis IV's father, the earlier king's descent from six gods is acknowledged, with a clear affirmation of the omnipotence of Amun of Thebes. Here, in the Dream Stela of Tuthmosis IV, Amun does not even rate a mention.

In this text we detect fundamental change. With the accession of Tuthmosis IV, it is the priests of Heliopolis who are in the ascendant, and the Theban Amun to whom lip-service is now paid. Close scrutiny of the titles and careers of the officials active during the reigns of Tuthmosis IV and Amenophis III confirms this conclusion: no longer are the state's key administrative posts held by members of the Amun priesthood; they have gone to more dependable subjects, including the viceroy of Nubia and other members of the military – and, more significantly, to men of northern stock.

PROMOTING THE SOLAR CREED

During the Old Kingdom, a millennium and a half before the New Kingdom, the divinity of the king had been an accepted reality, and his position within the proper order of things unassailable; in the interim, royal fallibility had been so frequently demonstrated that the image was now somewhat tarnished. The Hatshepsut episode, an outcome of ambitious priests meddling in the affairs of state, had done nothing to restore the shine.

Certain sections of Egyptian society with a vested interest in the realignment of temporal power evidently wished to set back the clock. Among their number were key, unnamed figures within the Heliopolitan priesthood. Anxious to re-establish the monarchy on a sounder theological footing, their goal was a return to the values of this purer past, when the king's godlike status was unchallenged and the principal power in the heavens was Re – the solar deity who had inspired the building of the pyramids, Egypt's greatest triumph. These were aspirations with which no ruler, anxious that control might be slipping slowly but surely from his grasp, could fail to concur.

The accession of Tuthmosis IV was a decisive moment, heralding a discernible increase of kingly interest in the solar cult – particularly at Giza, as we have seen, as well as at Re's cult centre, Heliopolis itself. Even in the south, at Karnak, the king's personal devotion to the sun god was marked by the erection of an immense obelisk (now standing in front of the church of St John Lateran in Rome), first quarried by Tuthmosis III but left unfinished for several decades. The Heliopolitan influence, however, is most clearly revealed in Tuthmosis IV's personal identification with the sun god: for the first time, we see pharaoh wearing in life the distinctive beaded *shebyu*-collar

Openwork wrist-ornament cut from a length of elephant tusk. Tuthmosis IV – wearing the short, 'Nubian' wig surmounted by a solar disc – despatches an Asiatic captive with his khepesh-*scimitar before the war-god Montu.*

and armlets of gold previously found only in a funerary context, and occasionally (as on an ivory wrist-ornament found by the Germans at el-Amarna) displaying on his head the disc emblematic of the sun god.

The most significant development of all, however, was the emphasis placed, from this time on, on a 'new' and highly honoured solar manifestation – the Aten. The Aten was not originally a god in its own right, but Re's most sentient aspect, the sun god's 'visible body' or light-energy. Occasionally, from as early as the reign of Amenophis II, this 'force' would appear as a disc sprouting a pair of arms, and consistently, following the accession of Amenophis IV-Akhenaten, the representation would be one of radiating beams terminating in hands presenting the sign of 'life' to the noses of the king and his family – and to them alone.

THE ATEN SCARAB

One important document relating to this new solar aspect, and an early, explicit reference to the Aten as an independent manifestation of solar divinity, is a large scarab, or beetle-form amulet, now in the British Museum. Scarabs were among the most popular of Egyptian protective charms, and possessed a powerful solar imagery in their own right: the beetle laid its eggs in a ball of dung, which it rolled along the ground with its legs in a motion reminiscent of the sun's journey through the sky; when the eggs hatched, new life was seen to spring forth from seemingly dead matter, completing the metaphor.

Large scarab of Tuthmosis IV inscribed with eight columns of hieroglyphic text celebrating the reception of Mitannian tribute – or even the arrival at court of a princess of that country. The last sentence alludes to foreigners being 'subjects to the rule of Aten forever'.

The text of the British Museum's scarab, arranged in vertical columns on the flat base, translates as follows:

> The princes of Naharin [Mitanni], bearing their gifts, behold
> Menkheprure [Tuthmosis IV] as he comes forth from his palace.
> They hear his voice like that of the son of Nut, his bow in his
> hand like the son of the successor of Shu. If he arouses himself
> to fight, with Aten before him, he destroys the mountain
> countries, trampling the desert countries, treading as far as
> Naharin and Karoy, in order to make the inhabitants of foreign
> lands like subjects to the rule of Aten forever.'

The authenticity of this text has been challenged on several occasions; despite its textual peculiarities, however, there seems little doubt that it is an ancient piece, with no evidence of recutting. It stands as an intriguing antecedent to the so-called 'commemorative scarabs' issued in several series both by Amenophis III and later by his son, Amenophis IV-Akhenaten, for presentation, we may assume, to favoured courtiers and as a means of publicizing specific events of the reign. Although the inscription probably commemorates the reception of Mitannian tribute in consequence of Tuthmosis IV's 'campaign' in the northern regions of his empire early in the reign, it may also mark the arrival at court of a princess of that country. Its real significance for us lies in the international context in which we find the name of the newly independent Aten for the first time invoked. During the reign to come, such mentions of the solar disc would increase in number and significance, both as a fully fledged god in the tomb of the architects Suty and Hor, and, more significantly, as a manifestation of the living king.

ATEN AS THE UNIVERSAL GOD

With the immense influx of slaves, merchants and foreigners of more elevated status as the 18th Dynasty progressed, Egypt had become an exceptionally cosmopolitan place; the innate suspicion of foreigners, heightened by the Hyksos experience 150 years and more previously, was gradually beginning to break down. In time, this influx of population intermarried with its hosts, and they, and their offspring, began to scale the ladders of integration and success – so much so that one of their number, Aper-el, under Amenophis III/Amenophis IV-Akhenaten would rise to the dizzy and unprecedented heights of northern vizier. Influences mingled – cultural, artistic and linguistic – with foreign cults such as those of Baal, Astarte and Reshep finding ready acceptance.

The official divinity of Egypt's empire remained Amun-Re, self-styled king of the gods, the composite deity representing the principal cultic traditions of both the south and north of the country; but his prominence was beginning to slip in the face of Heliopolitan revival. Amun and Re both were purely Egyptian manifestations of divinity, however, leaving the way open, in these newly international times, to a less partisan godhead. With the growing popularity of solar worship, the Aten begins to make an increasing contribution to this dialogue: a universal symbol, visible in all countries, it was evidently regarded as a particularly appropriate manifestation of imperial power – the solar manifestation with which pharaoh, in death, traditionally became one. And to promote the Aten as the empire's new, universal god, albeit tentatively, was to promote the status of kingship itself.

DEATH, BURIAL AND THE ACCESSION OF AMENOPHIS III

Tuthmosis IV died unexpectedly, long before he could celebrate his first *sed*-festival, or 30-year jubilee, and before, it is generally believed, the heir was of an age to be promoted as co-regent (but see below). Tuthmosis IV's skilful manoeuvrings had assured his son the inheritance of a 'great king': a land rich beyond compare, politically and administratively stable, and with borders stretching from Syria in the north to the fourth cataract of the Nile and beyond in the south.

The name of the successor was Amenophis (III), and he was the king's eldest surviving male offspring by a minor wife called Mutemwiya; like Tiaa before her, Mutemwiya seems not to have achieved the status of 'great royal wife' until the accession of her son. The young prince is shown as a child with his tutor, Heqaerneheh, in a well-known scene in the man's Theban tomb (TT64). (Heqaerneheh's father, Heqareshu, had himself been tutor to Amenophis III's own father, Tuthmosis IV.)

The tomb in which Amenophis III laid his father to rest was appropriately large and impressive, as Howard Carter, in his new role as Inspector in Chief of Antiquities for Upper Egypt, discovered when he located its entrance in 1903. That tomb is now numbered KV43 in the Valley of the Kings roster. Sparsely decorated, but large and well-cut, Carter found its parts strewn still with the broken remnants of pharaoh's original burial equipment. Blue faience *shabti*-figures (worker models for the Beyond) and amulets littered the ground of the burial chamber and its four subsidiary store chambers, together with statues of divinities carved in wood and liberally coated in black resin, wooden boxes and fragments of furniture, textiles, and vessels of faience, glass and hard stone. Notable among the king's military accoutrements was the body of an elaborately decorated wooden chariot. According to a graffito written in ink on one wall of the anteroom before the burial chamber, the king's burial had had to be restored during the reign of a later king, Horemheb, the work being carried out by two individuals – the treasurer Maya and his assistant Thutmose – of whose activities Carter would later find further traces in the tomb of Tutankhamun.

By the time of Carter's entry, the mummy of Tuthmosis IV himself was long gone: having survived the robbers, it was transferred to a new place of

Pharaoh Amenophis III, 'the Magnificent', Akhenaten's father: a fragmentary limestone relief from the tomb of the king's scribe Khaemhat, called Mahu, at Thebes (TT57). The king wears the shebyu-collar of massive gold beads, indicative of his solar divinity.

refuge at the end of the New Kingdom. Stripped of its jewels, rewrapped and roughly recoffined, the corpse eventually turned up in 1898 in the tomb of Amenophis II (KV35), the so-called 'second cache', which had been pressed into service as a hiding place for several of the displaced royal dead.

The interment of a king was a sombre and time-consuming affair, a mysterious and ritually vulnerable occasion of earthly and spiritual transition. It followed the traditional 70 days of the mummification ceremonies, during which the complex paraphernalia of the funerary ritual were prepared and set in place within the tomb in readiness for the crucial moment of departure from this world to the next. What happened to the equipment after this ceremony seems to have been a matter of little import, as the subsequent history of the Valley tombs would show: the machinery had served its purpose and sent the god on his way. With the reading of the final rituals and the heir's act of 'opening the mouth' of the Osiris-king with the ritualistic adze, the young successor, Amenophis III, could now assume the throne formally in his father's stead.

THE DIVINE BIRTH

The early years of Amenophis III's reign saw the Tuthmosid tradition of pharaoh as a superhuman warrior-athlete continue. 'But soon', as Pendlebury observes, 'the sloth which overtakes the Oriental who is born to the purple overcame him.' Henceforth – or, as the king might have put it, in these more sophisticated times – a greater emphasis would be placed upon pharaoh's superhuman link with the gods, and increasingly his oneness with the supreme creator, the solar divinity Re.

Despite the continued growth of Heliopolitan influence, however, the theological basis of Amenophis III's kingship, as recorded (in a manner comparable with that of Hatshepsut) in a series of reliefs on the walls of Luxor temple, was as divine child of Amun. These reliefs record how the royal mother Mutemwiya had been visited at night by the divinity and the future king conceived. The accompanying texts detail this meeting:

> 'When he had transformed himself into the majesty of this husband, the king of Upper and Lower Egypt Menkheprure [Tuthmosis IV], who gives life, he found her [Mutemwiya] as she was resting in the beauty of her palace. She awoke on account of the aroma of the god and cried out in front of his majesty. He went to her straightaway ... and caused her to see him in the form of a god.... She rejoiced at the sight of his beauty, and love of him coursed through her limbs. The palace was flooded with the god's aroma; all his fragrances were of Punt.
>
> Words spoken by Mutemwiya before the majesty of this august god, Amun-Re, lord of the thrones of the Two Lands: "How great is your power! ... Your dew permeates all my limbs." And then the majesty of this god did all that he desired with her.
>
> Words spoken by Amun-Re, lord of the thrones of the Two Lands, before her: "Amenophis-ruler of Thebes is the name of this child that I have placed in your body.... He shall exercise the beneficent kingship in this whole land.... He shall rule the Two Lands like Re forever."'

Why this renewed emphasis on Amun, given what we have discerned as a deliberate distancing from the Karnak cult by Amenophis III's predecessors? Perhaps, simply put, times had changed. Amun's political ambitions had been curbed: no longer did its priesthood claim the status of 'overseer of priests of Upper and Lower Egypt' or other key titles within the administration of the Egyptian state; while the king's own man, a northerner and sometime vizier of the south, Ptahmose, now held in check the temple of Amun as its high priest. The acknowledgment of Amun's paternity was something from which the prestige of the king, as much as the god, could be seen to benefit. Moreover, the cosmological theorizing of the day had recognized Thebes as the centre of the Egyptian universe; as important as its god, clearly, was the place itself.

THE MARRIAGE SCARAB

The situation following the death of Tuthmosis IV must have paralleled that both at the death of this king's own father and at the later elevation of Tutankhaten (Tutankhamun): since pharaoh was still a child, the reins of power will have rested in the hands of others. Quite who these controlling influences were is nowhere explicitly stated – but there are hints. Two, evidently, were the child-king's father- and mother-in-law.

A notable feature of the reign of Amenophis III was the issue of a series of large commemorative scarabs similar to that previously published by Tuthmosis IV to celebrate his Syrian 'triumph'. Evidently carved in more than one workshop, these were most probably put out on the dates they carry – though some Egyptologists argue that they were issued simultaneously after Year 11 of the reign to commemorate at one go the achievements of the king's first decade. As we learn from the first of these documents, by Year 2 of his reign the young Amenophis III had taken as great royal wife a girl of non-royal birth: Tiye, the daughter of a man named Yuya and the lady Tjuyu, whose principal estates were situated in Akhmim, 160 km (100 miles) to the north of Thebes.

The proclamation of this alliance was unprecedented, yet seems never to have attracted from Egyptologists the attention it merits. The text reads as follows:

> 'Living Horus, Strong bull appearing in Truth; he of the Two
> Ladies, Establishing laws, pacifying the Two Lands; Golden
> Falcon, Great of valour, who smites the Asiatics; King of Upper
> and Lower Egypt, Nebmaatre; son of Re, Amenophis – ruler of
> Thebes, who gives life; and the great royal wife Tiye, may she
> live. The name of her father is Yuya, the name of her mother
> Tjuyu. She is the wife of a mighty king whose southern
> boundary is at Karoy, whose northern at Naharin.'

As the issue of this, the so-called 'Marriage Scarab', reveals, by their mention Yuya and Tjuyu can have been no ordinary commoners, but individuals of

Large and well-preserved scarab of blue-glazed steatite. The base is inscribed with ten lines of hieroglyphic inscription publicizing the existence of Tiye, Amenophis III's principal consort. Surprisingly, Tiye's parents, Yuya and Tjuyu, are also mentioned – a reflection of that couple's enormous influence at court.

immense influence in Egypt at this time; and we may assume that it was in the interest of the child-king's supporters to acknowledge the couple's backing for the new regime in the most public manner possible. This conclusion finds confirmation in the fact that, in another issue of scarabs publicizing the king's marriage to the Mitannian princess Gilukhepa in Year 10, Tiye's parentage is once more, and quite gratuitously, emphasized. Whatever secondary wives the king might choose to take in, the text implies, the influence of Tiye and her family remained undiminished.

THE TOMB OF YUYA AND TJUYU

As was long ago suggested by the German scholar Hans Wolfgang Helck, the neutralization of the Egyptian priesthood was achieved at least in part by the increasing favour shown by the king towards certain elements within the military – a sector of society who, we may guess, were similarly uneasy about priestly ambitions. One of the military's key players, we now recognize, was Yuya. Before 1905, scholars knew little more about pharaoh's father-in-law beyond the bald statements conveyed by the two scarab texts mentioned above. And then, in February of that year, the American excavator Theodore M. Davis by chance uncovered the tomb of the man and his wife during the course of his digging in the Valley of the Kings. It was an extraordinary find, as the Egyptologist and Egyptian government representative Arthur Weigall recorded in a letter home to his wife:

> 'For some moments we couldn't see anything much, but as our eyes got used to the candle light we saw a sight which I can safely say no living man has ever seen. The chamber was pretty large – a rough hewn cavern of a place. In the middle of the room were two enormous sarcophagi of wood inlaid with gold. The lids had been wrenched off by the plunderers [in antiquity] and the coffins inside had been tumbled about so that the two mummies were exposed.... All round the sarcophagi – piled almost to the roof – were chairs, table, beds, vases, and so on – all in perfect condition.... In one corner a large chariot – quite perfect – as clean as a London hansom – lay; and by it a huge bedstead of inlaid wood something like Chippendale. Here, there was a group of lovely painted vases – here a pile of gold and silver figures. In one corner were some jars of wine, the lids tied on with string; and among them was one huge alabaster jug full of honey still liquid.... The room looked just as a drawing room would look in a London house shut up while the people were away for the summer. But with this terrifying difference – that everything was in the fashion of 34 centuries ago....
>
> [Gaston] Maspero, Davis and I stood there gaping and almost

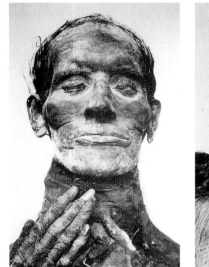

The extraordinary mummified faces of Yuya (left) and Tjuyu (right), parents of Tiye, Aanen and probably Ay, and influential father- and mother-in-law respectively of pharaoh Amenophis III, from their richly provisioned tomb (KV46) in the Valley of the Kings, discovered by Theodore M. Davis in 1905.

trembling for a time – and I think we all felt we were face to face with something which upset all human ideas of time and distance. Then we dashed for the inscribed objects and read out the names of Prince Auai [Yuya] and his wife Thuaie [Tjuyu] – the famous mother and father of Queen Tiy [Tiye]. They had been known so well and discussed so often that they seemed old friends.… But nobody had expected to see them as we looked at the mummies … [Tjuyu] with her hair still plaited and elaborately dressed, and … [Yuya] with his eyes peacefully closed and his mouth a little open.'

This tomb, now numbered KV46, was the most spectacular discovery made in the Valley of the Kings before Tutankhamun, having escaped with little more than a superficial plundering: it had been entered, three millennia previously, by workmen quarrying the adjacent tomb KV3 for a princely son of Ramesses III. The Ramessid intruders had naturally robbed their find, surreptitiously carrying off metals, precious and other-wise, as well as more mundane and easily negotiable items such as blankets and sheets; the possibility of removing the dead couple's perfumes and oils had also been entertained – the oil-jar lids had been roughly torn away – but abandoned when it was discovered that the contents had become rancid.

Despite these thefts, the treasures the plunderers had left behind were spectacular and, in the days before Tutankhamun so unrealistically inflated the world's archaeological expectations, provided an extraordinary and unexpected glimpse into the glory and sophistication of 18th-Dynasty court life. And, as icing on the proverbial cake, the occupants of the tomb, Yuya and Tjuyu, proved to be two of the finest mummies ever found.

THE ROYAL IN-LAWS

One intriguing feature of the burial discovered by Davis's team is the plethora of variant spellings of Yuya's name, a feature commonly taken to reflect the bearer's foreign origin, an interpretation seen by some to be supported by the mummy's striking features – of which more later. Given the family's close connections with the Middle Egyptian town of Akhmim, however, where Yuya's supposed father, Yey, held similar office, it seems improbable that the man was not a native Egyptian – though the family might conceivably have been of foreign ancestry. Yuya's principal title was 'father of the god', an intriguing designation of uncertain meaning borne by several high officials during the 18th Dynasty. In the case of Yuya, it can of course be construed literally, since he was the actual father-in-law of the king; for others, however, including Yey, it is difficult to demonstrate that the bearer, by virtue of his age or appointment (e.g. as royal tutor or adviser), enjoyed anything more than a father-like relationship with pharaoh.

Yuya's remaining titles fall into two groups: those reflecting sacerdotal obligations in his home town – 'priest of Min' and 'overseer of the cattle of Min, lord of Akhmim'; and those indicating his executive role at court – 'master of horse' and 'his majesty's lieutenant-commander of chariotry' – which titles have occasionally been cited as further indicators of Yuya's origins as a high-ranking Syrian *maryannu* (chariot warrior). Tjuyu's titles were 'king's mother of the great royal wife', 'lady of the harem of Min' and 'chief of the entertainers of Min', 'songstress of Amun' and 'chief of the entertainers of Amun', as well as 'songstress of Hathor'. In contrast with that of her husband, the appearance of Tjuyu's mummy is said to be wholly Egyptian.

Yuya and Tjuyu had other children besides Tiye, including a son, Aanen, whose filiation is mentioned twice on his mother's coffins. Aanen held important office as high priest of Re at Thebes, as the inscription on a large and impressive statue in priestly garb (perhaps originally from Amenophis III's mortuary temple at Kom el-Hetan) records:

> 'The hereditary noble and mayor, seal-bearer of the king of Lower Egypt, who may approach his lord, one great of love in the king's house, enduring of favours in the

Exquisitely carved shabti-*figure of wood, from Theodore Davis's 1905 find – a magical image intended to undertake agricultural work in the Beyond, if called, on Yuya's behalf.*

palace, the god's father, one pure of hands, the lector priest who knows the procession of the sky, chief of sightings in the great house, the *sem*-priest in Southern Heliopolis [Thebes], who gives offerings at their proper stations, who propitiates the gods with his voice, the second prophet of Amun, Aanen.'

Aanen's contribution to ensuing events is unclear, but probably significant; sadly, we are at present able to gather little information on this or any other historical matter from his only other notable monument, the wrecked Theban tomb (TT120) which, in death, was intended as his eternal home.

Most important of all, however, was the man assumed to be the third off-spring of Yuya and Tjuyu, the military officer Ay. He, like Aanen, would inherit Yuya's principal title, 'god's father', and – as events would show – every ounce of his political influence as well.

ALL THE KING'S WIVES

'Say to the king, my lord, my god, my Sun: Message of Shatiya, the ruler of Enishasi, your servant, the dirt under the feet of the king, my lord ... I herewith send my daughter to the palace, to the king, my lord, my god, my Sun.'

The mummies of Yuya and Tjuyu are not the only human remains to have come down to us from the reign of Amenophis III. The mummy of pharaoh himself also survives; like that of Tuthmosis IV, it was recovered from the 'second cache' in the tomb of Amenophis II (KV35) in 1898, though in a sorry physical condition – broken, rewrapped and placed in a new, modest coffin, and docketed in the course of several moves from hiding place to hiding place. Death, for Amenophis III, was far from becoming. The king's women – of whom, in life, there were many – would hardly have recognized him.

The body of Tiye, the daughter of Yuya and Tjuyu and Amenophis III's principal wife, has similarly been identified among the corpses of the second royal cache, in the guise of the striking, almost beautiful mummy of the 'Elder Lady'. The basis

The mummy of the so-called 'Elder Lady', discovered in one of the side-chambers of the tomb of Amenophis II in 1898. It has been suggested (on the basis of skull shape and hair analysis) that this striking corpse may be the mummy of Tiye herself – an attractive theory, but not all scholars are convinced.

Queen Tiye in later life: a small and exquisitely carved wooden head found at Kom Medinet Ghurab. The form of the headdress was altered in antiquity, perhaps to reflect a change in the queen's status following Amenophis III's death: a double Hathor plume with horned disc was added, and the original silver khat-*headdress covered with bead-embellished gessoed linen.*

for the identification, by a team led by American orthodontist and mummy specialist James E. Harris, was an examination of the corpse's skull, which proves to be similar in form to that of Tjuyu, and a comparison between its still-flowing, red locks and a sample from the package of Tiye's hair which had accompanied Tutankhamun to the grave. It is an equation which has since been challenged, but further scientific analysis will perhaps at some future date clarify the matter.

Tiye's status throughout her husband's reign was unassailable, and she would continue to be celebrated after Amenophis III's death during the first decade and more of the reign of her son, Amenophis IV-Akhenaten. For the first time in Egyptian history, the queen's name forms an integral part of the royal titulary – setting a significant precedent for the future: whenever Amenophis III is mentioned, Tiye is invariably mentioned also, even on the most minor of objects, including the faience *kohl*-tubes scattered like confetti to an adoring populace along with other cheap and cheerful items on festal occasions. And, like Amenophis III himself, the queen was the object of worship in her own right – most notably as the solar goddess Hathor, the king's divine partner, but occasionally in other guises also.

In emphasizing Tiye's position to this extraordinary degree, the 'party' of Amenophis III clearly had an aim in view: to promote the divine status of the royal family as an entity, if in a more discreet manner than the king's successor would choose to do. Yet it was a policy which reversed that assiduously pursued since Hatshepsut's disastrous usurpation of power. Why the change? As so often in ancient Egypt, there is far more going on than we can fully discern; but, given Amenophis III's youth and the likely beneficiaries of this new tack, the influence of Yuya and his family might reasonably be assumed.

Despite her power, Tiye appears not to have interfered with Amenophis III's evident fondness for female flesh (we know nothing of his taste, if any, in men) – for the king had several other, lesser consorts also. A number of these are known from not infrequent mentions in the official texts of the reign – including his daughters Sitamun and Isis, who functioned as great royal wife and royal wife respectively late in the reign. There were also, of course, several foreign princesses, a number of whom are referred to in the international diplomatic correspondence: a sister and a daughter of Kadashman-Enlil, king of Babylon; the previously mentioned daughter of the Mitannian king Shuttarna II, Gilukhepa, who travelled to Egypt accompanied by 317 handmaidens; Tadukhepa, a daughter of Shuttarna II's successor, Tushratta, whose personal baggage included a further 270 women and 30 male servants, as well as a king's ransom in bullion and other gifts; and an unnamed daughter of Tarkhundaradu, king of Arzawa in western Anatolia. These ladies appear but briefly on history's stage and disappear almost at once (perhaps concealed behind a new Egyptian name), drawn for good into the twilight world of the royal harem.

The concerns of Kadashman-Enlil, king of Babylon, for the fate of one of these 'lost' women, his sister, are alluded to by pharaoh himself in one of the Amarna letters (EA 1):

> 'I have just heard what you wrote to me about, saying: "Here you are asking for my daughter in marriage, but my sister whom my father gave you is already there with you, and no one has seen her so as to know if she is alive or if she is dead." ... If your sister were dead, what reason would there be for one's concealing her passing ...?'

In fact, the extraordinary luxury and respect with which such foreign princesses were treated was revealed by a discovery made by Egyptian locals in 1916 among the Theban cliffs. This was an intact though greatly flood-damaged tomb belonging to three minor Syrian wives of pharaoh Tuthmosis III: Menhet, Menwi and Merti (the last, interestingly, an early version of the name 'Martha'). All three had been buried in grand style, with masses of gold and silver jewelry, and vessels, cosmetic objects and other trinkets fashioned in a variety of precious materials. If their pampering in death reflected the luxury they enjoyed in life, Kadashman-Enlil's concerns were indeed without foundation.

The king's women of course fulfilled a variety of formal, ritualistic roles, but another and hardly less important function was to attend to the king's sexual gratification – and of such matters we are privy to rather more than good taste would strictly require. Several of these royal concubines are known from a *shabti* and from a group of fragments of canopic jars which had been unceremoniously dumped following a late-New Kingdom clear-out of one or more tombs in the Theban necropolis; they were turned up by local diggers at the turn of the century, and the texts first published by the French Egyptologist Georges Legrain in 1903 and 1904. The jar inscriptions shed an extraordinary light on the breadth of pharaoh's sexual tastes and proclivities – as both John R. Harris (who has very kindly allowed me to refer to his readings here) and Canadian Egyptologist Nicholas Millet have independently perceived. Harris's work in particular reveals how, in several instances among these texts, the harem-member's specialist sexual characteristics or 'skills' are stated in the most explicit terms: they include a common-or-garden case of excessive sexual zeal (the lady Tawosret), sado-masochism (the lady Sati, 'called "Miss Whiplash"'), with perhaps a touch of lap-dancing thrown in by the lady Takhat as an apéritif.

Yet pharaoh still had energy for more:

> 'To Milkilu, the ruler of Gazru: Thus the king ... Send extremely beautiful female cupbearers in whom there is no defect ...'

THE ROYAL CHILDREN

Amenophis III's principal children – those borne by the great royal wife Tiye – were at least six in number: the princes Tuthmosis and Amenophis; and several princesses, Sitamun, Henuttaneb, Isis and the little known Nebetah. The old view that Tutankhamun might have been a son of the royal couple is nowadays generally rejected. A further princess, the mysterious Baketaten who first appears in the reign of Akhenaten, may well be Sitamun parading under a new, Amarna-style name; or, more ominously, a late child of Amenophis III by Sitamun, since father–daughter incest (as we shall consider), for all the taboos, seems to have been one of the extraordinary features of the period. There were doubtless other, lesser offspring also, born to the women in the king's harem.

Tuthmosis, the king's eldest son and heir to the throne, is best known from his activities in the north of the country, at Memphis, where he held the office of *sem*-priest and high priest of Ptah. In this role, memorialized in a Serapeum relief-sculpture, Tuthmosis assisted Amenophis III in the obsequies of the first Apis bull, the god Ptah's earthly manifestation. Other monuments include an image of the princely mummy lying on a bier, and a miniature sarcophagus, now in the Cairo Museum, which Tuthmosis prepared for the burial of his pet cat – endearingly (and perhaps, at this early date, with some originality) named 'Pussy'. As others have remarked, the prince receives such extraordinary emphasis that this may reflect equally unusual talents – though, if so, he would not be spared long enough to put them to full use.

The sole evidence at this time of Tuthmosis' younger brother is a wine-jar docket, found among the ruins of Malqata palace and mentioning 'the estate of the true(?) king's son, Amenophis'. From subsequent developments, prince Amenophis appears to have served his princely 'apprenticeship' in the

Heliopolitan religious tradition, rather than in that of Memphis like his elder brother. He was named as formal successor at some date following Tuthmosis' death – which occurred, we may guess, just before the celebration of Amenophis III's first *sed*-festival in regnal year 30, since the role of the heir at this ceremony was played by a stand-in – the high official, Amenhotep son of Hapu. Prince Tuthmosis' death was an unexpected, and cruel, turn of Fate: it had never been anticipated that Amenophis (IV) would rule – and, for Egypt, it might have been very much better if he never had.

FOREIGN AFFAIRS

The reign of Amenophis III was characterized by an almost total absence of foreign conflict: now that the 'empire' was essentially stable and secure, beyond the occasional, staged bull- and lion-hunt (as recorded on two of the king's commemorative scarab series) and a minor insurrection in Nubia, there was little opportunity for pharaoh to demonstrate his physical prowess. As during the reign of his father, the principal arena for international posturing would be the diplomatic.

Amenophis III's foreign contacts were extremely wide-ranging, taking in the independent kingdoms of Babylon, Mitanni and Hatti, as well as the minor Syrian city-states; they also extended far into the Mediterranean itself – to Alashiya (ancient Cyprus), the principal source of much of the ancient world's copper, and beyond. While for the former group of contacts the evidence is primarily documentary – the Amarna letters – knowledge of the interaction between Egypt and the Mediterranean world at this period is for the most part archaeological. Of particular interest is a statue base uncovered in the ruins of Amenophis III's mortuary temple at Kom el-Hetan, inscribed with a series of 14 'name rings' which are clearly recognizable as Aegean toponyms. These names – including Phaistos, Mycenae, Ilios (Troy) and Knossos – have speculatively been identified as the itinerary of a diplomatic mission dispatched by the Egyptian king to further trade, with a series of large, blue faience plaques from Mycenae bearing Amenophis III's name mustered in support of the theory. Perhaps; but it seems altogether more likely that what the Kom el-Hetan base preserves is a simple statement of the *origins* of Amenophis III's Aegean 'tribute', conveyed on trading ships similar to that – dated by a gold scarab of Nefertiti – excavated over recent years and with extraordinary results by underwater archaeologist George Bass at Ulu Burun, off the Turkish coast.

THE AMARNA LETTERS

The Amarna letters, it will be recalled, were uncovered quite by chance by an Egyptian peasant woman digging among the ruins of this ancient city in 1887. Thanks to later excavation by Flinders Petrie and John Pendlebury, we now know their findspot to have been 'the house of correspondence of pharaoh, life! prosperity! health!' – the Egyptian foreign office. Though written in a non-Egyptian medium (on clay) in a foreign language and script (Akkadian cuneiform), recent analysis of the fabric of the tablets has suggested that a good proportion of the 380-plus texts were not originals, but copies actually prepared in Egypt, perhaps at Memphis, for internal circulation.

The archive as a whole opens around Year 30 of Amenophis III, continues through the reign of Amenophis IV-Akhenaten and closes at about the time the city was abandoned under Tutankhamun. The documents may be divided into two principal groups: the 'great king' correspondence, written directly between rulers during the last years of Amenophis III through to the first years of his successor; and (the bulk of the archive) the vassal letters – reports from the front by subject princelings, which document in exhaustive detail the shifting rivalries and petty disputes of the various local rulers of Syria-Palestine – most of these texts apparently somewhat later in date. In addition to the correspondence, the archive includes a handful of mythical texts, syllabaries and lexical texts. These will have been reference materials for the use of the Egyptian king's clerical staff, whose job it was, in this 'westernmost academy of the cuneiform world', to translate, copy and file letters received, and draft and file an appropriate response. For all its range and extent, however, it is obvious that the el-Amarna find represented no more than the discarded tip of a veritable iceberg of documentation which must once have existed and may still, in time, be turned up at the same site or elsewhere.

Because of their unusual nature, the Amarna letters were at first written off by scholars as fakes. As the assemblage passed from dealer to dealer, negative opinions on the antiquity of the lot began to mount up, and it was only when eventually shown to the colourful British Museum curator Ernest Alfred Wallis Budge (one of the few Egyptologists familiar with the strange cuneiform script) that their true significance was recognized – by which time a number, sadly, had already been lost to careless handling. Budge later recalled the moment of recognition in his memoirs:

E. A. Wallis Budge, seated behind his desk in the Department of Egyptian and Assyrian Antiquities at the British Museum. With his knowledge of the cuneiform script, Budge recognized at once the significance of the el-Amarna tablets, and secured for his institution as many as he was able.

'On the largest and best written ... I was able to make out the words
"A-na Ni-ib-mu-a-ri-ya," i.e., "To Nib-muariya [Amenophis III]", and
on another the words "[A]-na Ni-im-mu-ri-ya shar mâtu Mi-is-ri,"
i.e., "to Nimmuriya [Amenophis III], king of the land of Egypt".'

Budge 'felt certain that the tablets were both genuine and of very great historical importance'. It was the understatement of the decade: with the discovery of Amenophis III's mummy in 1898, pharaoh would be given a face and physical presence; now, to be going on with, archaeology had provided a voice and a personality.

THE WORKINGS OF INTERNATIONAL DIPLOMACY

'Say to Nimmuarea [Amenophis III], the king of Egypt, my
brother: thus Burra-Buriyash, the king of Karduniash [Babylonia],
your brother. For me all goes well. For you, your household, your
wives, your sons, your country, your magnates, your horses, your
chariots, may all go well.
    Just as previously you and my father were friendly to one
another, you and I should now be friendly to one another.
Between us, anything else whatsoever is not even to be
mentioned. Write to me for what you want from my country so
that it may be taken to you, and I will write to you for what I want
from your country so that it may be taken to me ...'

Reading the correspondence between pharaoh and his fellow kings is an eerie experience: gone are the bombastic phrases of glory and power familiar from the monuments, replaced by the wheedling negotiations and haggling of merchants – negotiations in which the desire for foreign female flesh, initiated by Tuthmosis IV and developed to a fine art by his son, played an important part. Significantly, however, the gift of women was a one-way trade: it was never reciprocated. As Amenophis III had loftily to remind one correspondent (probably Kadashman-Enlil of Babylon), eager for his own Egyptian princess: 'From time immemorial no daughter of the king of Egypt is given to anyone.' But gold was some consolation, as the reply from this same unnamed correspondent makes clear:

'As to the gold I wrote [to pharaoh] about: send me whatever is
on hand, as much as possible ... so I can finish the work I am
engaged on. If during this summer, in the months of Tammuz or
Ab, you send the gold I wrote to you about, I will give you *my*
daughter. So please send me the gold ...'

It was an unequal form of exchange, destined to continue, upon which pharaoh, still pre-eminent in international politics, poured undisguised scorn: 'It is a fine thing that you give your daughters in order to acquire a nugget of gold!' For gold was a commodity Egypt had in abundance; as Tushratta, king of Mitanni, and others were constantly to remark – here in a letter to Amenophis III – 'In Egypt, gold is more plentiful than dirt'.

BUILDING AND CONSTRUCTION

'It pleased his majesty's heart to make very great monuments, the likes of which never existed since the beginning of the Two Lands.' MORTUARY TEMPLE STELA OF AMENOPHIS III

In the absence of war, Amenophis III was able to devote his attention to making Egypt a worthy base for the richest and most powerful man in the world, a policy from which all the principal cities would benefit – but none more so than Thebes. Pharaoh had on his hands an abundant supply of craftsmen and administrators, and an ever-increasing surplus of funding. With these assets, Amenophis III determined to make Egypt's southern city outshine all others in glory and splendour as an appropriate reflection of his kingship. In this aim he largely succeeded, erecting here, in the chosen residence of his later reign, some of the most impressive monuments Egypt would ever see. The reason for this emphasis is suggested by the city's position at the literal centre of the greater Egyptian homeland (Egypt and Nubia): it was seen, by extension, as the very heart of the Egyptian universe – with all the ritualistic ramifications which that carried in its wake.

During the 37-year reign of Amenophis III, the face of Thebes was deliberately transformed from that of a provincial town to one enormous temple complex, principal stage for the enactment of the kingship, to vie in glory and prestige with Memphis, the ancient administrative capital of the country and its principal city throughout the dynastic period. Beyond Thebes, equally impressive individual structures were raised at sites including Memphis itself, Elkab, Letopolis, Hermopolis and Elephantine, as well as at Soleb, Sedeinga and Wadi el-Sebua in distant Nubia. The course charted by the king in his building programme, as characterized by Arielle Kozloff, was 'grand, original, and integrated', though subject to constant change, development and refinement, with monuments erected and dismantled without hesitation when appropriate or required.

The king's administrative base – planners, architects, scribes and artists – further expanded to accommodate the increased workload, and at its height perhaps even surpassed in numbers that employed for the grandiose architectural works of the Old Kingdom pyramid builders. In overall charge was the king's principal guide and mentor: the sometime vizier and 'scribe of recruits', Amenhotep son of Hapu – a man whose presence at court during Amenophis IV-Akhenaten's formative, princely years was to prove crucial to future developments in the realm.

KOM EL-HETAN: THE KING'S MORTUARY TEMPLE

Amenhotep son of Hapu is best known today for his achievement in the quarrying and transportation from Gebel el-Ahmar in the north of material for two monumental quartzite statues of the king, each over 21 m (69 ft) high when erected and weighing in excess of 700 tonnes. The roughed-out blocks were positioned at the entrance to pharaoh's Theban mortuary temple (Kom el-Hetan), where they were finally sculpted under the direction of Men, father to the sculptor Bek who would himself help formulate the distinctive Amarna art-style under Amenophis III's son and successor. Men's colossi were to stand as the focus of Amenophis III's new Thebes, as they still stand today as focus of the old. As the king recorded in a nearby inscription, 'Their [the statues'] height rises to heaven; their rays fall on the face like Aten when he shines at dawn.'

The modern name of these statues – the 'Colossi of Memnon' – derives from their erroneous association, in Classical times, with the defeated Ethiopian prince Memnon, son of Aurora, goddess of the dawn. The link came about as the result of an earthquake in 27 BC and the unearthly moans which were subsequently emitted by the northern statue, supposedly as it heated up at dawn. Interpreted as the plaintive call of Memnon to his mother, the noises ceased following Septimius Severus' repair of the monument in the 3rd century AD.

The temple for which these statues were originally commissioned was one of the greatest Egypt has ever seen, enormous in its physical scale (occupying an area of around 37 ha (91 acres), much of it intended to flood during the annual, rejuvenating inundation) and embellished with an immense range of the most refined sculptures, carved at every scale and in every stone then known to man – from limestone to obsidian – and cast from every precious metal. The inventory included quantities of divine statues, images of the gods with whom pharaoh was to merge in his *sed*-jubilee (see below) following a precedent set by the ancient 3rd-Dynasty king Djoser within his Step Pyramid complex at Saqqara. No expense was spared, as Amenophis III's stela inscription reveals:

'[It is] a monument of eternity and everlastingness, of fine sandstone worked

The principal administrator at Amenophis III's court, Amenhotep son of Hapu, shown as a scribe; the unrolled papyrus on his lap has been worn smooth by the touch of thousands of pious hands. Posterity was to cherish Amenhotep's memory as a sage, magician and holy man, and by Ptolemaic times he was worshipped as a god in his own right.

The Colossi of Memnon – all that now remains of the magnificent mortuary temple erected by Amenophis III on the Theban west bank. The statues were the creation of Men, father of the Amarna sculptor Bek whose pot-bellied physique is famously depicted on a sculpture now in Berlin.

with gold throughout. Its pavements are made pure with silver, all its doors with fine gold. It is very wide and great and decorated enduringly. It is adorned with this very great monument [the stela upon which the inscription is carved], and enriched with statues of the lord [pharaoh], of granite from Yebu [Aswan], of gritstone, and all kinds of costly stones, crafted in enduring workmanship.... It is equipped with a station of the lord [place where the king stood or sat during ceremonies], worked with gold and many costly stones. Flagstaffs are set up before it, worked with fine gold. It resembles the horizon of heaven when Re rises in it.'

As a reward for his achievements here and elsewhere, Amenhotep son of Hapu received the unparalleled honour of a fully fledged mortuary temple of his own, close to that of his master. Thanks in no small part to this endowment – which would long survive that of his royal master – posterity, both at Thebes and elsewhere, was to cherish Amenhotep's memory as a sage, magician and holy man; by the Ptolemaic period he was worshipped as a minor god. His popularity may be judged from the surfaces of his statues at Karnak, worn smooth by the touch of thousands of pious pilgrims eager for contact, however indirect, with the essence of a great – though perhaps, as we shall see, ultimately ill-fated – man.

KARNAK AND LUXOR

An inevitable beneficiary of Amenophis III's favour was Karnak, the palatial temple-residence of Amun at Thebes. Here, most notably, the king added the third pylon, or monumental gateway, together with its western approach-colonnade, as well as the tenth pylon – the clear aim of these developments being to emphasize the temple's two principal festal routes. Everywhere, throughout the complex, statue after statue was dedicated by the king – and never with more drama than in the temple of Mut. Here, several *hundred* human-size statues of the lioness-headed goddess Sekhmet were erected in row after neat row following their transfer from Kom el-Hetan across the river after the royal jubilee celebrations. Cost in these

Luxor temple today, as seen from the air. That part enclosing the 'holy-of-holies' – the rectangular, partially roofed section at the bottom – was constructed early in the reign of Amenophis III, while the broad sun-court and narrow processional colonnade seen in the centre were erected a short time later; the Opet Festival scenes which decorate the latter were completed under Tutankhamun. The two entrance pylons and first courtyard visible at the top are additions dating from the time of Ramesses II.

enterprises was no object – as may be gauged from the record of materials employed in the embellishment of one structure alone within the immense Karnak complex, the temple of Montu: electrum (a naturally occurring mix of gold and silver) – 3.25 tonnes; gold – 2.5 tonnes; copper – 420 kg (924 lb); beaten(?) copper – 10 tonnes; bronze – 1.5 tonnes; lapis lazuli – 567 kg (1,250 lb); turquoise – 98 kg (215 lb).

But Amenophis III's principal architectural triumph on the Theban east bank would be the temple of Luxor, birthplace of Amun, situated almost 3 km (2 miles) to the south and connected with Karnak by means of a processional way. Luxor would be the particular focus of Amenophis III's east bank building programme – and less, we may suspect, for its Amun association than for the crucial role it played in the promotion of the royal cult. The old temple of Tuthmosis III and Hatshepsut was demolished – to be replaced, in three distinct stages, by an entirely fresh building of fine sandstone, comprising the complex of the shrine proper, a large papyrus-columned court, hypostyle hall, and a colonnade with seven pairs of immense, 13-m (42-ft) high calyx-capital columns.

The temple of Luxor, still wonderfully preserved, was later extended by a further court during the reign of Ramesses II to complete the monument we see today; its 18th-Dynasty portions (the greatest achievement of the twins Suty and Hor, pharaoh's principal architects at Thebes) are the jewel in the Theban crown. And it was here, buried beneath the floor of the solar court, that one of Amenophis III's finest statues, of exquisite red, solar quartzite, would be disinterred in 1989 among the jumble of sculptures of the so-called Luxor cachette. In this statue, the king, 'the dazzling sun disc of all lands', is shown in the guise of the Heliopolitan solar divinity Re-Atum. The

Pharaoh Amenophis III: a statue in red quartzite from the Luxor cachette. A work from the end of the reign, the king is shown standing on a sledge to indicate his elevation to the ranks of the divine ancestors. The iconography of the piece, like the material itself, is wholly solar, with the crown appropriate for both the king and the Heliopolitan god Atum.

dedication is nominally to Amun; but, as the statue's texts make clear, it is the king, as solar deity, who gives and sustains life, even among the gods.

MALQATA

It used to be thought that the residence of the Egyptian king was attached to one or other of the principal temples – and, indeed, the larger temples do contain apartments which could be used by pharaoh during his visits. But these were not where the king actually lived – as the discovery of Malqata, the site of Amenophis III's mud-brick palace complex on the Theban west bank, revealed.

The Malqata palace was discovered by chance by the young Georges Daressy, newly appointed assistant to Gaston Maspero, Director of the Service des Antiquités and the Bulaq Museum, in the spring of 1888. Deciding to dig here a little, Daressy uncovered not only a number of rooms and a decorated royal dais, but several important sections of the original wall decoration also – at that time, and still, rare survivals of such domestic adornment. These preliminary explorations at the site whetted the appetite of others – including Percy Newberry and Robb de Peyster Tytus at the start of the 20th century; New York's Metropolitan Museum of Art between 1910

Well-preserved painted decoration on wall-footings uncovered at Malqata by the Metropolitan Museum of Art's Egyptian Expedition. Essentially untouched since its abandonment over three thousand years ago, Amenophis III's palace complex has proved an archaeological and historical gold-mine, yet to be exhausted.

and 1920; the University of Pennsylvania between 1971 and 1977; and, most recently, during the course of several seasons from 1985 on, a Japanese team from Waseda University in Tokyo. The principal discovery of this last mission was a wonderfully painted throne platform (since vandalized) at Kom el-Samak, beyond the Birket Habu lake-harbour, which had evidently been employed during one or other of the king's *sed*-festival celebrations.

What do we know about the site? Before the reign of Amenophis III, Thebes was visited but infrequently by pharaoh, and then primarily for festal reasons. Sometime before the occasion of his first jubilee, however, it seems that Amenophis III decided to make the southern residence his principal home. To that end, he began the construction of the Malqata palace and associated buildings, the development being tied in, chronologically, with the celebration of the three *sed*-festivals during the king's last decade.

Today, from the ruins, five principal areas can be distinguished: apartments for the king, with associated festival halls; apartments for the queen; apartments for the principal officials; a chapel to the god Amun; and a workmen's quarter. The settlement proper Amenophis III designated 'House of Nebmaatre splendour of the Aten', and following the celebration of the first jubilee in regnal year 30 it was known as 'The house of rejoicing'. The modern name of the site, 'el-Malqata', translates as 'the place where things are picked up' – reflecting the vast quantities of brilliant blue faience, characteristic blue-painted pottery and other artifacts with which the surface of the site, still not completely excavated, was for long years thickly strewn.

It is nowadays clear that Malqata was much more than a simple palace complex: occupying in excess of 32 ha (80 acres), it functioned as a city within a city. To judge from the painting-out of the Amun-element in his father's name among the interior decorations, occupation continued during the early part of Amenophis IV's rule until, following the 'heretic's' transfer to el-Amarna, the place will have fallen into disuse.

THE KING'S JUBILEES

Amenophis III celebrated three *sed*-festivals, or jubilees of kingly renewal, in or around regnal years 30, 34 and 37; and there is every indication, as we shall see, that he was actively involved in planning a fourth at the time of his death. In accomplishing the first of these demonstrations of his fitness to occupy the throne following three decades as king, Amenophis III was conforming strictly with tradition. The majority of kings who are recorded as having observed the ritual did so (or planned to do so) very much earlier in their rule; others, like Tuthmosis III, despite long reigns, appear not to have done so at all. The explanation for such anomalies still eludes us.

Indeed, the details of the *sed*-festival itself remain something of a mystery. The preparations, we do know, were long in the making, and involved the commissioning of everything from new structures in which the festival was to be enacted, to divine images and royal statuary of the finest quality,

The new, rebus writing of Amenophis III's throne name, 'Nebmaatre', on a mud wine-jar sealing from pharaoh's palace at Malqata. The king's name occupies the sun's place in the magical barque which daily traverses the sky.

jewelry and linens, as well as foods, wines and other provisions as offerings and for the accompanying banquets. For whatever reason, Amenophis III placed far more emphasis on the celebration of the *sed* than the great majority of his predecessors.

In contemporary texts it is stressed how vitally important it was that the various rites (of whose proper sequence we are still woefully ignorant) be carried out 'in accordance with the ancient writings' – a seeking after original truth (*maat*) which, developing gradually under Amenophis III, comes to dominate the reign of his son, Amenophis IV-Akhenaten. It is a tendency signalled in the solar element of the king's throne name (prenomen), 'Neb-maatre', which may be translated as 'possessor of the *maat* of Re'; and it has left its mark also in the archaeological record, in the king's restoration of the 'tomb of Osiris' at Abydos, as well as in an already ancient, Predynastic slate palette which was recarved with an image of the king and his queen at about this time. Interestingly, much of the research on which the jubilees and other aspects of the reign were based appears to have been entrusted to the wise man Amenhotep son of Hapu, the prime intellectual force of the reign. Amenhotep's own antiquarian leanings are apparent in his statues, which clearly hark back to Middle Kingdom originals.

The first of Amenophis III's jubilees is the best documented, with wine-jar dockets from Malqata (where the rites were celebrated) and reliefs and inscriptional evidence from the king's temple at Soleb in Upper Nubia, the ruins of the mortuary temple at Kom el-Hetan, the mortuary temple of Amenhotep son of Hapu, and the tombs of the king's high officials Khaemhat (TT57) and Kheruef (TT192). The second jubilee is known only from a series of Malqata jar labels; while the third is attested by further Malqata dockets as well as by scenes and inscriptions in the tomb of Kheruef.

As we know from other sources, the jubilee rites continued over an extended period, and took place in the presence of the gods of Egypt who were represented by their various cult statues. That the celebrations were memorable may be assumed from the quantities of food and drink consumed – calculated from the broken 'empties' – and from a rather peevish complaint from the king of Babylon, Kadashman-Enlil, that he had not been invited.

PHARAOH BECOMES A GOD

'Re-Horakhty, mighty bull who appears in *maat*, good god in true fact, the sovereign, ruler of the nine bows, dazzling sun disc for all lands ...' INSCRIPTION ON THE QUARTZITE STATUE OF AMENOPHIS III FROM THE LUXOR CACHETTE

If a layer of fog veils events on Egypt's earthly plane, theologically the situation is even worse, though it has over recent years clarified a little. That there had been important developments in kingship during the reign of Tuthmosis IV is hinted at here and there in the records; now, during the reign of Amenophis III, we may discern further change. For, having ascended the throne as a semi-divine being, pharaoh can be seen to have departed life at the end of almost four decades of rule already a fully fledged god, 'the dazzling sun disc (Aten)', complete with his own priesthood (one the anonymous owner of Theban tomb TT46). Hitherto, this had been a transformation achieved only after death.

As American scholar W. Raymond Johnson has demonstrated, this elevation can be dated to the period between the first jubilee (before which, in his various depictions, pharaoh does not wear the collar of heavy gold disc-beads – the *shebyu* – and armlets indicative of his transformed status) and the third (after which he does effect this new iconography) – that is to say, sometime during the king's fourth decade. More specifically, Johnson would argue for the transformation having occurred at the time of the first jubilee, after which the king's solar associations are indeed greatly emphasized. We see this emphasis in the adoption of a new rebus writing of pharaoh's throne name, 'Nebmaatre', which employs a figure of the king (*neb*) holding a feather (*maat*) and with a disc upon his head (*re*), and in the addition to the king's various temple structures at Luxor and elsewhere of solar courts. The transformation is actually articulated in the inscriptions, as Egyptologist Betsy Bryan has observed, where it is recorded not merely that the king decided to *join* the sun in his barque traversing the heavens: he actually *occupies the sun's place*.

For some, including Johnson, this elevation of pharaoh to the ranks of the gods imposed a necessary distancing from the realm of man – the implication being that the occasion of the first *sed*-festival was the time at which Amenophis III required and adopted a co-regent. The question of a co-regency between Amenophis III and his son and successor is a matter of intense and still unresolved scholarly debate, which we shall address in the next chapter.

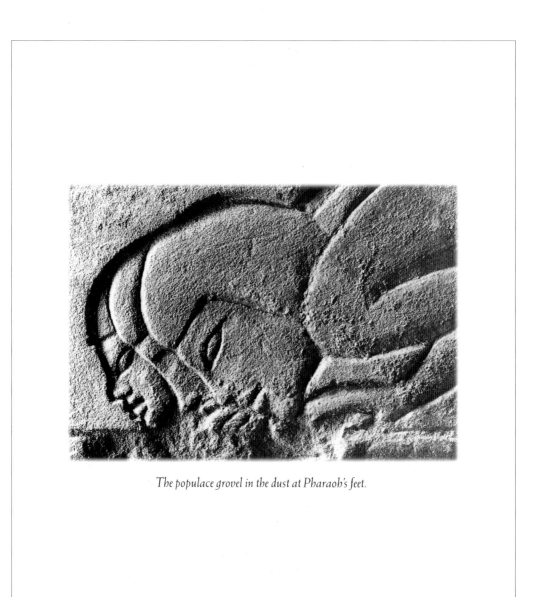

The populace grovel in the dust at Pharaoh's feet.

CHAPTER FOUR

REVOLUTION

LONG CO-REGENCY, OR SHORT?

One of the more curious features of ancient Egyptian kingly practice which has been referred to already in this book, though exercised quite inconsistently and (to the Egyptologist's frustration) leaving few obvious traces, is the system of co-regency – by which, in order to ensure a smooth transfer of power and control, the heir was appointed to rule as junior king during his father's lifetime. For the student of Middle Kingdom history, the problems inherent in managing the chronological implications of the co-regency phenomenon are mitigated somewhat by the existence of 'double datings' – that is to say, inscriptions which proclaim the regnal years of both the senior and junior ruler. In the New Kingdom, there are no such aids, and the Egyptologist has little option but to seek out less direct pointers to the existence and duration of the phenomenon in any given reign.

For those attempting to establish chronology and relationships both within and outside the royal family during the Amarna period, the possibility of a co-regency between Amenophis III and Amenophis IV is a matter of abiding concern. One instance of the uncertainties the situation throws up will suffice: in the absence of a co-regency, or the existence of only a short period of joint rule between the two pharaohs, the father of the 'king's son' Tutankhaten/Tutankhamun can have been none other than Amenophis IV-Akhenaten; if there was a long overlap of the two reigns, then Amenophis III, too, enters the frame as potential parent.

That Amenophis III and Amenophis IV might, for a time, have been associated on the throne has been argued, on and off, for a century and more. As long ago as 1935, the topic was described by Pendlebury as one of 'astonishing complexity', and the passing of the years has done little to simplify it, despite all the discussion the controversy has generated. For all the words, there remains a frustrating lack of incontrovertible proof one way or the other; we are left with no more than a mere balance of probabilities. An overview of the situation must, for obvious reasons, here suffice.

Given the unexpected death of Amenophis III's intended heir, Tuthmosis, and the unsettling effect which that development may have had on matters at court, the employment of the co-regency mechanism at this time would not, perhaps, be unexpected; and among those hints in the archaeological record that such a co-regency was at some stage in place is a famous scene on the third pylon at Karnak depicting a larger and smaller figure of Amenophis III and a second, erased king. Various explanations of these figures have been put forward, but the likelihood must be that what we have

Amenophis III and his ghostly (erased) companion in a relief on Karnak's third pylon. The balance of probability is that the latter, wearing the blue khepresh-*crown, is an image of the junior co-regent, Amenophis IV.*

before us is a representation of the senior king and his son and co-regent Amenophis IV.

If it is accepted that a co-regency between Amenophis III and Amenophis IV-Akhenaten probably did exist, what was its duration? Until recently, those advocating a long period of co-rule between senior and junior king tended to be in the minority. Thanks to the advocacy of W. Raymond Johnson, the case for a long co-regency has been skilfully argued afresh, primarily on the basis of perceived artistic synchronisms within the two reigns but with much collateral evidence presented in its support. For Johnson, the association between father and son may have begun as early as Amenophis III's Year 29, preparatory to the celebration of pharaoh's first *sed*-festival, which Johnson believes saw the elevation of the king to solar-divine status. The portraiture of Amenophis III prior to this jubilee, it is argued, resembles closely the pre-Amarna style employed by Amenophis IV at Karnak – which is quite different from the distinctive, youthful appearance of Amenophis III's final, newly 'transformed' state, a mode of representation which Johnson believes coincided with the son's adoption of the exaggerated naturalism of Amarna art. On the basis of these links, Johnson argues that the change in the junior co-regent's name from Amenophis IV to Akhenaten and the foundation of the city of Akhetaten coincided with the celebration of the senior king's second jubilee five years later; while the installation of the Aten in his new city took place three years after that, at the time of the third jubilee.

For the existence of a long co-regency, Johnson therefore puts forward a powerful case, but it is one which has yet to find wide acceptance. Egyptologists are by nature a conservative breed, and the caution of their reaction has no real bearing on the theory's intrinsic value. On the other hand, it remains to be explained how Johnson's ideas are to be reconciled with three of the few significant pieces in a sea of 'evidence' which may be marshalled in the co-regency debate.

The first of these is a docket scribbled in black ink in hieratic (a cursive form of the Egyptian hieroglyphic script) on the edge of one of the Amarna cuneiform tablets (EA 27), now in Berlin – a text which seems to set an upper limit for the duration of the supposed association of Amenophis III and his heir:

> '[Yea]r [...?]2, first month of winter, [day ...], when one [i.e. the king] was in the southern city [i.e. Thebes], in the mansion of Khaemakhet; copy of the Naharin [Mitanni] letter the messenger Pirissi and the messenger [Tulubri] brought.'

The conclusions to be drawn from this Amarna tablet are clear enough: first, from the content of the letter itself (see below), the docket was written but a short time after Amenophis III's death and Amenophis IV's accession to sole, internationally acknowledged rule; and, secondly, the dateline of the docket indicates by which regnal year of the successor-pharaoh the co-regency between the two kings had ended. Inevitably, however, the crucial portion of the docket has suffered damage. Despite former suggestions that the date might in fact be restored as '[Yea]r [1]2' – which would indicate that Amenophis IV succeeded to the throne only after a co-regency of some length, favouring W. Raymond Johnson's case – there now seems to be general agreement among Egyptologists that the actual reading of this date is simply '[Yea]r 2' – and this would indicate, at best, a relatively short period of joint rule.

The second contra-indication of a long co-regency is an extraordinary passage in one of the el-Amarna boundary stelae of Amenophis IV-Akhenaten's regnal year 5, to which we shall return a little later. In this text, the king refers to Amenophis III in the same breath as his other deceased ancestors – and this, as British Egyptologist John R. Harris observes, is a good indication that the father must, by this time, have been dead.

The third argument against a lengthy period of co-rule between the father and his son is the former's tomb, WV22. Here, the cartouched names of the

Hieratic docket scribbled in ink on the edge of one of the tablets (EA 27) uncovered at el-Amarna in 1887. The text reads: '[Yea]r [...?]2, first month of winter, [day ...], when one [i.e. the king] was in the southern city [i.e. Thebes], in the mansion of Khaemakhet; copy of the Naharin [Mitanni] letter the messenger Pirissi and the messenger [Tulubri] brought.' The date was formerly read as '[Ye]ar [1]2', and used to support the existence of a long co-regency between Amenophis III and his son and successor, Amenophis IV-Akhenaten.

king are presented in their full prenomen+nomen form, 'Nebmaatre Amenophis', rather than in the anti-Amun form favoured by his successor which replaces the birth name with a second 'Nebmaatre'. This, together with the fact that the 'Amen-' element survives throughout unscathed, suggests strongly that, at the time of Amenophis III's death, Akhenaten's persecution of the Theban god still lay in the future.

A short co-regency between Amenophis III and his son Amenophis IV-Akhenaten, therefore, is the option preferred here – and its relative merits will be revealed as our story continues to unfold.

THE FUNERAL OF AMENOPHIS III

> 'The god ascended to his horizon. The king of Upper and Lower
> Egypt Sehetepibre [Ammenemes I] flew to heaven and united
> with the Aten, the divine body merging with its maker. Then
> the residence was hushed; hearts grieved; the great portals
> were shut; the courtiers were head-on-knee; the people
> mourned.'

The above quotation, taken from a famous Middle Kingdom literary text known as the 'Tale of Sinuhe', describes the ultimate transformation of the royal being (in this case the 12th-Dynasty king Ammenemes I) – assimilation with the solar disc, or Aten. It was a transformation towards which Tuthmosis IV and Amenophis III had already made significant progress in life; and when the latter, in his 38th year of rule – fat, balding and ill-tempered as a result of badly abscessed teeth – at last became one with his ancestors, the son's politico-religious aspirations were provided, at a stroke, with a new and meaningful focus.

Since Amenophis III was the richest and most powerful ruler in the 14th-century BC world, his burial and the ceremonies surrounding the coronation of his successor must have been an awesome spectacle, with embassies from every corner of the known world in rich and colourful attendance. Once the embalming process had been completed and the solemn rituals associated with it, the funeral procession will have begun slowly to wind its way from the king's marvellously appointed mortuary temple towards the royal burial ground in the now-famed Valley of the Kings. A well-known scene in the burial chamber of Tutankhamun's tomb preserves a record of how, to the crowds massed on either side of the route, the cortège might have appeared: the innermost coffin containing the masked and bejewelled mummy of the king on its garland-bedecked sledge, symbolically dragged along by five groups of high officials whose number included the two viziers of Upper and of Lower Egypt. The whole had been preceded, we may suppose, by priests burning incense to purify the way, and was followed by columns of servants bearing the king's jewelry and other personal possessions and items of burial equipment which were to be buried with him.

The king's tomb

The tomb Amenophis III had prepared for this day was located in an annexe of Wadi Biban el-Muluk – the Valley of the Kings – known today as the West Valley. Work on cutting the sepulchre had, in fact, begun during the reign of his father, Tuthmosis IV – a revelation we owe to Howard Carter who, clearing the area in front of the entrance in 1915, uncovered a series of foundation deposits containing several small, blue faience plaques bearing the cartouches of this earlier king. Quite why Tuthmosis IV had begun work on a second tomb is a mystery yet to be solved; it is not impossible, however, that its excavation had been initiated with a co-regency between Tuthmosis IV and his son, if not a fact, then at least in view.

Amenophis III had intended the West Valley tomb not only for his own interment but for the burial of two of his wives also – Tiye, and most probably Sitamun, the daughter who, it will be recalled, not only functioned as queen towards the end of the reign but may have given birth to her father's enigmatic daughter, Baketaten. Since both queens survived their king, however – Tiye herself would live on until Year 14 of her son's reign – they were buried elsewhere: there seems to have been a reluctance to disturb the sanctity of the tomb once pharaoh's mummy was actually in place. Time would lessen such hesitancy, for the burial of Amenophis III was later cruelly disturbed when, at the end of the 20th Dynasty, the entire necropolis was ransacked by official salvage teams and the occupants of the royal tombs were carried off for reburial in a series of caches dotted around the necropolis. The badly damaged body of Amenophis III, as we have seen, eventually surfaced in the tomb of Amenophis II (KV35), uncovered by the Antiquities Service in 1898. The king was accompanied in this, his last resting place, by the mummified remains of 15 other kings and lesser royals whose tombs had been similarly pillaged by the ancient, post-Ramessid government commissions.

Following the removal of the king's mummy, the West Valley tomb of Amenophis III was abandoned and forgotten. It was first brought to light in the 1730s, visited by Bonaparte's expedition in 1799 and partially cleared by Theodore Davis's men during or after the first decade of the 20th century, before Carter moved in to explore the area. Work at the tomb was resumed in 1989 by a Japanese team from Waseda University in Tokyo. Taking up where Howard Carter had left off, the Waseda excavators began carefully sifting through what the salvage teams had discarded. And here, as one peruses the tomb's many hundreds of chopped up fragments, it is possible to discern a treasure even greater than Tutankhamun's, with slivers of the royal coffins still glinting with remnants of their original gilding, an exquisite lapis lazuli uraeus plucked, perhaps, from pharaoh's gold mask, and a mass of splinters and chippings from a range of the numerous royal and divine figures and other funerary objects intended to see Amenophis III safely into the beyond.

Even today, in its desecrated and gloomy state, the king's tomb leaves a powerful impression on the visitor: its scale is enormous, its cutting

Detail of a scene on the south wall of the well shaft of Amenophis III's tomb (WV22) in the western annexe of the Valley of the Kings at Thebes. The cartouches of the king are presented in the normal way, rather than with the throne name doubled as later favoured by his son; and they are intact. The implication is that Amenophis III was dead and buried before the Amun-persecution of Akhenaten's middle years began.

extraordinarily precise, and what survives of the wall paintings (after the mindless vandalism of 19th-century souvenir hunters) sublime. It was, once, a truly fitting sepulchre for Egypt's 'dazzling sun'.

Ageing Akhenaten: the body in Tomb 55

Amenophis III was dead and gone, buried by his second son, Amenophis IV. What do we know about the successor at this critical, early stage in his career? To answer perhaps the most basic question – that of his age – it is necessary to look first at yet another excavation in the Valley of the Kings, and one whose interpretation is absolutely crucial to the Amarna story.

As we have already seen, the wealthy American amateur Theodore M. Davis, digging in the royal burial ground in 1905, had had the enormous good fortune to alight upon the well-stocked burial of queen Tiye's parents, Yuya and Tjuyu. Two years later, excavating not far from this tomb, Davis's men discovered yet another important royal burial which was to enter the literature as 'The tomb of Queen Tiye'. It is a find better known today as 'Tomb 55', or, more prosaically, 'KV55', its current numbering in the Kings'

Valley sequence. The uneven publication of the discovery, and a long-standing belief among anatomists that the associated body was that of a relatively young man, have for years impeded a full and proper understanding of the burial – and the implications of this situation are serious.

As uncovered by Davis, Tomb 55 contained four principal items or groups of items – intriguing and seemingly contradictory clues to the identity of its occupant(s):

• the rotted remains of an exquisite coffin of gilded and inlaid wood, originally prepared for a woman before later being usurped for kingly use; its cartouches had been subsequently cut out and its face mask brutally ripped away with the evident aim of denying both the occupant's identification and future well-being;

• the panels of a large sepulchral shrine of gilded wood, inscribed for queen Tiye, its kingly scenes similarly censored at a later stage;

• a set of four usurped alabaster canopic jars, with stoppers carved to match the coffin and, again, the original text panels of the jars erased in antiquity;

• a set of four 'magical bricks', the spells of two at least incorporating the throne name of Amenophis IV-Akhenaten, 'the Osiris Neferkheprure-waenre'.

Excavation would in addition yield a number of smaller objects, some of which had spilled out from a series of broken wooden boxes sealed in antiquity with the name of Tutankhamun.

It was an odd assemblage which initially made little sense to the discoverers; but, requiring a title for his publication of the find, Davis opted for *The Tomb of Queen Tîyi*, Yuya and Tjuyu's daughter, on the basis of the name on the shrine and the mistaken opinion, early ventured by a passing medic, that the body appeared to be that of a woman.

In fact, the reality was much more complex, as Arthur Weigall, who had been supervising Davis's diggings on

The restored lid of the Tomb 55 coffin. Originally prepared for a woman, as the design and inscriptions show, the coffin had subsequently been adapted for kingly use; although the new owner's cartouches had been everywhere excised, and the gold portrait mask torn away, the epithets reveal him to have been Akhenaten himself.

The southern end of Tomb 55's single chamber, as first encountered. The dismantled sections of Tiye's gilded wooden shrine are propped up against the east wall, while the anonymous, water-damaged mummy lies on the rubble-covered floor beneath a niche containing four canopic jars with human-headed stoppers.

behalf of the Egyptian government since the Yuya-Tjuyu find, soon recognized. Weigall, throughout his life, argued energetically that the occupant of the altered and sadly abused but splendidly decorated coffin was in fact the owner of the tomb's 'magic bricks' – Amenophis IV-Akhenaten himself. And this king, he concluded, had originally shared the tomb chamber with the owner of the shrine, his mother, Tiye, before her body was later removed in antiquity by individuals hostile to the presence within of her 'heretic' son.

The weak link in Weigall's reconstruction was the estimated age at death of the Tomb 55 skeleton – which the anatomist Grafton Elliot Smith in 1912 put at 25 or 26 years. For an identification as Akhenaten, Weigall admitted, this was low, but not impossibly so, and for a time his analysis prevailed. Indeed, the examination of the mummy of Tutankhamun in 1926 appeared at first to support Weigall's case – the anatomy of it and the Tomb 55 corpse were so remarkably similar (we now know from analysis that the two bodies shared the same blood group also) that they must, in life, have been closely related.

With a re-examination of the Tomb 55 body by anatomist Douglas Derry a short time later, however, the argument seemed to collapse: the age at death of the corpse, Derry felt, was even lower than Elliot Smith had proposed – no more than 23. An identification as Akhenaten seemed out of the question; for, whatever his youth at the time of his accession, Amenophis IV could hardly have been a child of *such* immaturity – at worst, a mere six years of age – given the reforms upon which he was almost immediately to embark. For Derry, and for others since, the corpse was with far greater likelihood to be recognized as that of Amenophis IV-Akhenaten's shadowy successor, Smenkhkare. Although virtually nothing was known about this king, it had previously been speculated that he might be an elder brother of Tutankhamun; and with this new identification of the Tomb 55 body, so similar to that of his assumed brother, the hypothesis was seemingly confirmed. The circular nature of the argument ought to have aroused suspicion, as also the fact that *not a scrap* of archaeological or inscriptional evidence could be mustered from Davis's tomb to support Smenkhkare's association with any part of it.

Weigall's analysis of the archaeology, however, was very sound, and a review of the evidence today confirms his view that the Tomb 55 body ought indeed to be that of Amenophis IV-Akhenaten. It is equally clear, however, that Tomb 55 was not the original burial place of either this body or any part of the equipment buried with it: it had all been transferred from el-Amarna during the reign of Tutankhamun, as the group of small seal impressions found among the floor debris indicates. Tomb 55 was, in fact, a hasty reburial of mother and son, accompanied by a random selection of funerary items originally prepared for other and very different owners – most notably the coffin and canopic jars, which had once belonged to a secondary wife of Akhenaten named Kiya. We shall have more to say about this lady later on.

Despite the mongrelized nature of the funerary goods, this reburial within Tomb 55 had been carried out in a relatively disciplined manner, and had originally included substantially more equipment than that recovered by Davis. Its stripped and disordered state was the result of its rediscovery, two hundred years after Tutankhamun's day, during the quarrying of the overlying tomb of Ramesses IX. Evidently alerted to the existence of a void below by the hollow echo from their chisels, the Ramessid workmen had broken off their work to explore – and what they found had clearly horrified them. They acted accordingly. Tiye's mummy was removed from the defiling presence of her 'heretic' son for burial elsewhere – a possible candidate for her mummy, it will be recalled, turned up in the Amenophis II cache in 1898 – while the coffin and its occupant were consigned to the terrible oblivion of anonymity. The names were systematically cut out, and the identifying face torn away to destroy the eyes, nose and mouth and effectively deny the king's spirit sight, air and sustenance; for good measure, a stone was hurled at the coffin's head just before the party left. It was an attack, as we shall see, totally in keeping with the vilification of Amenophis IV-Akhenaten's memory during the Ramessid period.

So much for the archaeology. But what of the body and its problematic age at death? Joyce Filer seeks still to maintain its youth, but the fullest and most convincing examination of the Tomb 55 bones remains that of Fawzia Hussein and James E. Harris, reported on at the International Congress of Egyptologists in Cairo in 1988. These anatomists conclude that the skeleton is without doubt of male sex and belonged to a person 'of rather fragile constitution' who was closely related to Tutankhamun; the dentition is that of an individual in his mid-thirties, while anthropological standards and new X-rays (particularly of the long bones) suggest

The skull of the body from Tomb 55. Regrettably, bones were all that it proved possible for Davis to salvage of the water-soaked corpse; any mummified tissue visible at the time of the discovery rapidly fell to dust.

an age in excess of 35 years. Unless new evidence comes to light, it seems the impasse is in fact broken – in which case Akhenaten is found, and we are finally able to move forward.

THE YOUTHFUL SUCCESSOR

Physically, according to the anatomical examination published by R. G. Harrison in 1966, the body recovered from Tomb 55 is that of a man, tending slightly to the feminine and standing around 1.7 m (5½ ft) tall. The extreme physical deformity displayed in the early monuments of the king's sole reign is not present in the body itself; as we shall see, much of Amenophis IV-Akhenaten's art presented a deliberate exaggeration of reality, almost a caricature, intended to emphasize pharaoh's other-worldly status and the yawning void which separated him from ordinary men. We may guess that the famous statuette of the king in yellow limestone now in the Louvre more accurately reflects the king's appearance in life – and the similarity between the face of the person there depicted and that of Tutankhamun is as striking as that between the two mummies.

From Hussein and Harris's recent, revised estimate of the age at death of the Tomb 55 skeleton, it transpires that Amenophis IV ascended the throne as a teenager – and, if his actions in time showed flashes of undeniable brilliance, he would become known far sooner for his youthful arrogance. The comparison which has been drawn by Cambridge Egyptologist John Ray with the youthful Fatimid caliph el-Hakim (AD 996–1021), is an illuminating one: like Akhenaten,

> 'he [el-Hakim] is the son of a ruler known for his magnificence and liberality, he comes under the influence of a powerful female, his sister ..., he exhibits a growing religious mania which feeds on itself, and he also possesses an abstract sensitivity.... This intellectual ability goes hand in hand with arbitrary atrocities, unpredictable reversions of policy, rule by inner promptings, social upheaval and inhuman persecution of those who had incurred Al-Hakim's displeasure....'

The first hints of pharaoh's difficult character are revealed in his dealings with Tushratta. The following extract of a letter from the Mitannian king sets the scene:

'When my brother, Nimmureya [Amenophis III], went to his fate it was reported. When I heard what was reported, nothing was allowed to be cooked in a pot. On that day I myself wept, and I sat.... On that day I took neither food nor water. I grieved, saying, "Let even me be dead, or let 10,000 be dead in my country, and in my brother's country 10,000 as well, but let my brother, whom I love and loves me, be alive as long as heaven and earth"...

But when they said, "Napkhureya [Amenophis IV], the eldest son of Nimmureya and Tiye, his principal wife, is exercising the kingship in his place, then I spoke as follows: "Nimmureya, my brother, is not dead. Napkhureya, his eldest son, now exercises the kingship in his place. Nothing whatsoever is going to be changed from the way it was before ..."'

Tushratta's missive might be proposed as one of the great underestimations of history – did not the rest of this letter and others like it have so clearly as their almost desperate aim the desire to establish a rapport with the new pharaoh. For his fellow 'great kings', Amenophis IV was from the start to prove a problematic 'brother', as further correspondence from the Mitannian king reveals.

Yellow limestone statuette of Akhenaten now in the Louvre (restored below the knees). Originally one half of a dyad, the sculpture was acquired from Henry Salt during the early years of the 19th century. The first representation of the king to have been found in modern times, it probably remains the most true to life.

Cuneiform letter (EA 26) from the el-Amarna hoard of 1887, addressed to the widowed queen Tiye by Tushratta of Mitanni. 'You are the one who knows that I myself always showed love to [Amenophis III], your husband, and that ... your husband, on the other hand, always showed love to me.... Let your son ... cause me no distress whatsoever.... Let him treat me 10 times better than his father did, with love and evidence of esteem.'

The contents of Amarna letter EA 27 – the tablet bearing the Year 2 docket discussed above in connection with the co-regency problem – revolve essentially around the non-delivery of two solid gold statues, of Tushratta himself and of his daughter, Tadukhepa, which had possibly formed part of the latter's bride-price promised by Amenophis III before his death but never delivered. Tushratta, for whatever reason, was exceptionally keen to have these baubles, and the matter is raised again in a second letter. This second tablet is addressed by Tushratta to Amenophis III's widow, Tiye (EA 26), whom the Mitannian king is clearly approaching with a view to influencing her son – a curious strategy if the new king had *not* been less than fully adult.

Further confirmation of the king's youth is perhaps to be detected in Amarna letter EA 29, sent to pharaoh by Tushratta a short time later. Its irritated tone is revealing, and underscored by the Mitannian ruler's deliberate omission here and elsewhere of the title 'great king' – a designation which Tushratta none the less pointedly retains for himself. Tushratta writes:

'... the affair of my brother has now become a matter for
denunciation. For what reason has my brother's [...]. He is a man,
and he has taken his seat on the throne of his father now become
a god'

In the translation of ancient texts, much nuance is inevitably lost; but, reading between the lines, what the Mitannian king seems to be saying is: 'You're no longer a child, but a man; behave like one!' Tushratta's frustration with the situation, and with Amenophis IV's attitude, is almost tangible; and pharaoh's own determination to push the foreigner to the limit is further borne out by his continuing detention of the Mitannian king's messengers. The situation was so dire as to prompt Tushratta's step-by-step recapitulation, with gritted teeth, in this same letter, of the good relations which had formerly existed between the two countries – prior, that is, to the new king's accession. Sadly, we do not have a copy of pharaoh's reply – but perhaps there never was one.

Tushratta could perhaps take heart from the fact that he was not the only foreign ruler experiencing difficulty with Amenophis IV: Suppiluliuma, the Hittite king, was clearly having similar problems – as other letters (EA 41 and EA 42 – if the intended recipient of the latter was indeed Amenophis IV) reveal:

> 'And now, as to the tablet you sent me, why did you put your name over my name? And who now is the one who upsets the good relations between us, and is such conduct the accepted practice? My brother, did you write to me with peace in mind …?'

What was the reason for pharaoh's tiresome behaviour? Demonstrably, he considered his fellow great kings and their petty dealings beneath contempt. His eyes, as time would show, were set on higher things.

NEFERTITI

> '… she who satisfies the Aten with a sweet voice and with her lovely hands bearing the sistra' INSCRIPTION FROM THE TOMB OF THE GOD'S FATHER AY

In the few early representations of Amenophis IV which now exist, the king is shown without the woman who would dominate the coming years – Nefertiti. This is remarkable, since the fact that the couple's first and third

The royal consort, Nefertiti, shown in the highly mannered style of Amenophis IV-Akhenaten's first years of rule; a solar ray before her face terminates in a human hand holding the sign for 'life'. The style, size and material of the block – sandstone – identify it as coming from the Aten temple-complex erected at Karnak early in the reign, subsequently razed by Akhenaten's successors.

daughters, Meritaten and Ankhesenpaaten, were, by the end of the reign, seemingly old enough to bear children themselves would indicate that their mother, Nefertiti, was at its start already queen. Although this absence may be no more than an accident of survival, if Amenophis IV was acting as co-regent at this time, the conclusion might be that in any period of joint rule there was room for only one publicly acknowledged queenly presence – and that was Tiye, who is shown in company with her son in this capacity on a number of occasions. The fact that Nefertiti is not acknowledged as queen before the introduction of the new Atenist style might, therefore, be a further indication that Amenophis IV's revolution began only after his father's death.

Nefertiti's parentage remains a mystery. The pale skin and slender, haughty looks of the Berlin portrait which so attracted Hitler might well support the foreign origin which the queen's name, 'The beautiful one is come', ostensibly implies. Indeed, it is not at all surprising that an identification with Tadukhepa, daughter of Tushratta of Mitanni, should have been proposed, and on more than one occasion. The arguments raised against the equation, however, are several. They include the later occurrence at el-Amarna (in the tombs of Panehsy, Maya and elsewhere) of a 'queen's sister' of Nefertiti named Mutbenret/Mutnedjmet – the reading is contested – as well as the fact that Nefertiti had her own Egyptian (wet-)nurse whose existence, in the context of a newly arrived, pubescent Tadukhepa, would be similarly difficult to explain.

In fact, on present evidence, the probability is that Nefertiti was Egyptian born and bred. Her nurse was none other than Tiy – to be distinguished by the

The loyal servant: the god's father Ay and his wife, Tiy, receive faience(?) and gold collars as gifts from Akhenaten and his queen. The scene is from the official's tomb at el-Amarna (no. 25); the royal benefactors are shown in Lepsius's copy on page 17.

spelling from Amenophis III's principal consort, Tiye – who was the wife of Ay, likely brother-in-law to the old king Amenophis III and uncle of Amenophis IV. Might Ay have been Nefertiti's father? On analogy with the status of Ay's supposed father, Yuya, it is conceivable that Ay too wished his title 'god's father' to be construed literally as father-in-law to the king; it was certainly a label by which he himself set great store, since it would later be incorporated in his kingly nomen, almost in support of his claim to the throne. But, if Ay was Nefertiti's father, why is Tiy identified merely as 'nurse'? Perhaps she was simply a later wife of Ay, rather than Nefertiti's actual mother.

Certainly, if Ay did father Nefertiti, he would have been continuing the tradition of marrying into the royal household upon which his family's fortunes seem at least in part to have been based. The high favour he enjoyed as a mere executive officer of the new regime (see below) would also be explained, as also his subsequent allocation of a large and impressive tomb at el-Amarna – to say nothing of his future elevation to the kingship itself. The further implication would be that Mutbenret/Mutnedjmet was another offspring, with both daughters (half-)sister to Ay's supposed son, Nakhtmin – in whom Ay, as pharaoh, would later invest heavily his hopes for the future.

The religious impulse

'Gods had come and gone. Pharaohs had patronized one and then another as in Christian times kings would patronize some favourite saint without alarming the Church. Amen [Amun] was fast set. He might be hated and envied by the priesthood of Ra [Re] whom he had ousted from power, but no Pharaoh would be so mad as to turn against the bringer of victory. But they had reckoned without the possibility of a fanatic.' John Pendlebury

Amenophis IV's politico-religious beliefs were to change the face of the ancient world. But what was their source? Who were his teachers? The Heliopolitan priest Aanen, his uncle, may have been one, but we know virtually nothing of the man beyond his titles; another influence is noted by the 3rd-century BC historian, Manetho, through his later redactor, Josephus. This is how Josephus records the start of the Amarna era:

'This king [Amenôphis], he [Manetho] states, conceived a desire to behold the gods, as Ôr, one of his predecessors on the throne, had done; and he communicated his desire to his namesake Amenôphis, Paapis' son, who, in virtue of his wisdom and knowledge of the future, was reputed to be a partaker in the divine nature. This namesake, then, replied that he would be able to see the gods if he cleansed the whole land of lepers and other polluted persons. The king was delighted, and assembled all those in Egypt whose bodies were wasted by disease: they numbered 80,000 persons. These he cast into the stone-quarries to the east of the Nile, there to work segregated from the rest of the Egyptians. Among them, Manetho adds, were some of the learned priests, who had been attacked by leprosy. Then this wise seer Amenôphis was filled with dread of divine wrath against himself and the king if the outrage done to these persons should be discovered; and he added a prediction that certain allies would join the polluted people and would take possession of Egypt for 13 years. Not venturing to make this prophecy himself to the king, he left a full account of it in writing, and then took his own life....'

A confusion in detail, as in so much of Manetho that has come down to us, is apparent; as Josephus himself observed, 'so long as Manetho followed the ancient records, he did not stray far from the truth; but when he turned to unauthorized legends, he either combined them in an improbable form or else gave credence to certain prejudiced informants.' The subsequent excision from official Egyptian 'histories' of all mention of Amenophis IV-Akhenaten and his successors perhaps goes some way towards explaining the garbled nature of Manetho's version of events: he will have been dependent largely upon hearsay.

The names of the royal protagonists are clear enough. The first of these, 'Amenôphis' will be Amenophis IV himself, with 'Ôr', in this instance, his father as Horus, the primeval king. For Josephus, the former was 'a fictitious person', since Manetho 'did not venture to define the length of his reign, although in the case of the other kings he adds their years precisely'; other explanations for this omission are possible, however – not least the heretic pharaoh's later execration.

The real interest in this extract of Manetho is the mention of 'Amenôphis, Paapis' son', who is none other than the venerable Amenhotep son of Hapu, the great builder, administrator, wise man and student of the arcane who had served Amenophis III with such distinction and transformed the face of Thebes and much more

A hauntingly realistic sculptor's model in plaster from the el-Amarna workshop of Thutmose. It is now plausibly identified as the face of Amenhotep son of Hapu – the wise counsellor of Amenophis III who, Manetho records, was driven to suicide during the reign of that pharaoh's son and successor.

besides. That the sage lived on into the reign of Amenophis IV is generally ignored, but perhaps reflected in the existence of two plaster portraits among the collection of art works in the studio of the sculptor Thutmose at el-Amarna (see below) – their likely attribution pointed out to me by W. Raymond Johnson. Amenhotep son of Hapu's initial influence on the new king helps to explain the philosophical continuity between the reigns of this official's two masters. As Manetho shows, however, it was a philosophy which Amenophis IV chose from the very beginning to interpret in his own distinctive manner.

THE KARNAK TEMPLES

Pharaoh, by tradition, stood as interlocutor between regions divine and the world of men – a god, Re, in life the incarnation of Horus, in death one with Osiris and the imperishable stars. During the reign of Amenophis III, belief in the divinity of pharaoh had been elevated to new and (for the 18th Dynasty) unprecedented heights – slowly, deliberately, and with a clear purpose in view: to re-establish kingly authority. This was an aspiration which his son would share, pushing faster and ever more strongly to restore the prestige of the king to the unassailable position it had occupied at the very start of Egyptian history. But where Amenophis III had been patient in his ambitions and content to follow the wise counsels of others, Amenophis IV was a young man in a hurry – impulsive, emotional and overly confident in his ability.

Amenophis IV's devotion to the solar religion – his own, élitist version of it, which again harked back to the distant past – appears fully developed at the very start of the reign. Pharaoh, it is clear, was a man with a mission; of rare intelligence, recognizably well-tutored in the theological minutiae and thoroughly versed in the arcana of the temple archives, despite his age he was certain in his beliefs and determined to share them. One manifestation of this youthful confidence was the enormous building programme upon which the king embarked early in the reign – most notably at Thebes, before the eastern and western entrances of Amun's great Karnak complex.

In recent decades, the documentation relating to the Karnak structures has been greatly expanded by the computerized study of a collection of the several tens of thousands of sandstone blocks from the period (decorated for the most part in painted sunk relief) used as fill in the construction work of those kings who later dismantled the Amenophis IV structures. The man behind this programme of study, the Akhenaten Temple Project (ATP), was an American, Ray Winfield Smith, and the scholar who has brought the idea to fruition is Canadian Egyptologist Donald B. Redford. Complementary work on related blocks has been carried out independently, and with equally interesting results, by the Centre franco-égyptien at Karnak.

The Karnak reliefs are of two basic sizes: the first, a series of larger blocks inscribed for Amenophis IV and carved in traditional style which are now

The small, decorated, component blocks of Amenophis IV-Akhenaten's dismantled Karnak temples were reused as convenient fill-material in the construction work of later pharaohs. Here we see the interior of the ninth pylon at Karnak, erected by Horemheb, and the neat rows of talatat *which form its core.*

known to have come from the king's southern gateway at Karnak; and a second, in many ways more interesting series of smaller blocks of half-cubit length – their small size not necessarily to facilitate handling, as some have thought, but to recall the smaller, 'purer' format employed at the 3rd-

Dynasty Step Pyramid complex of Djoser. These smaller blocks are generally referred to as *talatat* – a term (perhaps of Italian origin) used in Islamic architecture and believed to refer to their three-handbreadths' size. Although Egyptologists have been aware of the *talatat* since the early years of the 19th century through the studies of Émile Prisse d'Avennes and Karl Richard Lepsius, until the work of the ATP their context remained uncertain. Piecing together the elements of this immense jigsaw (most of the pieces of which had lost their edges, making the joins less than apparent) has shed important new and unexpected light on a previously little-known period of Amenophis IV's reign.

The work of reconstruction has to date resulted in the joining of more than 20 per cent of the *talatat* blocks, and has revealed the original existence at Karnak – now, significantly, referred to as the 'Upper Egyptian Heliopolis' – of a series of temples erected by Amenophis IV and his consort, Nefertiti, in honour of the Aten. The dismantling of these temples had begun already in the reign of Tutankhamun, and the process continued under Horemheb; the brightly painted blocks were thereafter reused as fill for building works at the same site – in the construction of the second, third, ninth and tenth pylons as well as in the foundations of the great Hypostyle Hall. Other blocks of the same type, found reused at Luxor temple in the Ramesses II pylon and at Medamud by later, 19th-Dynasty kings, prove similarly to have originated from Amenophis IV's dismantled Karnak structures.

Slow and painstaking work by archaeologists, occasionally computer-aided, has resulted in the successful reconstruction of a number of scenes which once decorated the Aten complex at Karnak. This particular wall, still preserving impressive amounts of the original colour, is decorated with bustling views of daily life in the temple storerooms, workshops and brewery.

The great bulk of the Karnak blocks was brought to light during the 1920s and 1930s; sadly, the documentation of their original arrangement, which would have been immensely helpful in the reconstruction of the monuments, was inadequate, and much additional confusion was caused during their removal and subsequent storage. Despite these difficulties, the years of study by Redford's team in particular have been crowned with great success, in that it has been possible not only to reconstruct a number of key scenes but to demonstrate convincingly that the temples from which the *talatat* originate were four in number, erected for and after a *sed*-jubilee celebrated by Amenophis IV. The Karnak monuments may be listed as follows:

• *Gemetpaaten* ('The Aten is found'), the largest of the temples, represented by blocks recovered from the foundations of the Hypostyle Hall at Karnak and from within the second and ninth pylons. From the tentative attempts at representing the 'revolutionary' new art style and the presence of a single daughter, Meritaten, this presumably was the first monument commissioned by the king, perhaps in Year 2; further, as a result of excavations carried out at the site from 1975 on, we now know that it was the original home for 28

Henri Chevrier's excavations in progress at the site of Akhenaten's extensive temple complex at Karnak. The colossal sculptures the Frenchman's work brought to light – shocking in their extreme, early Amarna style – had been dismantled and buried, like the buildings they adorned, following pharaoh's death.

*Seen from below – the angle at which Amenophis IV-Akhenaten's
Karnak colossi were intended to be viewed – the peculiar
distortion of the king's face is far less apparent; the impression is
one of unadulterated power. The early form of the Aten's name,
contained in a pair of cartouches, is inscribed in raised
plaquettes on the arms and on the torso.*

bases and 25 magnificent but sadly frag-
mented royal colossi first discovered by Henri
Chevrier in 1925. The structure's location, to
the north of the temple of Amun, was presumably balanced on the south by the
king's palace; this structure is mentioned in the texts but, since it will
have been of mud-brick construction, no traces survive;

• the temples *Rudmenu* ('Enduring in monuments') and *Tenimenu*
('Exalted in monuments'), structures perhaps commissioned
around Year 3 and conceivably
erected in the vicinity of the ninth
pylon, where their component
blocks were found;

• the temple *Hutbenben*, 'Mansion of the
benben-stone', the stone which was the cultic focus of the Heliopolitan sun-
cult. An addition to the *Gemetpaaten*, the sole officiant depicted in this
structure's decorative scheme is Nefertiti, whose role as the female element
in the worship of the Aten was clearly of fundamental importance. The
temple, which incorporates in its scenes a second daughter, Meketaten, was
erected in about Year 4.

In the solar design of its architecture – as no doubt in other ways – the
Atenist religion was indebted to many aspects of the Heliopolitan cult. The
temples of the Aten were open to the sky, bright and airy – in complete contrast to the dark, secluded inner recesses of Amun's cult, thick with incense
and redolent of mystery and the unknown. The open nature of the Aten
temples points up another difference: namely, that there was no need of a
cult image, since the god was visible constantly throughout the hours of
daylight. As a result, much of the daily routine of the old religion could
be dispensed with, and the Aten's priesthood was correspondingly smaller.
Its prime function now, it seems, was the presentation of daily offerings
and their retrieval after the divinity had taken his fill. More importantly, the
role of the priests was established, once again according to *maat* or 'proper
order', as mere 'servants of the god' – their principal, of course, being
pharaoh himself.

THE JUBILEE OF THE ATEN

Though similar temples were subsequently raised at el-Amarna, Heliopolis, Memphis, Hierakonpolis, Nubian Sesebi and elsewhere, the Karnak structures stand at the heart of the Atenist revolution; and it is these early monuments – and more particularly their documentation of the mysterious jubilee which Amenophis IV-Akhenaten celebrated after only his second or third regnal year – which hold the key to an understanding of events at this time.

The principal question the Karnak temples pose is this: why did Amenophis IV decide to celebrate a *sed*-festival so far in advance of his 30th year of rule? In fact, the usual three-decade lead-in before a king's first jubilee was often flouted, and for reasons which are not at all apparent. The explanation which will be explored here, however, is that the timing of Amenophis IV's *sed* was influenced not by the regnal years of his own reign, but by those of his father.

A precise correlation between the *sed*-festivals of Amenophis III and those of his son cannot be proposed with absolute conviction, since the figures as they stand do not quite add up; but the suspicion that Amenophis IV's jubilee coincided with either the third *sed* of his father or with the occasion of a fourth jubilee which had been planned for Amenophis III's 40th or 41st year, is difficult to shake off.

If Amenophis III did not live beyond his 38th regnal year, as Egyptologists usually assume, a correlation with the third jubilee would necessarily imply a brief period of co-rule between the two kings; a correlation between Amenophis IV's *sed* and a projected fourth *sed* of Amenophis III would not. If, however, Amenophis III lived on for a year or two *after* the celebration of his third jubilee and his highest attested year 38 – which is not inconceivable –

Block from Karnak with the remains of two scenes from the sed-festival celebrated early in the reign. On the left Akhenaten is shown making offerings to the Aten, while on the right the king is shown in close-fitting festal robe flanked by deeply bowing priests; in both scenes it is pharaoh alone who is bathed in the life-giving rays of the solar disc.

both the brief co-regency which seems indicated by other features (see above) *and* the equation with this unachieved fourth *heb-sed* of Amenophis IV's first jubilee might be accommodated. The arguments are both complex and speculative, but the possibility seems to offer a way forward.

Interestingly enough, a parallel to 'jubilee by proxy' has been recognized in the *sed*-festival reliefs of Tuthmosis IV at Amada: since this king died after a relatively short reign, leaving no other evidence to suggest he celebrated a jubilee in his own right, it has been proposed that the ritual recorded at Amada had, in fact, been celebrated on behalf of his predecessor, Amenophis II. If this is so, then Amenophis IV at Karnak was following in his grandfather's footsteps, celebrating this jubilee on the deceased Amenophis III's behalf – though with an added spin given to the proceedings, as we shall see, by Amenophis III's solar aspirations.

The jubilee reliefs of Amenophis IV reconstructed by the ATP have added considerably to the surviving corpus of depictions of this ancient rite (from Abu Ghurab, dating from the reign of the 5th-Dynasty king Niuserre; from the Karnak temple of Khonsu, Soleb, and the Theban tomb chapels of Khaemhat (TT57) and Kheruef (TT192), from the reign of Amenophis III; and from the festival hall of Osorkon II at Bubastis), the aim of which was to confirm and revitalize pharaoh in the presence of the gods and of the people.

Yet the Amenophis IV celebrations differ markedly from these other *sed*-festivals of which we know: here, at Karnak, the only divinity mentioned is Aten – Amun, Ptah, Thoth, Osiris and the other great gods before whom the rites are traditionally enacted and whose multiplicity Amenophis III indeed celebrated are conspicuously absent; nor is Amenophis IV anywhere shown running the traditional course to demonstrate his physical fitness to rule. Interestingly, too, while the courtiers attending the festival celebrations of Amenophis III are mentioned by name, those taking part in the son's *sed* are identified only by their office.

Not improbably (to judge from the 'earlier proclamation' of the el-Amarna boundary stelae, discussed below), further rejuvenation rituals were envisaged, to be celebrated at intervals following this first, Karnak jubilee at the new capital the king was about to establish at el-Amarna in Middle Egypt. Direct evidence is admittedly slight – a single Hermopolis block, now in the Metropolitan Museum of Art in New York, which bears part of a chair-carrying scene paralleled in the king's *sed*-festival reliefs at Karnak. But a theoretical scheme of repeated jubilees celebrated at el-Amarna at intervals as the reign progressed might prove to link in with various 'key' stages in the development of the Atenist revolution – stages which will reveal themselves in due course.

ART AND HISTORY

If, as we assume, Amenophis IV did in fact rule for a spell as co-regent with his father, then the monuments suggest that the son's revolutionary aspirations were held in close check during that time. He first appears – in the

Theban tombs of the high officials Kheruef (TT192) and Ramose (TT55), perhaps on the occasion of his investiture as co-regent – in pure Amenophis III style, like a child dressed by his parents, as a miniature adult, a mirror image of his father. He is permitted to embark upon a restricted programme of construction work at Karnak, using conventional-sized blocks, to build a temple dedicated to his personal god; and here too, in the earliest reliefs, the young king is shown in a wholly conventional manner, the only concession to his individuality being a gentle acknowledgment of plumpness. The Aten itself, in its earliest Karnak manifestation, displays the same orthodox appearance: shown as a traditional, falcon-headed god wearing the solar disc with encircling uraeus, the divinity is distinguished from a dozen similar gods by his mantra alone – 'Re-Horakhty who rejoices on the horizon in his name of Shu (light) which is the sun disc (Aten)'.

Other monuments of Amenophis IV's early years are known, each commissioned in the same conservative spirit – including damaged rock stelae at Zarnikh, opposite Esna, and Aswan, and the enormous inscription cut into the rocks at Gebel el-Silsila. Undated, this last records an expedition sent out by the king to quarry a block of golden-yellow quartz-sandstone. This was to be carved as the *benben*, cultic focus of the Karnak temple which the king, 'first prophet of Horakhty', was in process of building. The vignette of the stela is again carved with a scene in traditional style and shows Amenophis IV offering to Amun-Re beneath a winged solar disc.

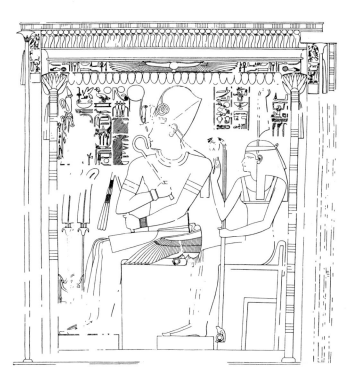

The Theban tomb of Ramose (TT55), Amenophis III's vizier, was in the process of decoration at the time of the old king's death, and illustrates the suddenness of the change accompanying Amenophis IV-Akhenaten's accession to sole rule. On the left, as youthful co-regent, the son is represented in the staid, formalistic manner of his father's later years; on the opposite page, in the revolutionary style which would soon become familiar – a scene of Amenophis IV and his consort, Nefertiti, showered with 'life' and 'dominion' by the rays of their solar god, the Aten.

Change, when it came, was sudden, and the most likely explanation is that parental shackles had been removed – that Amenophis III, in short, was now dead. The moment of transition is captured, dramatically, within a single monument – the tomb of Amenophis III's southern vizier, Ramose, a relative of Amenhotep son of Hapu. Although much of the tomb's carved relief decoration is executed in the senior king's elegantly formal style, with his death the restraining hand of decorum is removed and we witness, virtually overnight, fully formed, the imposition of Amenophis IV's relaxed and naturalistic vision, not only on the king and his chief queen, Nefertiti – who are sketched standing in the 'Window of Appearance' beneath the protective, life-giving rays of the Aten – but also upon poor Ramose himself. Whether the official was pleased with Amenophis IV's efforts, which in one instance are balanced provocatively with the old on the opposite side of the same wall, history does not relate; but the styles of the father and his newly independent son make strange bedfellows today, and must have caused a few raised eyebrows in antiquity too. The tomb was, in any case, never completed – perhaps because the workforce had been transferred to more pressing works either locally or at the new capital, Akhetaten (below); perhaps because Ramose died – conceivably of shock. Another tomb displaying similar

A sandstone block from Karnak preserving the remains of two scenes. On the left, the Aten is seen in its earliest manifestation – not as a rayed solar disc but in anthropomorphic form with a falcon's head. The fragmentary scene on the right shows Amenophis IV himself, in the style current during his father's reign.

stylistic juggling was also left unfinished: that of the steward Parennefer (TT188), a younger, more flexible man, evidently, to whom the king would grant a new sepulchre (no. 7) at el-Amarna later in the reign.

Significantly, this sudden change of style coincides with the erection at Karnak of the structures necessary for the celebration of the *sed* it is proposed Amenophis IV was now preparing to celebrate on behalf of his deceased father. This was clearly an event of superlative importance – for it marked, I would suggest, the culmination of Amenophis III's solar divinization.

AMENOPHIS III: THE ATEN REVEALED

With the celebration of the Karnak jubilee, a significant change occurred in the manner in which the Aten was represented. The old, falcon-headed god disappears, replaced by the new, hieroglyphic form seen in the Ramose reliefs: the soon-to-be ubiquitous solar disc extending rays of life and dominion to the noses of the pharaoh and his queen. Accompanying this new depiction of the god is the same didactic name we encountered in the earliest of Amenophis IV's representations of the god – the mantra which lays such particular emphasis on the light which, for the new pharaoh, was

considered the true essence of the solar theology. Now, significantly, this mantra is contained within two cartouches (*left*), supplemented by a formula indicating that the Aten is a god who celebrates *sed*-festivals. It is as if the Aten were a king – which is how, in effect, the god was henceforth regarded.

The regal status of Amenophis IV's solar cult is articulated for the first time on the occasion of the Karnak jubilee celebrations, and, as a result, its nature stands clearly revealed: the Aten and Amenophis III are one and the same, the king's solar divinity now formalized, in death, in an abstract iconography appropriate to his newly disembodied state. But much more than this: uniting with the disc in the beyond in the time-honoured fashion, Amenophis III is but one royal essence among many. The cult of the Aten has become the cult of kingship itself – the final act in the gradual and deliberate reassertion of kingly power sparked by Hatshepsut's abasement, a century earlier, to the Amun priesthood. The homophony discerned by Gerhard Fecht between the ancient pronunciation of Aten ('Yati') and the Egyptian for 'my father/forefather' ('yata') – expressions which dominate the inscriptions of the period – was clearly much more than an amusing play on words.

TRUE REVOLUTION

The adoption of the new iconography was accompanied by a series of revolutionary changes which would entail the reversal of every aspect of Egyptian life, from modes of religious worship to language and terms of address. The name attached to the fourth of Amenophis IV's temples at Karnak, the *Hutbenben*, 'Temple of the *benben*-stone', underlines the radical nature of these changes, and the king's evident desire to present them as a return to first principles and the unsullied (and unpoliticized) religious 'purity' first expounded in the solar worship of earliest times. Yet, for all its claims to having been sourced in the far-distant past, the emphasis of the regime would henceforth be on the new, the fresh, the concrete, the here and now. This was true revolution. Time, in a sense, was redundant; everything had been stabilized by the final transformation of Amenophis III to the godly sphere, and the formal establishment of his and his ancestors' worship now that the son had ascended the Egyptian throne.

Kingship past, present and future were as one, indivisible, divine; and the office – in theory, at least – was more powerful now than it had ever been. As a reflection of this new reality and his anointed role as the Aten's 'chief of seers' and 'high priest', pharaoh changed his name: no longer Amenophis, 'The god Amun is content', from Year 5 he was known as Akhenaten, 'He who is effective on the Aten's behalf'. Akhenaten was now his father's sole representative on earth, and their co-regency was set to continue.

Courtiers cringe in the dust at the feet of the all-powerful king – in fear as much as in respect. A sandstone talatat *block from one of Amenophis IV-Akhenaten's dismantled Karnak structures.*

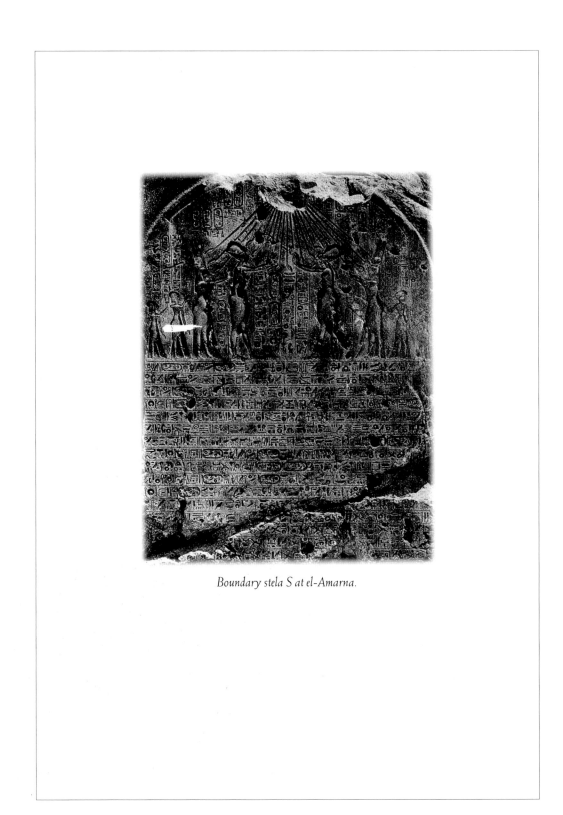

Boundary stela S at el-Amarna.

CHAPTER FIVE

THE MOVE TO EL-AMARNA

'Then said [Akhenaten]: "Bring me the king's companions and
the great ones of the palace, the supervisors of the guard, the
overseers of works, the officials and all of the court in its
entirety". So they were led into him at once, and they lay on
their bellies in his majesty's presence, kissing the ground before
the great god. Then said his majesty to them: "Behold Aten! The
Aten wishes to have [a city] made for him as a monument with
an eternal and everlasting name …"' EXTRACT FROM THE EARLIER
PROCLAMATION OF THE EL-AMARNA BOUNDARY STELAE

Further change was in the air. Within a very few years of his father's death,
Amenophis IV-Akhenaten decided to abandon both Memphis, Egypt's
administrative capital, and Thebes, its religious heart, to their officials and
their priests; pharaoh's domain, he decreed, would henceforth be ruled from
a new city dedicated exclusively to the new deity: Akhetaten, 'Horizon of
the Aten'. According to the inscription on a chair belonging to the necropolis worker Nakhy, 'servant in the Place of Truth on the west of
Akhetenaten [sic]', this was a designation which had originally been applied
to Thebes itself. But Thebes had evidently proved unworthy of its new god,
and was now to be abandoned for good. The move, characteristically impulsive and peremptory – we shall consider why later – was nevertheless an
opportunity for the king to crystallize his vision.

The new Akhetaten was to be built far from the southern city, on virgin
land in an unoccupied, easily policed
desert bay in the eastern cliffs which
border the Middle Egyptian Nile. Here,
at the modern site of el-Amarna, in the
very centre of the country, the Aten and
its high priest would reign supreme,
unchallenged by any other god. It was
an act of high drama, and for most
Egyptologists today the doing of a religious maniac. But change tends not to

*Akhenaten bestows gifts from the 'Window of
Appearance' at el-Amarna – a detail from the
highly stylized relief decoration of a courtier's
tomb (that of Parennefer, no. 7).*

happen without a reason – particularly change as fundamental as this. It was a situation which history would witness again, and on more than one occasion; and one later recurrence, in a very different part of the world, perhaps has something to teach us.

Japan: the foundation of the Heian state

'The rivalry between the throne and the temple, the struggle between priest and king for power ... is a characteristic of *all* nations ...' Leslie White

Some two thousand years after Akhenaten's birth, towards the end of the 8th century AD, on the opposite side of the globe, the Japanese imperial court took the radical decision to abandon the existing capital at Nara and move, lock, stock and barrel, to a new site elsewhere. There would be two attempts at the shift: first stop, in 784, was a site known as Nagaoka, located to the southwest of present-day Kyoto; and this move was followed, a decade later, by a second transfer to the site of Kyoto itself, then named Heian-kyo. For Japanese historians, the abandonment of Nara marks the start of a flourishing new era, the Heian period; what interests the Egyptologist is less this future glory than the dynamic behind the move.

Japanese society at this time was dominated, and would continue to be dominated for some years to come, by the influence of a single family: the Fujiwaras. The strength of the Fujiwara clan depended upon two factors: first, various key positions they held within the government structure had, during the course of time, become hereditary; and, secondly, the tradition had grown up of marrying-off Fujiwara daughters not only within the imperial family but to the very emperor himself.

The jealousies and intrigues Fujiwara prestige generated at court were considerable, and beginning to pose a real threat to stability; matters were made worse by an extraordinary rise in the wealth and political power of the Buddhist temples and their personnel, and an attendant jostling on the part of the priests themselves for worldly influence and control. It was a situation which clearly could not be allowed to continue.

With the accession of a new and capable emperor, Kanmu (who owed his own rise to a Fujiwara plot involving the removal of an inconvenient rival prince), the problem was addressed by upping sticks. It was a clever ruse: by it, the troublesome priests were abandoned in Nara, while the drain on time, effort and money required to build the new capital provided a more than adequate distraction to those among the aristocracy inclined to make mischief. When this mischief continued, in 794 the process was repeated, and the capital moved yet again, to another site geographically close-by but physically more remote; and this time it worked. With the aristocracy cut off from their economic base, and the priesthood left behind in their temples, power was again concentrated firmly in the hands of the emperor.

Although the cultures of Egypt and Japan are separated by a great distance in time, space, and much else besides, the parallels between Kanmu and the Amarna experience are striking: for 'Fujiwara' substitute 'Yuya family'; for 'Buddhist priesthood', 'Amun priesthood'; for 'Kanmu', 'Akhenaten'; for 'Nagaoka' and 'Heian-kyo', 'Akhetaten'. What the Japanese experience points up is that the Amarna revolution, albeit born from particular circumstances, would follow a historically familiar course – and one dictated less by theological insanity than by court intrigue and politics.

POLITICS AT THE EGYPTIAN COURT

Life in the upper reaches of the Egyptian state will perhaps always have been a Machiavellian affair, though until the days of Hellenistic Greek rule under the Ptolemies (332–30 BC) the records are frustratingly silent on the political deeds and misdeeds of the country's élite. Only occasionally in dynastic times does the curtain lift to reveal the extremes and possible dangers of court life – and, when we are able to take a peek, it becomes clear how much we have been missing. Plotting was clearly endemic, and the sly administration of poison, the 'accidental' bump on the head, the surreptitious sliding of a knife between the divine ribs – these were all too often the grim realities of the Egyptian political system.

An informative glimpse of the frail reality behind the god-like mask of dynastic rule is afforded at the start of the 12th Dynasty, during the reign of its founder, Ammenemes I (1991–1962 BC). This king, who hailed from Elephantine in the south, was not of royal stock but had served as vizier to Nebtawyre Mentuhotep. Nebtawyre was the second successor of Neb-hepetre Mentuhotep, who had achieved the reunification of a divided north and south following the disruptive years of the First Intermediate Period (2134–2040 BC). Ammenemes himself came to the throne under dubious circumstances; it was clearly a difficult time, and, in a move which has intriguing parallels with our story, early in his reign he abandoned the existing capital city, Thebes, for a new site in the vicinity of el-Lisht – Itjtawy. As the Japanese experience suggests, this was no whim on the king's part, but a determined attempt to consolidate power in the face of continuing opposition. For Ammenemes I, in personal terms, the ploy failed; and, unlike the Japanese emperor Kanmu, he would have no second chance for it to succeed. As the spirit

Ammenemes I, founder of the 12th Dynasty. Faced with continuing opposition from vested interests in Thebes and Memphis, the king decided to found a new capital city at Itjtawy. By abandoning Thebes for el-Amarna, Akhenaten was employing the same stratagem.

Extract from the 'Teaching of Ammenemes I', inscribed in hieratic on two joining amphora sherds from el-Amarna house M 50.31 – one of only two literary texts known from the new city. The lines are those which describe the assassination of Ammenemes I by his bodyguard – lines memorialized for their topicality, perhaps, following an attempt on Akhenaten's life? Or as a thought for the future?

of the king recalls in an extraordinary literary composition known as 'The Teaching of Ammenemes I to his Son Sesostris':

"'It was after supper, night had come. I was taking an hour of rest, lying on my bed, for I was weary. As my heart began to follow sleep, weapons for my protection were turned against me, while I was like a snake in the desert. I awoke at the fighting, alert, and found it was a combat of the guard. Had I quickly seized weapons in my hand, I would have made the cowards retreat in haste. But no one is strong at night; no one can fight alone; no success is achieved without a helper. Thus bloodshed occurred while I was without you, [my son Sesostris]; before the courtiers had heard that I would hand over to you; before I had sat with you so as to advise you. For I had not prepared for it, had not expected it, had not foreseen the failing of the servants.'"

The reference is oblique, acknowledging the delicacy of the subject-matter, but it is clear that the king had been killed – in the tradition recorded by Manetho, at the hands of 'his own eunuchs'. Ammenemes I's ghostly advice to his son was clear and to the point:

"'Beware of subjects who are nobodies, of whose plotting one is not aware. Trust not a brother, know not a friend, make no intimates – it is worthless! When you lie down, guard your heart yourself, for no man has adherents on the day of woe. I gave to the beggar, I raised the orphan, I gave success to the poor as to the wealthy; but he who ate my food raised opposition, and he whom I gave my trust used it to plot …'"

This was a teaching Akhenaten evidently knew well – of extant texts, not only are the majority of New Kingdom date, but the 'Teaching of Ammenemes I' is one of only two literary texts reported from el-Amarna. Ammenemes' fate Akhenaten was determined to avoid. The move to Middle Egypt, we may be sure, had at its roots far more than fanciful religious experimentation: for pharaoh, its architect and driving force – as for Ammenemes I before him – it was a fight for very survival. And this, indeed, is what is hinted at today in the sadly battered series of documents known as the boundary stelae.

THE AMARNA BOUNDARY STELAE

The ancient site of Akhetaten was demarcated by a series of great boundary stelae, of which a total of 15 have been recorded. The first of those discovered on the west bank, by the French traveller Claude Sicard in 1714, is known as stela A; the first of those on the east bank is stela U, which was observed in 1840 by Anthony Charles Harris, an Alexandria-based English merchant travelling in company with George Gliddon – the latter soon to establish himself as a successful lecturer in matters Egyptological on the American circuit. But it was to be Karl Richard Lepsius, leader of the Prussian expedition, following in Harris and Gliddon's footsteps a short time later, who first publicized in the *Denkmäler* the important inscriptions the monuments carried. Not until 1908 would Egyptologists be provided with a full text, thanks to the labours of Norman de Garis Davies; and now, almost a century later, a new and more reliable edition of these important inscriptions has been published by the American scholars William J. Murnane and Charles C. van Siclen III.

Practically everything we know about the founding of Akhetaten, and the reasons for Amenophis IV's abandonment of Thebes, is

El-Amarna boundary stela A, located on the west bank of the Nile just south of Tuna el-Gebel, together with its attendant, rock-cut sculptures of Akhenaten and his family – a drawing made in 1827 by Robert Hay (shown in Turkish dress on the right), an early visitor to the site.

recorded on these important, rock-cut stelae. In terms of their contents, the monuments fall into two main groups: the three stelae of the first group (designated M and X, plus a later rescript, K), are dated to Year 5 of Akhenaten's reign, and carry a text known as the 'earlier proclamation' delivered in early April of that year; the second group, comprising 11 stelae (A, B, F, J, N, P, Q, R, S, U and V) are dated to Year 6, with either one or two supplemental texts dated to Year 8, essentially confirming and amplifying the oath previously made. A further 'boundary stela', smaller and with a very poorly preserved and seemingly anomalous text, is designated L. It is not impossible that further boundary markers will in due course be uncovered by the shifting sands or by an eagle-eye scrutinizing some wind-worn rock face – and this would indeed be helpful, since the texts of the known series are riddled with lacunae and obscurities.

The earlier proclamations, on stelae M, X and (in its probable original form) K, were each positioned to the rear of a niche just over 1 m (3 ft) wide; the emplacement of K was apparently later cut back to incorporate attendant, three-dimensional carved images of the king and queen and two princesses. This was the impressive form of architectural setting continued for the later proclamations. Most of the boundary stela sculptures are now destroyed, but fragments can be recognized today (from their characteristic fossil-bearing stone) in several museum collections around the world, including the Ägyptisches Museum in Leipzig, the Fitzwilliam in Cambridge and the Matsuoka Collection in Tokyo.

THE DEDICATION

The significance of the boundary stelae lies not in their striking architecture but in their historical content as official proclamations of royal policy – presented for the first time in the contemporary mode of speech known as Late Egyptian – at three critical points in Akhenaten's reign.

Following a lengthy opening paragraph setting out the recently adopted official titulary of the new solar triad – Aten, Akhenaten and Nefertiti (see below) – the narrative begins as follows:

> 'On this day [Year 5, fourth month of the growing season, day 13], when one [i.e. the king] was in Akhetaten, his majesty appeared on the great chariot of electrum – just like Aten, when he rises in his horizon and fills the land with the love and the pleasantness(?) of the Aten. He set off on a good road towards Akhetaten, his place of the primeval event, which he [the Aten] made for himself to set within it daily, and which his son Waenre [Akhenaten] made for him – being his great monument which he founded for himself; his horizon, in which his circuit comes into being, where he is beheld with joy while the land rejoices, and where all hearts exult when they see him.'

Akhenaten and Nefertiti steal a kiss in the great royal chariot of electrum. The vehicle is closely similar to those discovered by Howard Carter in the tomb of Tutankhamun in 1922.

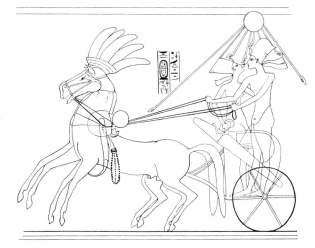

A description is given of the oblation made by the king to his god, before the inscription recounts how Akhenaten had his courtiers brought before him:

> 'Then said his majesty to them: "Behold Aten! The Aten wishes to have [...] made for him as a monument with an eternal and everlasting name. Now it is the Aten, my father, who advised me concerning it – namely Akhetaten. No official had ever advised me concerning it, nor had any people in the entire land ever advised me concerning it, to tell me to make Akhetaten in this distant place. It was the Aten, my father, who advised me concerning it, so that it could be made for him as Akhetaten. Behold, I did not find it provided with shrines or plastered with tombs or porticoes(?) ... or covered with ... or with the remnant of anything which had happened to it... Behold, it is pharaoh – life! prosperity! health! – who found it, when it did not belong to a god, nor to a goddess; when it did not belong to a male ruler, nor to a female ruler; when it did not belong to any people to do their business with it.... I found it abandoned....
> It is the Aten, my father, who advised me concerning it, saying: 'Behold, fill Akhetaten with provisions – a storehouse for everything!', while my father [Aten] proclaimed to me: 'It is to belong to my majesty, to be Akhetaten, forever and eternity..."'

The king then declares, on oath, that the Aten's wish will be carried out – and that the burden for carrying this project is to fall upon those in attendance: 'Make Akhetaten as an estate of the Aten, my father, in its entirety – for I have made it as a memorial, whether belonging to my name or belonging to her name, namely the great royal wife Nefernefruaten-Nefertiti, or belonging to his [the Aten's] name forever and eternity.' It was to be a city controlled, on the god's behalf, by the king and queen alone. The Aten desires, and the king acts – precisely the situation mirrored by the king's new name, 'Akhenaten': 'He who is effective on the Aten's behalf'.

With the king's remarks the courtiers obsequiously concur:

> '"May his lordship govern from Akhetaten. May you conduct every land to him [the Aten]. May you tax the towns and islands

for him. Every city down to … every … belonging in its
entirety to the Aten, acting in accordance with what he
himself ordains … '"

Having established the role of his people, Akhenaten goes on to define
the precise boundaries of the Aten's new domain:

"'Since he casts [his rays] on me, bestowing life and dominion
forever and eternity, I shall make Akhetaten for the Aten, my
father, in this place. I shall not make Akhetaten for him south of
it, north of it, west of it or east of it. I shall not go past the
southern stela of Akhetaten toward the south, nor shall I go past
the northern stela of Akhetaten downstream, making Akhetaten
there. Nor shall I make it for him on the western side of
Akhetaten; but I shall make Akhetaten for the Aten, my father,
on the eastern side of Akhetaten – the place which he himself
made to be enclosed for him by the mountain, on which he may
achieve happiness and on which I shall offer to him …'"

This is the predestined location of the Aten's city, echoing the form of the
hieroglyph depicting the sun rising above the eastern horizon; no one else –
whether it be the queen, the official classes or the common people – had
influenced the Aten's choice, made manifest through the king. Nowhere else
would Akhenaten choose to live.

THE MOTIVATION

A listing of what were to be the new capital's principal features (considered
further below) is then rudely interrupted by the following interjection:

"'As for the … in Akhetaten [= Thebes?]:
– it was worse than those things I heard in regnal year 4;
– it was worse than [those things] I heard in regnal year 3;
– it was worse than those things I heard [in regnal year 2;
– it was] worse [than those things I heard in regnal year 1];
– it was worse [than] those things [Nebmaat]re [Amenophis III]
heard;
– [it was worse than those things which … heard];
– it was worse [than] those things which Menkheperre [Tuthmo-
sis III] heard;
– [and it was] worse [than] those things heard by any kings who
had ever assumed the White Crown [i.e. controlled the south]!'"

This change of tack is of extraordinary interest. Not only does it confirm the
suspicion that the text recorded in the boundary stelae is a near-verbatim

Stela S – one of the best-preserved of the el-Amarna boundary texts, with its lunette containing mirror-image scenes of the king and his family in adoration of the Aten. Carved after Year 6 of Akhenaten's reign, it contains a version of the 'later oath', with a supplemental 'repetition' dated to Year 8.

record of the king's speech – in which case we have preserved here a rare insight into Akhenaten's rhetorical style; but the outburst presents Akhenaten's justification for the move from the first, Theban Akhetaten – characteristically opaque when first expressed and now, thanks to later damage, all the more so. The sentences which follow are fragmentary, and preserve little connected narrative. What is clear, however, is that these 'things' were 'against my father' and 'offensive'. Had society scoffed at pharaoh's revolutionary beliefs? Had Akhenaten taken offence? Or are we to discern in these words something far more serious – that there had been a direct challenge to pharaoh's authority within Upper Egypt?

As other sources indicate, pharaoh and the Amun priesthood had been in uncomfortable alliance for a number of reigns, though tensions had apparently eased somewhat under Amenophis III. Had old enmities now resurfaced with the accession of a strong-minded son who brooked no opposition? Had Akhenaten's determination to reimpose *maat* – for him, the rightful dominance of pharaoh – so upset Egypt's vested interests that events had now taken a more serious turn?

As the unhappy fate of Ammenemes I demonstrates, Egypt had in the past been no stranger to court intrigue of the most dangerous kind; while a nasty, harem-based conspiracy against the 20th-Dynasty king Ramesses III confirms that such threats were to continue well after Akhenaten's time. The wording of the boundary stelae decree is exceptionally strong – too strong, it would seem, for anodyne explanation – and powerfully stated. The provocation, clearly, had been a serious one.

Had there, in short, been an attempt on the life of the royal person? What could have been *worse* than regicide? If Akhenaten had narrowly escaped assassination – and his subsequent persecution of the Theban god does indeed suggest a grudge of considerable magnitude – then he was now moving cleverly and decisively to outflank the opposition.

Pharaoh and his new city bathed in the life-giving rays of the Aten – a scene in the Amarna royal tomb.

CHAPTER SIX

UTOPIA

EXODUS

That Akhenaten's theological designs should have provoked resistance from the Amun priesthood is hardly surprising; yet, ironically, as we now see, it may well have been this very resistance which hardened the king in his resolve and prompted the decision to desert Thebes for pastures new.

For the heralded move, the king must have been able to count upon a substantial degree of support, and this seems to have been supplied by at least two elements within the country. One of these was the military, the class to which Yuya had belonged and among which his probable son, Ay, now exercised influence. Thanks to the conquests of his ancestors, pharaoh had long been able to call on a standing army, and its upper echelons were bound to the palace by an unquestioning personal loyalty resulting from their shared upbringing as 'children of the *kap*' (royal nursery). It was a military whose massed ranks Akhenaten took every opportunity to celebrate in temple reliefs, first at Thebes and later at el-Amarna, and the respect is reciprocated as the troops, who are everywhere, bow almost double before their royal master.

The second area of support, we may venture, came from the younger generation who supplied Akhenaten's 'new men' – starred individuals like the overseer of prophets of all the gods, Parennefer, and the chancellor Maya. These and others among the royal retinue claimed to have owed their rise to the new king's favour alone – and we are inclined to believe them; as creatures untainted by family ties and obligation to the old system, they will have been eager to carry out Akhenaten's will. For more ordinary youngsters, it will all have been viewed as a fashionable and exciting adventure, a contrast to the staid and perhaps stale atmosphere of conservative Thebes. For the new generation, pharaoh was hero of the hour, the man who had re-established true order on the Egyptian world. There was energy in the air; the people believed.

HORIZON OF THE ATEN

The virgin stretch of land Akhenaten chose for his new city was located on the eastern bank of the Nile within the 15th Upper Egyptian nome or district, some 320 km (200 miles) south of Memphis, the administrative capital of the country, and 400 km (250 miles) north of Thebes, the New Kingdom's religious and economic heart. It was a choice dictated by several factors, one of which, clearly, was the site's suggestive topography with its notched cliff reminiscent of the hieroglyph *akhet*, 'horizon', through which the sun god was reborn each morning. Politically neutral (by its absence of occupation), el-

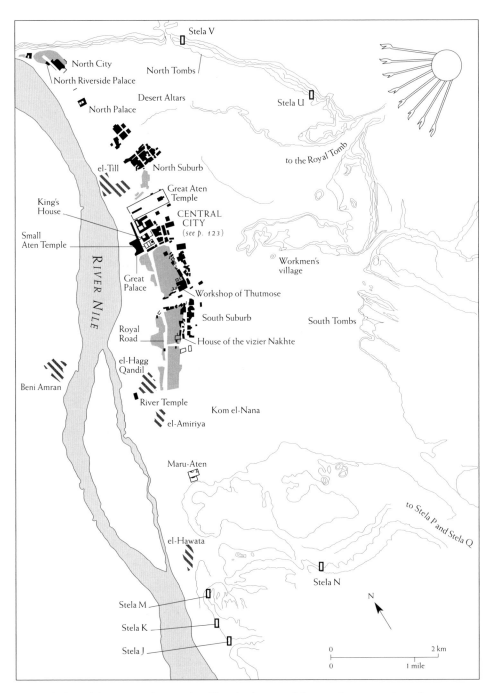

The bay of el-Amarna, showing the ribbon development of the city along its north-south spine, the 'Royal Road'. Focus of the settlement was the Central City, with the Small and Great Aten Temples, the Great Palace and the busy administrative quarters. Above and below were dormitory settlements, while to the east, in the cliffs, were located the tombs of the royal family and Akhetaten's highest officials.

Amarna was also well-suited topographically, as equidistant between these established cities, to combine their roles of administrative and economic control. For the monarch himself, it was a centrality which may have held a deeper significance: for, whereas Thebes appears to have owed its new prominence under Amenophis III to its position as the literal centre of the *greater* Egyptian homeland (Egypt proper and Nubia down to Soleb and Sedeinga), the site chosen for Akhetaten was precisely midway between Egypt's *traditional* borders – the Delta in the north and Elephantine in the south.

Here, perhaps, we have a first clue to one of the characteristics of Akhenaten's reign: his demonstrable lack of interest in the 'empire' abroad (to the inexorable decline of which we shall later return). Despite the universality of the Aten and the official dogma propounded in the Great Hymn to the Aten (discussed below) that all men are equal regardless of skin colour, and despite the occasional burst of energy expended abroad, notably in the south (a campaign against Ikayta, and the erection of a temple at Sesebi deep in the Sudan), we are left with a lurking impression that pharaoh considered the lands beyond Upper and Lower Egypt essentially an irrelevance – foreign, impure, and their inclusion within Egypt's borders not in accordance with the earliest concept of *maat* which he saw it as his mission to reimpose.

LAYING OUT THE CITY

"'At Akhetaten in this place shall I make the House of Aten for the Aten, my father;
– at Akhetaten in this place shall I make the Mansion of the Aten for the Aten, my father;
– at Akhetaten in this place shall I make the Sunshade of the great royal wife Nefernefruaten for the Aten, my father;
– in the Island of the Aten, whose jubilees are distinguished at Akhetaten in this place shall I make the House of Rejoicing in Akhetaten for the Aten, my father...
– And at Akhetaten in this place shall I make for myself the residence of pharaoh – life! prosperity! health! – and I shall make the residence of the great royal wife ...
– Let a tomb be made for me in the eastern mountain of Akhetaten, and let my burial be made in it, in the millions of jubilees which the Aten, my father, decreed for me. Let the burial of the great royal wife Nefertiti be made in it, in the millions of years which the Aten my father, decreed for her. And let the burial of the king's daughter Meritaten be made in it, in these millions of years ...
– And let a cemetery be made for the Mnevis bull in the eastern mountain of Akhetaten, so that he may be buried in it. Let there be made tomb chapels for the chief of seers, for the god's fathers of the Aten, and the ... of the Aten in the eastern mountain of Akhetaten, so that they may be buried in it ...'"

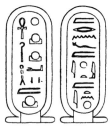

This is how the early boundary stelae define the form Akhetaten was to take. Work seems to have begun almost at once. The force which carried out the project, like that which had laboured at Karnak in previous years, is largely anonymous, but was doubtless a combination of the usual conscript labour, the military (of whom there are representations carrying out such tasks in the *talatat*), and (from the distorted echoes of truth in Manetho's record) Egyptian and foreign slaves also.

Drawing on the existing infrastructure, with the banks of the Nile supplying mud for bricks and the local cliffs and quarries in the north the limestone with which the cores of most of the principal structures were faced, some three or four years after foundation the new settlement appears to have been ready for the formal installation of its king. The likelihood is that this installation was the occasion for the promulgation of a new, 'purified' (abstract) form of the Aten's name: 'Re, horizon ruler, who rejoices on the horizon in his name of Re the father, who has returned as the sun disc' (*above left*). And with this installation, as we shall see, came the terror.

Akhenaten's construction programme has been studied in detail by Egypt Exploration Society architect Michael Mallinson. It evidently began with the erection of the two boundary stelae M and X, one to the north and one to the south, the mid-point between these serving to define the central axis of the city. On this axis, Akhenaten erected the first altar, initially a simple sacred grove (the future Small Aten Temple), with a small palace (the King's House) to its northern side; at the termination of the axis – at the same distance east–west as the stelae are north–south – he would establish his tomb. A second temple erected to the north (the future Great Aten Temple) and two other important palace complexes to the north (the North Palace)

and south (the South Palace) seem to have been positioned by reference to key distances along the processional routes at Thebes (Karnak–temple of Mut; Karnak–Luxor).

In the second discernible stage of development at el-Amarna, the first simple shrines were replaced with stone sanctuaries bounded by enclosure walls, their form based on the small stone temples of Amenophis III at Karnak, but open to the sky in the manner of the Heliopolitan sun temples. Again, certain

A master-relief recovered from the royal tomb of el-Amarna, gridded to facilitate transfer of the design to the tomb wall. The scene is a familiar one: the king, queen and royal daughters make offering to the Aten, which bathes the royal family in its life-giving rays.

correlations in the dimensions of the el-Amarna structures and earlier building-works at Karnak and at Heliopolis have been recognized by Mallinson. The conclusion which has suggested itself to him is that Akhetaten's two principal temples were in fact symbolic substitutes for the two main Re shrines at Heliopolis and Karnak – those of Re-Horakhty and Amun-Re. For Mallinson, the king's aim was evidently for the new capital to unite the essence of the two cult centres within a single ambit.

The final stage in setting out the city saw the symbolic nature of the structure extended and clarified, with 12 more stelae erected to establish the final boundaries across the Nile river and into the desert. Now, for the first time, we begin to discern the amazing rationale behind the kingly scheme. By joining up the dots, so to speak, Mallinson has been able to show that the proportions of the Great Aten Temple, when projected out, replicate those of the city limits – revealing the hidden truth that the entire foundation had in fact been conceived as one vast temple. What is more intriguing still, however, is the focus of this 'temple': the Amarna royal tomb, located beyond the break in the eastern cliffs through which the Aten was reborn each day.

The Amarna royal tomb as source of all life at el-Amarna: a computerized reconstruction showing how the boundary stelae were intentionally positioned to replicate the plan of the Great Temple. The focus of that 'temple's' worship is clear – the royal tomb, from which the Aten (and kingship) is reborn each and every day.

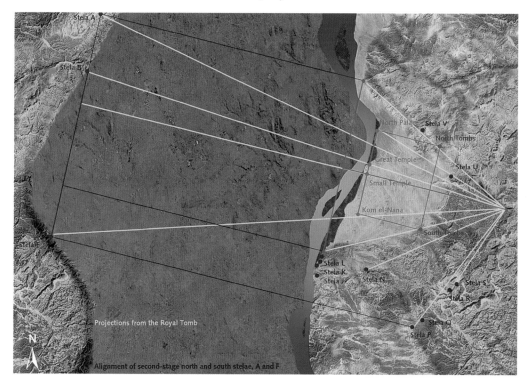

In this light, Akhenaten's vow not to extend beyond the limits set by the boundary stelae becomes easier for us to understand; as does his stated desire that, wherever he die, he be interred within the royal tomb. With the royal tomb as the *raison d'être* of Akhenaten's architectural scheme, our newly discerned basis of Amarna religion – the kingship itself – finds extraordinary confirmation. In this new theology, the royal tomb is the sepulchre not only of Akhenaten himself: as the place of the Aten's rebirth, it represents the burial place and point of daily resurrection of *every* king of Egypt, past, present and future, who has or will ultimately become one with the solar being. Akhenaten's much-vaunted worship of a single god was nothing of the sort; it was ancestor-worship writ large, emphasizing the divine power of the kingship with a will and determination not demonstrated since the days of the pyramids.

THE AMARNA BOUNDARY STELAE

Designation	Location	Content	Date
A	west bank	later proclamation	Year 6
		'repetition of oath'	Year [8]
		'another oath'	Year [8]
B	west bank	later proclamation	Year [6]
		'repetition of oath'	Year 6
		'another oath'	Year 8
F	west bank	later proclamation	Year [6]
		'repetition of oath'	Year 8
J	east bank	later proclamation	Year [6]
		'repetition of oath'	Year [8]
K	east bank	earlier proclamation	
		(rescript)	Year 5
L	east bank	[anomalous]	Year ?
M	east bank	earlier proclamation	Year [5]
N	east bank	later proclamation	Year [6]
		'repetition of oath'	Year 8
P	east bank	later proclamation	Year 6
		'repetition of oath'	Year [8]
Q	east bank	later proclamation	Year [6]
		'repetition of oath'	Year [8]
R	east bank	later proclamation	Year 6
		'repetition of oath'	Year 8
S	east bank	later proclamation	Year 6
		'repetition of oath'	Year 8
U	east bank	later proclamation	Year 6
		'repetition of oath'	Year 8

Designation	Location	Content	Date
V	east bank	later proclamation	Year [6]
		'repetition of oath'	Year [8]
X	east bank	earlier proclamation	Year [5]

AKHENATEN'S CITY

'Tell el-Amarna is a city of mud brick. Only in very exceptional
circumstances was stone used. The brick is merely sun-dried,
and ... [in] a country where rain is exceedingly rare ... will last
for ever ...' JOHN PENDLEBURY

New capitals had been established before, and would be founded again in
Egypt and elsewhere. But Akhenaten's was a shift carried out in some style.
The new Akhetaten was envisaged on a heroic scale, enclosing an area of
over 200 sq. km (77 sq. miles), much of it agricultural land on the west bank
of the Nile, housing a population which has been estimated at between
20,000 and 50,000 souls.

By Year 9 it was ready for its official inauguration – and, to judge from the
number of wine-jar dockets of this date recovered from the site, it must have
been quite a party. Akhetaten was rich beyond compare, amply funded from
the start by its king and with further investment to come as the wealth of the
old gods was in due course redirected to benefit the new. And this money
worked wonders. If the trees and bushes so commonly represented in the
reliefs reflect a true reality, Akhetaten was a green and pleasant land, well
watered by its many wells – a notable feature of Amarna town planning – and
as far removed as can possibly be imagined from the arid wasteland it
appears today. Let us consider what, of this city, Time has left to us.

North City

The so-called 'North City' is a self-contained area at the northern edge of the
site of el-Amarna, incorporating an administrative complex of mud-brick
courtyards and storage magazines. To the south have been identified large
domestic villas for the city's élite – though, intriguingly, these do not include
the highest officials of the administration who, like the vizier Nakhte, as
excavator Barry Kemp notes, appear to have 'lived almost as far away from the
king as [they] could'. These villas border the northern continuation of the
simply swept but still impressive Royal Road, which linked the North City
with the Central City. To the west of this road stand the ruins of the fortified
structure today referred to as the 'North Riverside Palace' – a square-towered
construction decorated with scenes of the royal family and now for the most
part lost as a result of the Nile's changed course; for Kemp, this was 'the principal royal residence at Amarna'. A little further south is the 'Great Ramp'
which perhaps represents the remains of a bridge over the Royal Road.

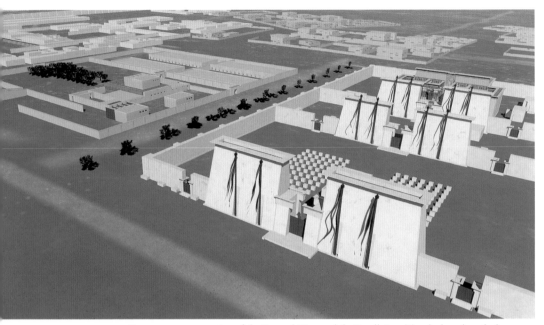

Computer reconstruction of the Central City and the Small Aten Temple, based on the latest excavations at the site. Open to the sky, behind the first pair of gleaming white pylons with their poles and streamers may be seen row upon row of altars arranged to receive offerings.

North Palace

Another self-contained element of the city was the 'North Palace' (which, though also originally siding the river, is to be distinguished from the North Riverside Palace). Situated in an isolated location to the south of the Great Ramp on Royal Road, the North Palace is famous today for two things: first, its exquisite wall paintings depicting marsh life (which suggested to Pendlebury that it might originally have been 'a kind of Zoological Gardens where the King could watch animals and birds and satisfy his love of nature'); and, secondly, its assumed role as the place of refuge of queen Nefertiti following her supposed 'disgrace'. It was, as we shall reveal, the dwelling of a queen, but the queen in question was a lesser wife of Akhenaten named Kiya – of whom more later – and not Nefertiti herself. Kiya's inscriptions and images here were subsequently altered, however, for a new occupier at the end of the reign: Akhenaten's daughter-queen, Meritaten.

North Suburb

The North Suburb, now extensively excavated, has revealed itself as a residential area which was still growing in extent at the time el-Amarna was abandoned under Tutankhamun. Laid out in a far less systematic manner than the official quarters of the city (below), with a few notable exceptions the houses are also smaller, more densely packed and of lower social status than those in the corresponding South Suburb. Unlike the royal family, whose lives were remote and detached, the different classes of ordinary folk mingled freely here as elsewhere at el-Amarna. 'Suburb' in fact conveys a misleadingly sleepy impression of its original character. As Barry Kemp points out: 'Quite apart from the rubbish that filled every open space … the houses were busy centres of private manufacture as well as of the storage and handling of farm produce. They were generators of part of the city's economic substance.'

One of the most familiar of the North Suburb 'villas' is that excavated by the EES in 1929 – T36.11, which is a typical example of the dwelling type. Access was gained to its grounds (originally surrounded by a 3-m (10-ft) high, crenellated mud-brick boundary wall) by means of a keepered gate. Such gates were frequently supplied with jambs and/or a lintel bearing the owner's name and official titles, though sadly most of these identifying texts had been carried off in antiquity for reuse. At the end of the entrance path lay the domestic chapel dedicated to the Amarna triad of Aten-king-queen, and beyond that the gardens. Following the path round to the right, however, the visitor was led through into a small courtyard and the domestic quarters proper – labelled by the excavators as porch, vestibule, four-pillared north loggia, four-pillared central room (with clerestory windows), two-pillared west loggia and, leading off from the central room, the single-pillared women's quarters. Around this formally decorated, central core of rooms were arranged half a dozen bedrooms and store chambers, and bathrooms, with stone fitments and occasionally a toilet with comfortably shaped seat. A second storey in such houses may not have been uncommon, though naturally enough little evidence has survived. Abutting the boundary wall lay the various service buildings – servants' quarters, kitchens, stables, kennels and granaries. The regular orientation was to the east, and for a reason, as Pendlebury, the excavator, would note: 'an East wind is a rarity, and unless things have changed very much in three thousand years it was better to be in the windward of your servants and food.' In common with all the dwellings at el-Amarna, the wooden furniture and other valuable portables of T36.11 had gone, carried off at the time the city was abandoned. But it is not difficult, from the reconstructions which have been

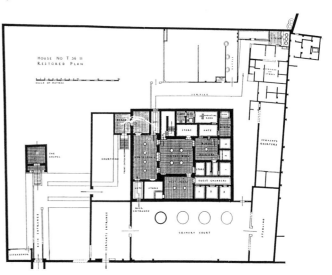

Restored plan of house T36.11 in the North Suburb of el-Amarna, excavated by John Pendlebury in 1936. The general design of a central chamber surrounded by a series of smaller rooms tended to be constant, the distinction between the homes of the rich and less so being primarily one of scale.

made, to visualize the house occupied and peopled with its elegant proprietor and his family and servants, equipped with low stools and chairs draped with elegantly coloured textiles. And comfortable, too, as Pendlebury observes: 'A prince might have a dozen columns in his entrance hall and a few more rooms, a poor man was content with a hovel consisting of a central room with mere cubby-holes opening off it, but the principle of a main living-room surrounded by others to keep it cool is invariable.'

Central City

The ancient administrative heart of Akhetaten is today referred to as the Central City. It was situated on a slight rise; in antiquity bordering the Nile, it was known as the 'Island of the Aten distinguished of jubilees'. This was the only part of the site to be laid out on a grid, and the planning is impressive: self-contained blocks located according to their function and divided by straight streets. Much of the southern area of the Central City is now under cultivation, and remains to be excavated.

The focal point of this administrative district was the end section of the Royal Road, with the principal structure the Great Palace ('The house of rejoicing in Akhetaten') (2; numbers refer to the plan, p. 123), positioned on the waterfront and beautifully appointed with painted pavements (of which Flinders Petrie uncovered the remains in 1891, later destroyed), and courtyards, of which the largest was once equipped with colossal statues of the king. Equally striking must have been an annexed building erected by Akhenaten's

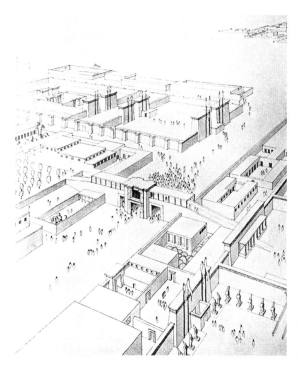

successor, with its maze of columns and wall-to-wall coloured faience. Here, in the Great Palace, open to the sky and to his god, pharaoh would receive foreign envoys – and, as their kings would complain, not always with the best of grace: 'Why should messengers be made to stay constantly out in the sun and so die in the sun? If staying out in the sun means profit for [pharaoh], then let [the messenger] stay out and let him die right there in the sun – but for [pharaoh] himself there must be a profit.'

Reconstruction (by Egypt Exploration Society architect Ralph Lavers) of the Central City as it once appeared, looking from north to south. In the centre is Royal Road, with the Small Aten Temple and King's House to the left, and the Great Palace on the right. On the bridge is the 'Window of Appearance' from which Akhenaten is so frequently seen in the reliefs bestowing the royal favour.

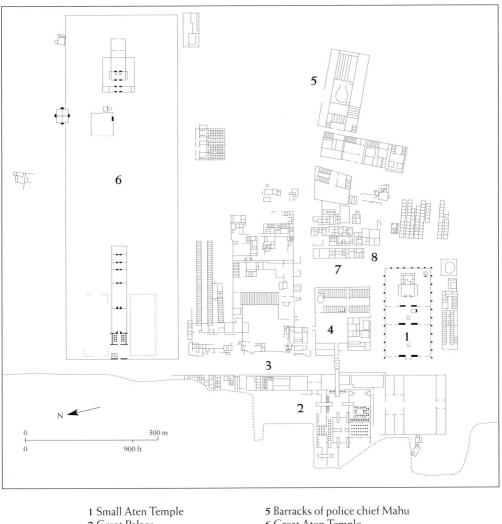

N

0 ——— 300 m

0 ——— 900 ft

1 Small Aten Temple	5 Barracks of police chief Mahu
2 Great Palace	6 Great Aten Temple
3 Royal Road	7 Records Office
4 King's House	8 'House of Life'

Simplified plan of the Central City area at el-Amarna.

In this same area of the Central City, connected to the Great Palace by a bridge, was another, more practical royal residence – the King's House (4), comprising three separate elements: a palace; a courtyard; and magazines. This was the place where pharaoh met with his ministers, as well as the probable location of the 'Window of Appearance' so frequently encountered in the reliefs. From here the king bestowed upon his loyal subjects collars and other gifts of gold to symbolize the divine light of the sun, as well as provisions – the frequent depiction of this act emphasizing the dependence of the populace (or, at least, the court) on pharaoh's continuing beneficence. Clearing a ruined side chamber in the King's House in 1891–92, Petrie uncovered fragments of the marvellous fresco painting preserving an exquisite image of the king's youngest daughters (p. 20). And servicing this house and the other institutions was a range of mud-brick magazines, the barracks of the police chief Mahu (5), and administrative offices (including the Scriptorium, or 'House of Life', and the famous Records Office (7)), together with a restricted dormitory sector whose rubbish mounds yielded to Petrie's diggers much imported Mycenaean Greek pottery testifying to an extensive, continuing trade between the two cultures at this time.

The enormous Great Aten Temple ('House of the Aten in Akhetaten') (6) was located on the opposite side of Royal Road from the Great Palace; although originally faced with stone, most of this was robbed out in antiquity and only mud-brick cores and foundations now remain to trace out its plan on the ground. This structure contained new versions of the *Gemetpaaten* ('The Aten is found') shrine and the *Hutbenben* ('Mansion of the *benben*-stone'), first erected at Karnak. Measuring some 730 m (2,395 ft) in length and 229 m (750 ft) wide, the Great Temple was the nerve centre of the Aten cult at el-Amarna. Perhaps never completed, its ancient appearance was that of a vast open space enclosing a mass of regularly laid out altars of mud-brick, 365 each for Upper Egypt and for Lower Egypt. Upon these altars offerings from the two geographical domains were made to the Aten daily, before the food reverted to the priests and populace after the god had had his fill. Dedications of cult furniture, such as *situlae* (ritualistic buckets) were also made, and occasionally in the names of private individuals.

For all their physical openness, this and other Atenist temples were probably as remote from the people as Egypt's traditional shrines. Though detailed drawings in the Egyptians' peculiar perspective-less style were provided on the walls of the temples and the Great Palace and in the tombs, and have been explained by some scholars as an attempt to demystify the structures, they more probably, in traditional fashion, served simply to guarantee their functioning into eternity. These representations of the principal

The sanctuary of the Great Aten Temple at el-Amarna, as depicted in a block transported from the city for reuse at el-Ashmunein (Hermopolis Magna) across the river. Statues of the king with tables of offerings and tall, trumpet-shaped stands with burning incense flank the principal altar, which is piled high with offerings of food and flowers.

(Above) Two torsos of fine, indurated limestone discovered (together with a mass of smaller fragments) by Howard Carter while working for Flinders Petrie in the vicinity of the Great Aten Temple in 1891. The subjects are (left) Nefertiti, clad in pleated, diaphanous robe, and (right) Akhenaten. Each is embellished with pairs of cartouches containing the early form of the Aten's name; both statues originally held offering tables.

Amarna temples show them to have been embellished with numerous standing statues of Akhenaten and Nefertiti (and occasionally of other individuals also, including Amenophis III, Tiye and Akhenaten's 'other' wife, Kiya), facing towards the focus of the city – the royal tomb – and holding in their hands a flat offering tray. By chance, the smashed remains of 17 or more of the Great Aten Temple's statues, carved in the exquisite indurated limestone of Qau, had been dumped unceremoniously beyond its boundary by later wreckers, and were here uncovered by Howard Carter in 1892. Wonderfully carved to a superb finish, they must, when intact, have been among the finest sculptures of the reign.

Located 500 m (1,640 ft) to the south of the Great Aten Temple, to the rear of the King's House, was the Small Aten Temple ('Mansion of the Aten in Akhetaten') (1). Mallinson's interpretation has been mentioned above; by

Akhenaten presents a table of offerings to the solar deity: a small, limestone statue from an el-Amarna house-shrine, excavated by the Deutsche Orient-Gesellschaft in 1911. The modelling is in the more moderate style favoured later in Akhenaten's reign, and, like the Louvre sculpture (p. 85), probably gives a good impression of the king's appearance in life.

its alignment with the royal tomb, the presence of a 'robing room' and its own 'Window of Appearance', this structure was equated by previous commentators with the royal mortuary temple of old, where the king's cult was celebrated both before and after death. It too had been largely constructed in stone, though again this had been later robbed-away to leave the substantial brick core noted by the *savants* of Napoleon's Egyptian expedition in 1799.

South Suburb

Less than 50 per cent of the area to the south of the Central City has so far been excavated. This, the South Suburb, like its northern equivalent, was essentially a residential quarter, though with some administrative buildings; it appears to be somewhat earlier in date than the North Suburb, which may represent a settlement overflow testifying to the success of the foundation during its early years. The occasionally higher social status of the South's inhabitants is apparent not only from the larger floor area of the villas and the frequency of walled gardens but from the increased evidence of stone jambs and lintels carrying the name and principal titles of the house owners, many of whom are well known – the priests Panehsy and Pawah, for example, the vizier Nakhte and the general Ramose. The most famous of the villas excavated here, however, is that belonging to Thutmose, one of a number of sculptors who had settled in this sector. Thutmose's house doubled as a studio for the production of royal portraits – an amazing collection of which, as recounted in Chapter 1, was uncovered here by the Germans in 1912, including the famous one-eyed bust of Nefertiti now in Berlin (see p. 24).

'River Temple'

The so-called 'River Temple' was first excavated by the Egypt Exploration Society in 1922 close to the modern village of el-Hagg Qandil, and was recently re-examined by the Egypt Exploration Society. Once believed to provide the only evidence of continuous occupation on the site from the 18th Dynasty through until the 26th Dynasty – several hundred years after the heretic's city had been formally abandoned – it is now recognized as in fact a very late structure merely incorporating Amarna stone.

Kom el-Nana

The ruins of Kom el-Nana, close to the modern settlement of el-Amiriya, were for many years described as a Roman camp. Excavations by Barry Kemp on behalf of the Egypt Exploration Society have now revealed a large stone temple of Amarna date, in part surrounded by a formal garden of small trees and a range of service buildings including a bakery – clearly another self-supporting institution. As Kemp observes, 'It says much for our ignorance of the Amarna Period that the existence of this major building, still without its original name and ownership being known, should have remained unknown until so recently.'

Maru-Aten

Maru-Aten, the ancient name of a site which has now entirely disappeared beneath the ever-encroaching cultivation, comprised two large, walled areas each enclosing a series of shrines and solar altars, or 'Sunshades', assigned to various of the royal women, with gardens and a small lake. The pavements, as frequently at el-Amarna, were painted with marsh scenes, substantial portions of which have been recovered in the course of excavations. The surviving blocks of the structures here are of great historical interest: in common with those from the North Palace, they reveal the usurpation by Meritaten of texts and images originally prepared not for Nefertiti, as once assumed, but for the shadowy Kiya.

The desert sites

The desert areas to the east of the city proper have preserved a number of monuments from the period, linked by an ancient criss-cross of still-visible tracks; these had been made and would be followed by the ancient police presence whose role, perhaps initially to guard against the incursions of desert outlaws and other undesirables, not improbably broadened in time to one of keeping the city's population in. One of the most significant of these outlying sites is that today known as the Desert Altars; this consists of a series of buildings erected just below the North Tombs, perhaps for the 'reception of foreign tribute' in Year 12 of the reign (below). Other features of interest include the Workmen's Village, a settlement of 64 houses of regular form contained within an enclosure wall with outlying chapels. This village appears to have been occupied well into the reign of Tutankhamun, its workers' role having perhaps included the preparation, servicing, safeguarding and eventual dismantling of the royal necropolis. A second settlement of similar nature not far distant has been dubbed the Stone Village.

The royal tomb (Amarna tomb no. 26)

At the very start of his reign, while Amenophis IV still entertained hopes that Thebes itself might successfully be transformed into 'Horizon of the Aten', pharaoh appears to have planned for his eventual burial within the confines of the Valley of the Kings, close to his father, Amenophis III. The son's original tomb is probably to be recognized today, on the basis of cutting and size, as the unfinished sepulchre now designated WV25, though a tomb later employed for the burial of Ay as king, WV23, is another possible contender. Work on Amenophis IV's Theban tomb had clearly advanced but a small way, however, when the decision was taken to abandon Thebes for good. Items of burial equipment which may have been commissioned at this early date would eventually find their way into the tomb of his son and successor, Tutankhamun.

The form Amenophis IV's Theban tomb was intended finally to take is unclear, but the sepulchre he excavated for himself at el-Amarna (Amarna

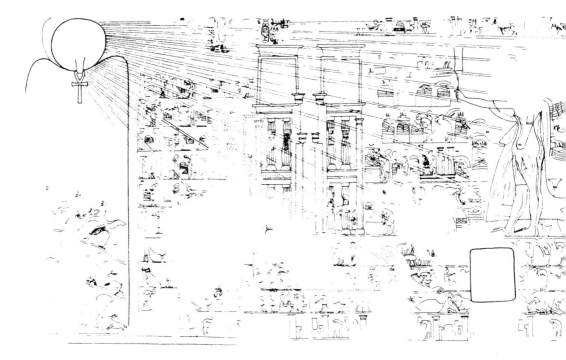

tomb no. 26) off the Wadi Abu Hasa el-Bahri deep in the eastern cliffs, an hour's ride and more from the Northern Tombs, differs markedly from the Theban sepulchre of his father, Amenophis III. Although the tomb was never completed, it is assumed that the cranked turn to the left of his predecessors had been abandoned in favour of a single corridor on a straight axis, interrupted by two flights of stairs with a central 'slide' to facilitate the introduction of the sarcophagi. Egyptologists Geoffrey T. Martin and Mark Lehner were the first to suggest that this new form of royal tomb, as originally conceived, might have been intended to allow uninterrupted access to the sun's rays. Mallinson's revelation that the royal tomb served as focus of the architectural scheme at el-Amarna indicates, in fact, that the beams of divine energy were perceived as travelling in the opposite direction – flooding *out* of the tomb and on to the city. The dynamic is graphically represented in sunk relief on wall A of room *alpha* – by chance one of the better-preserved scenes in the royal tomb.

From the presence of the nearby Amarna tombs nos. 27–30 (see below), it was clear that Akhenaten originally intended the site as a new Valley of the Kings, fulfilling the funereal aspects of his boundary-stelae pledge by preparing in the surrounding cliffs a whole series of independent, subsidiary burial-places for the various members of the royal family. The intended occupants will have included his mother Tiye, the great royal wife Nefertiti and his daughters.

With the early deaths of the king's second child, Meketaten, and his secondary wife, Kiya, however, the decision was taken to quarry a further

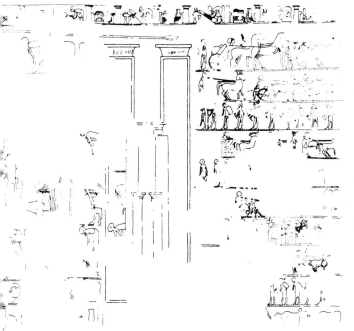

This scene on wall A of room alpha in the Amarna royal tomb is one of the most revealing of any to have survived from the period. In it the solar disc is seen to rise on the eastern horizon to shed its life-giving rays on Akhenaten's city – visual confirmation of Michael Mallinson's theory which would have the royal tomb as focus of the entire site.

suite of chambers on the north side of the entrance corridor of the king's own tomb, just above the stone-cut staircase before the tomb's protective 'well'. Wall reliefs in rooms *alpha* and *gamma* suggest that both wife and princess died in childbirth. A third phase of development within the tomb is represented by the curiously meandering corridor of undeniably royal form cut in this same wall closer to the entrance. The probability is that this 'royal tomb within a royal tomb' was intended to contain the burial of Nefertiti, following an increase in her status at court (see below) – though the possibility, if slight, cannot be ignored that Akhenaten may have been planning for the eventual reinterment here of his father, Amenophis III.

Like rooms *alpha* and *gamma*, the royal tomb's principal chamber, E, had also ultimately been employed, though in the original design of the tomb the room had been a mere pillared hall some distance from the intended holy of holies. It was evidently pressed into service at the death of the king's mother, Tiye, fragments of whose sarcophagus were cleverly and independently identified a few years ago by Edwin C. Brock, Marc Gabolde and Maarten Raven; the fragments had been recovered by Barsanti and later by the EES and others, together with the smashed up remains of the king's granite coffer, canopic chest and a whole mass of stone *shabti*-figures and other scraps. Akhenaten's burial had followed within a few years of his mother's, at which point two of the four rock-cut pillars and a section of the floor were removed to make sufficient space for his shrines and the chamber finally sealed.

Conceived as the powerhouse of the king's new religion, the royal tomb was of immense importance as the creative source of all life at el-Amarna. Indeed it may well have been this, its driving role, which would require the dismantling of its 'machinery' and the transfer of its occupants for a 'neutralized' reburial at Thebes following the abandonment of the Atenist dream under Tutankhamun.

Subsidiary burials (Amarna tombs nos. 27–30)

Despite the Amarna regime's denial of animal worship in the persecution which was to follow the move to el-Amarna (below), one creature, by virtue of its solar associations, did initially find official favour – the Mnevis bull, incarnation of the creator god Atum. Archaeologists believe that the animal was stabled during life in the North Palace; in death, according to Akhenaten's earlier proclamation, it would be favoured with a burial in the eastern cliffs of the new capital.

Although the location of the projected Mnevis cemetery has never been identified, the skull and several bones of a bull or ox were observed in 1980 by Geoffrey T. Martin and Mark Lehner in a side wadi off the Wadi Abu Hasa el-Bahri, sticking out of a dump of material excavated (presumably by the Pendlebury expedition) from tomb 28. The resemblance in plan of this tomb to the 18th-Dynasty Apis burials discovered at Saqqara in the 1850s is striking. Given this similarity, it is at least possible that these meagre remains represent not funerary offerings, as the finders initially assumed, but the actual remains of the Mnevis itself.

The adjacent, unfinished tomb no. 29, of typical royal design – though, lacking a sarcophagus slide, evidently of second rank – is that tentatively assigned to Akhenaten's youngest daughter, Nefernefrure; her apparent exclusion from the royal tomb would suggest that she died after her father.

Of the remaining royal-wadi tombs, we know virtually nothing.

THE ROYAL BURIAL GROUND AT EL-AMARNA: WHO WAS WHERE?

No.	Occupant/intended owner	Description
26	Akhenaten; Tiye; Meketaten; Kiya; Nefertiti-Smenkhkare?	elaborated royal type
27	?	royal type, steps with sarcophagus slide, unfinished beyond first corridor
28	Mnevis bull?	private type, three chambers
29	princess Nefernefrure?	royal type, steps, unfinished beyond fourth corridor
30	?	private type, small, unfinished

The private tombs (Amarna tombs nos. 1-25)

'The interest of the [private] tombs lies in the series of vivid
pictures they give us of life in the new city, and particularly in
the representations of public buildings and ceremonies which
they show. Carelessly and hastily carved as many of them are,
the new spirit of realism is strikingly evident.... In one scene
Nefertiti is devouring a whole chicken, Akhenaten is gnawing at
a large bone wrapped around with strips of meat.... In another
scene they are discussing a goblet of wine that is about pint size
and the King leans back slightly as it goes down ...' JOHN
PENDLEBURY

Strange to say, apart from the occasional *ad hoc* interment within the city
limits, no trace of a dedicated cemetery for the ordinary classes has ever
come to light at el-Amarna. Though several private *shabti*-figures belonging
to these people have survived, the whereabouts of the actual burials remains
one of the enduring mysteries of the site. Perhaps, as Pendlebury believed,
their principal cemetery 'is to be looked for on the Western bank, for tradition dies hard and for countless generations the Western desert had been the
last resting-place of the people.' But it is equally likely that, for all the city's
wealth and undoubted energy, to serve at this remote court for many felt like
exile. With insufficient time for a real sense of permanence to develop, close

*The royal family at table: Akhenaten attacks a mutton joint while his queen, Nefertiti,
chews on a duck or chicken; the third figure, on the right of the scene, is the king's mother, Tiye.
Three princesses are also shown, together with two servants who make ready further
delicacies for their royal master.*

links will have continued to be maintained with home-towns – where Amarna influence will have been much watered-down – and it is perhaps to these local towns and villages, in time, that the ordinary people tended to retire for burial among their ancestors.

The bulk of the non-royal tombs at el-Amarna, therefore, are those of Akhetaten's high officials. These were cut in the cliffs to the east of the city, in two distinct and perhaps ranked groupings: those known today as the Northern Tombs, 25 in total and a good walk from the North City, which must have been intended for the king's closest advisers and most favoured associates; and the Southern Tombs, 18 in number and a similar distance from el-Hagg Qandil, which from the officials' titles were prepared for the executive and administrative arms of the court. It is interesting to note that the large and impressive tomb of the god's father Ay, son of Yuya and Tjuyu, brother to queen Tiye and Aanen, and quite likely Nefertiti's father, is located among the southern group – explaining, perhaps, Ay's ability to step back from the regime following its collapse: he had simply been following orders.

The most impressive of the Northern Tombs are those of Huya, Meryre I and Panehsy; the best of the Southern group those of Ay and Mahu. The significance today of these and their fellows lies in the scenes, both in finished sunk relief and in preliminary ink sketches, which decorate their walls. In these scenes, contrary to earlier practice, the tomb owner is shown on a relatively small scale, with the bulk of the space given over to depictions of the royal family. Many of the scenes are of significant historical value: interior views of the Great Aten Temple (in the tomb of Meryre I); a sculptor's workshop (in the tomb of Huya); Nefertiti's sister Mutbenret/Mutnedjmet with her two dwarves (in the tombs of Panehsy,

Polychrome faience shabti-figure of the god's father Ay. The findspot of the piece, which has been in private hands for around a century, is not recorded; whether it was intended for the man's el-Amarna tomb, or as a votive image dedicated elsewhere, remains uncertain.

Maya and elsewhere); the 'visit' to el-Amarna of queen Tiye (the tomb of Huya), and the Year 12 'reception of foreign tribute' (commemorated in the tombs of Huya and Meryre II); and a unique representation of the mystery Amarna pharaoh Smenkhkare and queen Meritaten (in the tomb of Meryre II p. 168).

The abundant inscriptions which accompany such scenes are of both secular significance, providing numerous hints to the identities and evolving status of the various key players in the drama, and, of course, religious interest, the most notable contributions in this sphere being the famous hymns to the Aten in the tombs of Huya, Ahmose and Ay. Scenes of the deceased before the traditional funerary gods are wholly absent, in keeping with the 'purified' nature of Akhenaten's new religious scheme. They are replaced by images of the king and his queen, often making abundant offerings to the Aten – from which the deceased might, in due course, hope to benefit – as well as the gifting to the regime's principal officers of gold collars and other rewards for loyalty from the 'Window of Appearance'.

Before their desecration and decay brightly painted and architecturally imposing, these tombs inspired at least one Classical visitor to express in a scribbled graffito his admiration for the 'skill of the sacred masons'. They were, indeed, the highest of all expressions of royal favour and, as products of the state workforce, they followed a similar design, described by Pendlebury:

> 'In plan they are of essentially the same type as the rest of the
> XVIIIth Dynasty tombs at Thebes. There is a forecourt from
> which a door leads into a large Hall the roof of which is
> sometimes supported by "papyrus columns" left in the solid
> rock. The other feature is a chamber containing a statue of the
> owner of the tomb reached either directly from the Hall or via a
> corridor and anteroom. The grave shaft varies in position but is
> most frequently in the front Hall.'

Both their size and the quality of the carving (though this was compromised somewhat by the poor local stone) amply reflect the importance of the intended owners. For all their high rank, however, it remains a curious fact that mentions of these officials beyond the confines of their sepulchres are rare and generally inconsequential. The exception is Tutu, whom we encounter on several occasions as a royal envoy in the Amarna letters; and of course the god's father Ay, who comes into his own following the accession and early demise of his ward, the tragic Tutankhamun.

Most of the Amarna tomb-chapels appear to have been abandoned unused with the return to Thebes under Tutankhamun; certainly, little in the way of recognizable burial equipment has ever been brought to light here. More interestingly, not one is finished – even the earliest. This gives us, perhaps, our first clue to the Amarna regime's failure and ultimate collapse: compromised by financial mismanagement, the economy early began to fail. Before long, funds would run out altogether.

ADVISERS AND INTELLECTUALS: THE NORTHERN TOMBS

No.	Name	Principal titles
1	Huya	overseer of the royal harem overseer of the double treasury of the great royal wife steward in the house of the great royal wife Tiye
2	Meryre [II]	royal scribe steward overseer of the double treasury overseer of the royal harem of the great royal wife [Nefertiti] chief of the *menesh*-boat
3	Ahmose	true royal scribe fanbearer on the right of the king steward in the house of Akhenaten overseer of the court of justice
4	Meryre [I]	great of seers of the Aten in the house of Re fanbearer on the right of the king

No.	Name	Principal titles
5	Pentju	royal scribe king's chief first servant of the Aten in the mansion of the Aten in Akhetaten chief physician the two legs of the lord of the Two Lands chamberlain one who approaches the person of the king chief of chiefs noble of the first rank among the sole companions
6	Panehsy	first servant of the Aten in the house of the Aten in Akhetaten second prophet of the lord of the Two Lands Neferkheprure-waenre [Akhenaten] overseer of the double granary of the Aten in Akhetaten overseer of cattle of the Aten

PHARAOH'S EXECUTIVE ARM: THE SOUTHERN TOMBS

No.	Name	Principal titles
7	Parennefer	royal craftsman, pure of hands overseer of all the craftsmen of the king overseer of all the works of the king in the house of the Aten foremost of commoners one who accompanies the lord of the Two Lands in every place overseer of prophets of all the gods
8	Tutu	chamberlain first servant of Neferkheprure-waenre [Akhenaten] in the house of the Aten in Akhetaten first servant of Neferkheprure-waenre [Akhenaten] in the *wia*-barque

The site of the northern group of officials' tombs at el-Amarna, high in the cliffs overlooking the city. They were intended – to judge from the six which are actually inscribed – for the king's closest advisers.

135

Interior of the rock-cut tomb-chapel of Akhenaten's chamberlain, Tutu, no. 8 among the southern group of tombs at el-Amarna: the papyrus-columned transverse hall, looking north. Like all of the Amarna private tombs, it is unfinished and seems never to have been employed.

No.	Name	Principal titles
[8	Tutu]	overseer of all craftsmen of the lord of the Two Lands overseer of all works of his majesty overseer of silver and gold of the lord of the Two Lands overseer of the treasury of the Aten in the house of the Aten in Akhetaten chief spokesman of the entire land
9	Mahu	chief of police of Akhetaten
10	Ipy	high steward royal scribe overseer of the great harem of pharaoh steward of Memphis
11	Ramose	royal scribe steward of Nebmaatre [Amenophis III] scribe of recruits general of the lord of the Two Lands
12	Nakhtpaaten	vizier
13	Neferkhepruhersekheper	mayor in Akhetaten
14	Maya	general of the lord of the Two Lands overseer of the house of pacifying the Aten(?) steward of Waenre [Akhenaten] in Heliopolis overseer of all works of the king royal scribe

No.	Name	Principal titles
		scribe of recruits
		overseer of cattle of the temple of Re in Heliopolis
		fanbearer on the right of the king
15	Suty	standard-bearer of the bodyguard of Neferkheprure-waenre [Akhenaten]
19	Sutau	overseer of the double treasury of the lord of the Two Lands
23	Any	true royal scribe
		scribe of offerings of the lord of the Two Lands
		scribe of offerings of the Aten
		steward of the house of Aakheprure [Amenophis II]
24	Paatenemheb	royal scribe
		general of the lord of the Two Lands
		overseer of works in Akhetaten steward
25	Ay	god's father
		fanbearer on the right of the king
		overseer of all the horses of the lord of the Two Lands
		true royal scribe
		chief of archers

EL-AMARNA, THEBES – AND THE KINGLY AIM

Akhenaten's new city at el-Amarna was a settlement established from the very beginning according to a carefully thought-out geometrical scheme, in its details semi-standardized and – perhaps for the very reason that it was, in a sense, Akhetenaten (sic) at Thebes rethought and refounded – in the scheme's overall feel not dissimilar to that imposed on the southern city by Amenophis III. As Michael Mallinson has noted: 'One can say that Akhenaten was combining at Amarna the basic concept of Karnak, the scale of landscape transformation familiar to him from his father's great works at Malkata [Malqata], and the broader Theban topography laden, as it was, with religious associations.' Even the now-abandoned route of the Opet Festival, with its procession of Amun, Mut and the child-god Khonsu along the sacred, designated way from Karnak to Luxor, had its equivalent at el-Amarna: the still-impressive, 40-m (130-ft) wide connecting highway of Sikket el-Sultan – the Royal Road. And along it the 'new' sacred triad of Aten-Akhenaten-Nefertiti would now solemnly progress, the former in the sky above the people's heads, the latter on earth in their chariots of gleaming, solar gold.

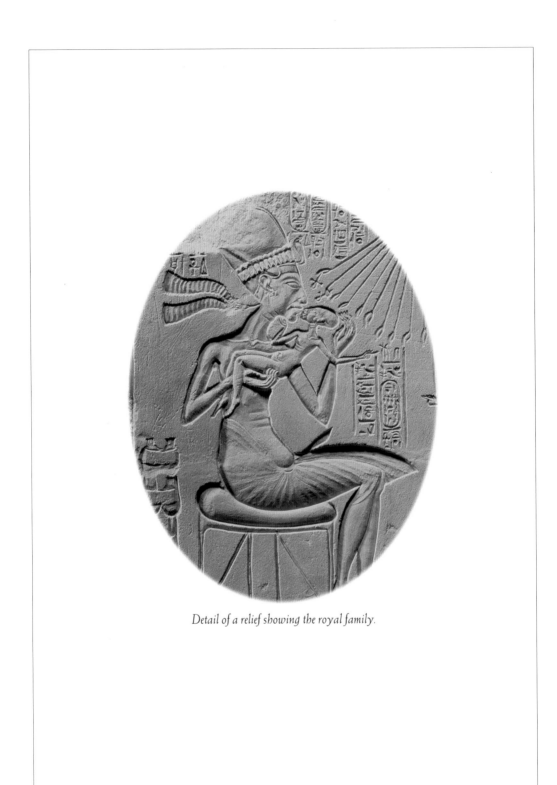

Detail of a relief showing the royal family.

CHAPTER SEVEN

RELIGION, ART —TERROR

'LIVING ON TRUTH'

An epithet employed by Akhenaten from the very start of his reign was *ankh em maat*, which translates as 'living on truth' but might better be understood as 'living according to the proper order'. This is the underlying theme of the king's 17-year rule: his aim, it is clear, was to return to first principles, to purify – ruthlessly, as we shall see, by whatever means necessary – a way of life he believed had strayed from its true course. The unifying characteristic of the regime was therefore change.

Akhenaten's version of *maat* placed particular emphasis on actuality and the here and now – in Amarna art; in the abandonment of Osiris and belief in a world beyond; in the modernizing of language – what was spoken was what was now written. But in practice change occurred at every level of life, from a preference for the use of small blocks in the king's building works at Karnak (an acknowledgment of Egypt's earliest and therefore 'purest' form of architecture, as seen at the Step Pyramid of Djoser) to the imposition of a novel designation for an office as mundane as that of chief vintner. No aspect of *maat* was too large or too small to receive pharaoh's personal attention.

For the people themselves, the intellectual beauty of pharaoh's creative spirit will have meant little. To an existence previously filled with celebration of the divine, the predictable cycle of the morning birth and evening death of the sun god now provided life's only rhythm. The festivals of the past which had divided the year and provided the stops and starts which powered day-to-day living were removed; and they do not seem to have been replaced – despite the fact, as Barry Kemp has observed, that 'worship of the sun provides a ready-made set of calendrical feasts [in the form of] the solstices and equinoxes'. The progress of the king along the Royal Road, however splendidly orchestrated, offered but a poor substitute.

None the less, the citizens of el-Amarna and Egypt generally seem to have struggled to accommodate their king's vision, glorifying not only publicly but in private letters the new reality as they once had the old – but, we may guess, ultimately with little conviction. The populace were grateful for their fine town and what for many will have been a superior standard of living, with well-designed accommodation and a secure income; but, given the magico-religious basis of medicine and so many other aspects of daily life, their need for the old gods was practical as much as spiritual. The constancy of this need is underlined by the not infrequent discovery at el-Amarna (and not always in post-Akhenaten contexts) of illicit images of the old gods – including Thoth, Ptah and, not surprisingly, Bes and Thoeris, the deities of the hearth.

THE NEW RELIGION

> '... all that we have of [Akhenaten] is contemporary and goes
> back to the man himself. His teaching is revealed to us by him
> alone, with no intermediaries, and it is subject to falsification
> only by modern interpretations' ERIK HORNUNG

Akhenaten's worship of the Aten has been variously characterized as religiously, intellectually or politically inspired. Probably it was all three, though the precise proportions of the mix are open to interpretation.

Pharaoh first articulated his beliefs at the very start of the reign, at Karnak, where the fragments of a key speech have been reconstructed by Donald Redford and the Akhenaten Temple Project:

> 'Look, I am speaking that I might inform you concerning the
> forms of the gods; I know their temples and I am versed in their
> writings, namely the inventories of their primeval bodies and I
> have beheld them as they cease to exist, one after the other,
> whether consisting of any sort of precious stone or [...] – except
> for the god who begat himself by himself [Atum] ...'

Graven images, the king pronounced, were man-made, albeit produced in accordance with age-old, prescribed patterns; the reality was that they came and went, no matter how precious and incorruptible the material. The only eternal was the originator of it all – the primordial god Atum, immanent in the solar disc, the Aten, which was reborn each and every day without fail. And within this sun, as other evidence suggests, in Akhenaten's belief resided the very essence of kingship itself.

Akhenaten identified the place of the Aten's rebirth, both on cosmological and topographical grounds, in the very centre of his realm, where he chose to locate his tomb, the focus of his new city, Akhetaten. The siting of this tomb, and of the lesser cemeteries associated with it, on the east rather than the west bank of the Nile, was new and intentional: it served to emphasize the living nature of the kingship as it manifested itself each day in the form of the dawn sun. The contrast with the traditional emphasis on the Osirian west, with its negative connotations of sunset, finality, death – for the Egyptians, contrary to popular belief, were no less fearful of, and depressed by, the cessation of life than ourselves – was striking and deliberate.

Initially, at least, Akhenaten's emphasis on life rather than death, on the here and now rather than the gloomy morrow, will have struck a popular chord – as the Inyotef Song, now recognized as a creation of this time, attests:

> 'Make holiday,
> Do not weary of it!
> Lo, none is allowed to take his goods with him,
> Lo, none who departs comes back again!'

The Great Hymn to the Aten.
Though extracts from this
evocative literary composition
are preserved in a number of
tombs at el-Amarna, the
fullest version occurs in the
tomb of the god's father Ay,
arranged in 13 vertical
columns above kneeling
images of the tomb-owner
and his wife.

Eat, drink, and be merry, was the Atenist cry – live for the moment.

The superficial appeal of the new religion is evident from the sentiments expressed in the 'Great Hymn to the Aten', a composition found in its fullest form in 13 vertical columns of hieroglyphic text in the tomb of the god's father Ay at el-Amarna, an inscription partially destroyed in 1890 but fortunately preserved in a copy made by Urbain Bouriant in 1883/84. As the most

explicit exposition of the Atenist vision to survive, and of particular significance in that it is a work deemed to have been penned by Akhenaten
himself, it is here quoted in full, after the translation of W. J. Murnane:

'Beautifully you appear from the horizon of heaven, O living
Aten who initiates life –
For you are risen from the eastern horizon and have filled every
land with your beauty;
For you are fair, great, dazzling and high over every land,
And your rays enclose the lands to the limit of all you have
made;
For you are Re, having reached their limit and subdued them for
your beloved son;
For although you are far away, your rays are upon the earth and
you are perceived.

When your movements vanish and you set in the western
horizon,
The land is in darkness, in the manner of death.
People, they lie in bedchambers, heads covered up, and one eye
does not see its fellow.
All their property might be robbed, although it is under their
heads, and they do not realize it.
Every lion is out of its den, all creeping things bite.
Darkness gathers, the land is silent.
The one who made them is set in his horizon.

But the land grows bright when you are risen from the horizon,
Shining in the disc in the daytime, you push back the darkness
and give forth your rays.
The Two Lands are in a festival of light –
Awake and standing on legs, for you have lifted them up:
Their limbs are cleansed and wearing clothes,
Their arms are in adoration at your appearing.
The whole land, they do their work:
All flocks are content with their pasturage,
Trees and grasses flourish,
Birds are flown from their nests, their wings adoring your ka;
All small cattle prance upon their legs.
All that fly up and alight, they live when you rise for them.
Ships go downstream, and upstream as well, every road being
open at your appearance.
Fish upon the river leap up in front of you, and your rays are
even inside the Great Green sea.

O you who brings into being foetuses in women,
Who makes fluid in people,
Who gives life to the son in his mother's womb, and calms him
by stopping his tears;
Nurse in the womb, who gives breath to animate all he makes
When it descends from the womb to breathe on the day it is born –
You open his mouth completely and make what he needs.
When the chick is in the egg, speaking in the shell,
You give him breath within it to cause him to live;
And when you have made his appointed time for him, so that he
may break himself out of the egg,
He comes out of the egg to speak at his appointed time and goes
on his two legs when he comes out of it.

How manifold it is, what you have made, although mysterious in
the face of humanity,
O sole god, without another beside him!
You create the earth according to your wish, being alone –
People, all large and small animals,
All things which are on earth, which go on legs, which rise up
and fly by means of their wings,
The foreign countries of Kharu [Syria] and Kush [Nubia], and
the land of Egypt.
You set every man in his place, you make their requirements,
each one having his food and the reckoning of his lifetime.
Their tongues differ in speech, their natures likewise. Their skins
are distinct, for you have made foreigners to be distinct.
You make the inundation from the underworld,
And you bring it to the place you
wish in order to cause the subjects to live,
Inasmuch as you made them
for yourself, their lord entirely,
who is wearied with them,
the lord of every land, who rises
for them,
The disc of the daytime, whose awe-
someness is great!
As for all distant countries, you make
their life:
You have granted an inundation in

'All flocks are content with their pasturage, Trees and grasses
flourish ... All small cattle prance upon their legs': a polychrome
faience tile from el-Amarna.

143

heaven, that it might come down for them
And make torrents upon the mountains, like the Great Green
(sea), to soak their fields with what suits them.

How functional are your plans, O lord of continuity!
An inundation in heaven, which is for the foreigners and for all
foreign flocks which go on legs;
And an inundation when it comes from the underworld for the
tilled land [Egypt],
While your rays nurse every field:
When you rise, they live and flourish for you.
You make the seasons in order to develop all you make:
The Growing season to cool them, and heat so that they might
feel you.

You made heaven far away just to rise in it, to see all you make,
Being unique and risen in your aspects of being as 'living Aten' –
manifest, shining, far yet near.
You make millions of developments from yourself, you who are a
oneness: cities, towns, fields, the path of the river.
Every eye observes you in relation to them, for you are Aten of
the daytime above the earth.
When you have gone, nobody can exist.
You create their faces so that you might not see yourself as the
only thing which you made.

You are in my heart, and there is none who knows you except
your son, Neferkheprure-waenre [Akhenaten],
For you make him aware of your plans and your strength.
The land develops through your action, just as you made them
[people]:
When you have risen they live, but when you set they die. You
are lifetime in your very limbs, and one lives by means of you.
Until you set, all eyes are upon your beauty but all work is put
aside when you set on the western side.
You who rise and make all creation grow for the king, as for
everyone who hurries about on foot since you founded the land,
You raise them up for your son, who issued from your limbs, the
king of Upper and Lower Egypt, lives on *maat*,
The lord of the Two Lands, Neferkheprure-waenre,
Son of Re, who lives according to *maat*, lord of diadems,
Akhenaten, great in his lifetime;
And the great royal wife, his beloved, the lady of the Two Lands,
Nefernefruaten-Nefertiti – may she live and be young forever
continually.'

Even in scholarly translation, the beauty of this hymn with its celebration of 'god as life' is self-evident – and, for the Judaeo-Christian world, much discussed resonances between the second stanza and the biblical Psalm 104 add to its appeal:

'Thou makest darkness, and it is night: wherein all the beasts of the forest do creep forth.
The young lions roar after their prey, and seek their meat from God.
The sun ariseth, they gather themselves together, and lay them down in their dens.
Man goeth forth unto his work and to his labour until the evening.
O Lord, how manifold are thy works! In wisdom hast thou made them all: the earth is full of thy riches....
Thou hidest thy face, they are troubled: thou takest away their breath, they die, and return to their dust.
Thou sendest forth thy spirit, they are created: and thou renewest the face of the earth.'

Reading this composition, the extent of Amenophis IV-Akhenaten's devotion to his god and the sincerity of his vision can hardly be questioned.
Or can they?

INTERPRETING THE HYMN

The Hymn's substance is little enough on which to build a new religion, and what is more the sentiments expressed are not particularly new: some motifs have been identified among the much earlier Coffin Texts, while other elements are found expressed in a virtually identical manner in a pre-Amarna hymn to the god Amun (Papyrus Bulaq 17); and this is to cite but two of Akhenaten's recognized sources. How are we to interpret such borrowings?

The standard answer is that Akhenaten's Hymn reflects in its composition common philosophical themes prevalent at that time in the Egyptian and Near Eastern cultural heritage, themes to which the king had clearly been exposed and from which he inevitably drew inspiration. This is undoubtedly so. But we sense also an air of deliberate contrivance, of familiar elements having been cynically combined and repackaged with a particular end in view. As James Allen has recognized, the worship of the Aten 'has less to do with man's relationship to god than with his understanding of the fundamental nature of reality'. And the nature of this new reality stands starkly revealed in the final stanza: 'There is none who knows you [Aten] except your son, Neferkheprure-waenre [Akhenaten]. For you make him aware of your plans and your strength'. This concept, too, refers back to earlier models (the text known as 'König als Sonnenpriester') which ascribe knowledge of the heavens and celestial bodies and their movements to the king alone; but here it is taken to a practical extreme. Not only did pharaoh's religion seek to deny the existence of other gods, whose representatives had fomented opposition to his will, but to the new god – itself a mere abstraction – only the king himself has direct access. The resultant dynamic is a revealing one: Akhenaten and his family worshipped the Aten, while the populace worshipped them. Whatever pharaoh's own personal beliefs – and they remain elusive – Atenism itself was in practice little more than a pragmatic instrument of political control. To quote James Allen again: 'The god of Akhenaten's *religion* is Akhenaten himself.'

It is hardly surprising, therefore, that Donald Redford should characterize 'the new concept of deity that Akhenaten produces' as

> 'rather cold. His Disc created the cosmos ... and keeps it going;
> but he seems to show no compassion on his creatures. He
> provides them with life and sustenance, but in a rather
> perfunctory way. No text tells us that he hears the cry of the poor
> man, or succours the sick, or forgives the sinner. The reason for
> this as for all other conspicuous absences in the new cult is simply
> that a compassionate god did not serve Akhenaten's purpose.'

Indeed.

THE ATENIST TRIAD

Ancient Egyptian religion had from the earliest times displayed a natural inclination to the arrangement of its gods in groupings of threes, or 'triads'. Following the model of Osiris-Isis-Horus, the triad later took on a 'familial' pattern of father-mother-child, and several cities worshipped their own particular variations on this theme: for example, Amun-Mut-Khonsu at Thebes, and Ptah-Sekhmet-Nefertum at Memphis. It was a metaphor upon which Akhenaten, in an endeavour to explain the new system, would early draw.

The Amarna icon, comprising Aten, Akhenaten and Nefertiti, represented a new approach to the concept of the divine family. Each of the three was equated with one of the principal members of the primary Heliopolitan mythology: the Aten was identified with the creator-god Atum; Amenophis IV-Akhenaten with Atum's self-seeded offspring Shu; and queen Nefertiti with the goddess Tefnut, who was Shu's female twin, theological equal and equivalent. With the birth of the king and queen's six daughters – Meritaten, Meketaten, Ankhesenpaaten, Nefernefruaten-tasherit, Nefernefrure and Setepenre – Akhenaten's earthly version of the Heliopolitan Ennead (the nine gods of creation) would be complete.

The new royal-divine family dominated every aspect of life, first at Thebes and then at el-Amarna, parading in public procession along Royal Road, or besporting themselves in the 'Window of Appearance' of their palace, rising in it like the sun on the horizon (to employ an Atenist simile) to reward their loyal subjects. And when the ordinary people returned home, it would be to shrines containing a small sculptural image or stela – not of the usual domestic deities (though such, as observed, were still popular among ordinary folk), but of this same royal family, from whom all prosperity, both material and spiritual, was deemed to flow. The spurious, imposed nature of this worship is reflected in its speedy decline following Akhenaten's death.

THE ROYAL IMAGE

The manner in which the royals were represented in the domestic-shrine stelae was relaxed and informal: the solar orb bestowing its life-giving rays upon a rather louche-looking king who, a selection of his children variously draped about him, affectionately chucks his wife under the chin. Whether such images accurately reflect the truth of a happy family man at peace with his god, with himself and with the world is a matter of opinion. Given what we are beginning to discern of the Amarna system, the likelihood is that this is how the king *wished* to be perceived – as far from the reality of dictatorship as possible. Many modern parallels could be cited – the Führer patting his dog, Stalin with his reassuring pipe, the beatific Mao Tse-Tung.

In Akhenaten's 'new look', these striking changes in composition and gesture, which treat in an extraordinarily open manner much that had been private and sacrosanct, are facilitated by the adoption of a novel canon of proportions. The concept of eternity is abandoned in favour of an obsessive attention to a detailing of the here and now; previously differentiated, heaven and earth were now one and the same. What, in short, we see on the reliefs is not idealism but a perverted reality – and a reality which, for the first time in Egyptian art, we are supposed truly to believe. The 'look' as applied to Akhenaten himself is irresistibly described by Cyril Aldred:

The royal family: Akhenaten, Nefertiti and their three eldest daughters, Meritaten, Meketaten and Ankhesenpaaten, beneath the life-giving rays of their god. The physical intimacy of this and other Amarna scenes is remarkable; it is attributed, by one recent commentator, to pharaoh's deficient eyesight – a symptom of the Marfan's Syndrome from which she believes he and his offspring may have suffered.

Akhenaten and Nefertiti take their ease: the queen, wearing the cap-crown characteristic of her later years, holds a bouquet of two mandrakes and a lotus to the nose of her king who, suggestively, employs a staff – reminiscent of the numerous staves found in the tomb of Tutankhamun – for support.

'The King was now represented with a receding forehead, a lined and haggard face, a long nose, thick lips, slanting eyes, a hanging overgrown jaw, and hollow cheeks…. His neck was shown as lean and arching, emerging from pronounced collar-bones…. His breasts were prominent, his paunch pendulous, his buttocks large, and his thighs inflated above spindle shanks.'

A courtier at the gallop, carrying his master's sandals. The chariot, first introduced into Egypt during the Hyksos period, revolutionized Egyptian warfare and was the principal means of transport at el-Amarna (along the neatly swept 'Royal Road') for both the royal family and their highest officials. An interesting feature of this relief is the rare, full-face representation of the nearside horse.

The sensitivity of Amarna art is nowhere better evoked than in this exquisite sculpture of two hands from a composite statue of the king and, presumably, his queen Nefertiti. It comes from house P49.6, excavated by the Germans in 1911-12; the material is a red quartzite.

How different from the image of heroic king so assiduously cultivated by Amenophis II! Gone, too, is the studied elegance of Amenophis III and of Amenophis IV's earliest years. And all quite deliberate: for, if we are to believe the protestations of the king's chief sculptor, Bek, 'the disciple of his majesty', it was pharaoh himself who originated the style.

Amarna representation had as its principal aim and effect the distancing of pharaoh and his followers from the ordinary people, who are shown in the same scenes in a relatively normal fashion. Frighteningly impressive in works such as the Karnak colossi found by Henri Chevrier in 1925, it served to separate the believers from the rank and file, associating the loyalists more closely with the divinity of their leader and his equally distorted family. As time went on, this extremism would soften and diminish – Aldred believed as a consequence of Bek's death and the adaptation of his style by other masters, including Thutmose; and soon after the accession of Tutankhaten the new iconography would be abandoned altogether, though its influence would continue to be seen in the finer details of Egyptian art for generations to come.

THE PHYSICAL REALITY

For the German Egyptologist Walther Wolf, writing in the 1950s, the Amarna art style was one of 'sick ugliness and nervous decadence'. It is an interesting description, and, since the king's extreme form of representation must, to some extent, have drawn on reality, it is clearly worth reviewing whether it had any discernible basis in physical fact.

Several attempts to determine Akhenaten's pathology have been made in the past – best-known being Grafton Elliot Smith's proposal (subsequently taken up by Cyril Aldred) that pharaoh had been a victim of 'Froehlich's Syndrome' (adiposogenital syndrome), an endocrine disorder whose physical manifestations supposedly have much in common with the manner in which Akhenaten is depicted. As a diagnosis, however, it is flawed in two important respects: first, most sufferers are mentally retarded; and, second, one of the features of the Froehlich's disorder is impotence. Clearly Akhenaten had no deficiencies in either department, and the possibility has now, rightly, been dismissed.

In consequence of the failure of the Froehlich's hypothesis, such long-range diagnoses are now considered by most mainstream Egyptologists as little more than wild surmises and generally ignored. One subsequent casualty is a relatively recent article, in the *Journal of the Society for the Study of Egyptian Antiquities*, by Canadian scholar Alwyn L. Burridge. The paper was acknowledged with a truly deafening silence, despite the fact that Burridge puts forward an intriguing case. She has gathered an extensive, and indeed superficially attractive, body of evidence to suggest the possibility that Akhenaten suffered from a rare (1 in 10,000) genetic disorder known as 'Marfan's Syndrome'. Detailed analysis of the Tomb 55 skeleton and related bodies will, it is hoped, in due course prove or refute the hypothesis, but, in the meantime, 'The precise collection of anomalies' discernible in representations of the king, Burridge maintains, is simply 'too consistent to be mere co-incidence.'

Among the outward effects of Marfan's Syndrome (which is caused by a single, dominant, abnormal gene and involves no mental or reproductive impairment) are the following, as Burridge conveniently summarizes:

A classic case of Marfan's? In this early representation of the Amarna royal family on a balustrade section from Akhetaten, the features the ancient artist has chosen to exaggerate correspond closely to those which characterize the syndrome.

- tall stature, slender bones, long face, high palate, narrowly spaced teeth
- elongated extremities, slender spidery fingers and toes (arachnodactyly)
- arm span exceeds height
- spinal anomalies: exaggerated angulation of the neck and spine (kyphosis)
- curvature of the spine (scoliosis), congenital absence of one half of a vertebra (hemi-vertebra)
- funnel chest (pectus excavatum) or pigeon chest (pectus carinatum)
- prominent shoulder blades (winged scapulae), prominent clavicle (collarbone)
- wide pelvic girdle
- deficiency and often localized distribution of subcutaneous fat
- hypermobility of joints, backward curvature of the knee in normal stance (genu recurvatum), flat feet
- abnormally elongated skull (dolichocephaly)
- chin protrudes beyond the forehead when viewed in profile (prognathism)
- deformity of outer ears
- hypogenitalism
- connective tissue weakness and hernias, defective development of tissue (muscular hypoplasia) and poor muscle tone (hypotonia)

As Burridge observes, virtually *all* of these are features exaggerated in representations of Akhenaten (and to a lesser degree in those of his family) – in a syndrome which occurs over a considerable range of severity and requires 'Only two of the above symptoms … to confirm a diagnosis'. That Akhenaten was a potential sufferer of Marfan's is a possibility which, if true, carries much in its wake – not least that he (and his offspring) would have been susceptible to sudden death in consequence of a weak cardiovascular system and, by virtue of keratoconus (abnormally cone-shaped corneas, which are actually discernible in a number of the king's representations), 'likely blind for most of his adult life'.

If Burridge's diagnosis is in time shown to have any basis in fact, a great deal that has hitherto gone unexplained would fall neatly into place: Manetho's report of Amenophis IV-Akhenaten's desire 'to see the gods' – perhaps a literal wish; his adherence to the Aten – perhaps the only divinity whose pyramidal rays he was able dimly to discern; his skill in music – traditionally a vocation of the blind – which is manifest in the Great Hymn to the Aten; the extraordinary physical intimacy of the royal family in Amarna art, with the sense of touch everywhere emphasized; pharaoh's physical weakness, reflected in his not-infrequent use of a crutch or stick (note the enormous number of sticks in the tomb of his son, Tutankhamun); the early and still unexplained death of Tutankhamun himself (see below); and the skeletal deformities – found in Marfan's – which are seemingly apparent in at least one of the boy-king's foetus-offspring.

But who within the king's family might have introduced the syndrome? The answer may have been inadvertently suggested some years ago by an article in the sensationalist *National Enquirer*. The tabloid published a photograph purporting to show the extraordinarily well-preserved body of 19th-century United States president Abraham Lincoln – whom few (including the *National Enquirer*) realized had been a Marfan's sufferer. Of course the identification was a spoof. The face was of Yuya, Akhenaten's odd-looking grandfather – but the resemblance to the Marfan's president was striking.

DECLINE AND FALL

'When I was young, [pharaoh] brought me into Egypt. I served the king, my lord, and I stood at the city gate of the king, my lord.... And indeed, now that I have placed the ... yoke of the king, my lord, on my neck, I carry it.' LETTER OF YAKHTIRU, A VASSAL MAYOR

The Amarna period was not a time of growth for the Egyptian empire, though the 'imperial' system was, of course, still in place and functioning, albeit to reduced effect. Egypt's southern dominions, which fell under the direct supervision of the Nubian viceroy, the king's son of Kush, seem to have suffered least, remaining relatively – if not totally – stable; we have (from Buhen and Amada) evidence of a campaign there in Year 12 of the reign, most probably in pursuit of gold to finance the king's dreams. In the north, where day-to-day control in Syria-Palestine was left in the hands of vassal rulers, the situation was very different.

Many of these northern vassals had themselves been educated in Egypt (and were therefore sympathetic to the controlling power) or had children hostage at pharaoh's court to guarantee their parents' continuing loyalty. Up until the death of Amenophis III, the system had worked tolerably well: though there would always have been a certain fluidity along the northern-most border, the vassals had, by and large, maintained order in the areas under their charge, and pharaoh (either in person or through his agents) had had to trouble himself with little beyond an annual, late-summer foray to maintain the *status quo* and collect the taxes levied in his name.

From the start, however, Amenophis IV-Akhenaten had shown that he cared little for affairs beyond the Nile valley, for warfare, or for the ways of international diplomacy. For all the fine universalist talk of the Great Hymn to the Aten, the king's interests and concerns revolved wholly around the home country. Perhaps even foreign trade was a reliance pharaoh was doing his best to reduce. Experimentation in the domestic production of glass ingots, for example, was well under way at el-Amarna, as archaeo-technologist Paul Nicholson has demonstrated. In part, clearly, this was to service an increasing demand; but the development may indicate also a longer-term desire on the king's part to achieve independence in this and in other areas of supply – an extension of that drive for self-sufficiency reflected, at a different level, in the king's enormous well-digging programme at Akhetaten.

Pharaoh's determined, almost pathological lack of interest in the world outside inevitably took its toll on Egyptian prestige abroad. Our basic source is the Amarna correspondence. The precise chronology of the vassal letters is disputed, but it is difficult to avoid the conclusion that they chart a gradual and inexorable decline in pharaoh's hold on his northern dominions; with Mitanni and Hatti now at war, these subject kinglets, quarrelsome at the best of times, found themselves spiralling into a state of anarchy. The pleas for a reimposition of order come from all quarters, including Akhenaten's fellow 'great kings': Burra-Buriyash of Babylonia, for one, wrote with some concern, drawing pharaoh's attention to the robbery on Egyptian territory of several important caravans (EA 7–8). The pleading of pharaoh's underlings for military support to pacify an increasingly lawless situation was similarly growing.

The more opportunistic of Egypt's vassals inevitably took advantage of the situation. The best known today is Abdi-Ashirta and his son, Aziru, local rulers of Amurru in northern Syria, who, in league with the 'Apiru' (a pejorative term applied to those who rejected Egyptian control), were clearly playing both ends against the middle. Akhenaten was warned repeatedly of this duplicity by Rib-Hadda of Byblos, 'footstool for your feet' – one of pharaoh's more loyal vassals. 'May the king, my lord, know that the war of Abdi-Ashirta against me is severe, and he has taken all my cities …'; and later, despairing of ever receiving Egyptian assistance, 'you are going to come into an empty house. Everything is gone'. The king's detached response was merely to complain that Rib-Hadda 'writes to me more than all the other mayors'. Modern commentators have tended to share the king's irritation, viewing Rib-Hadda's outpourings as hysterical cries of 'wolf!'. They were not. The mayor of Byblos repeated his panicked pleas for military aid both to the king and to his representative, Amanappa (Amenopet) – and the number of letters sent on a common theme offers a chilling glimpse of the slim odds Rib-Hadda estimated for their eventual arrival. These and other warnings were ignored; Rib-Hadda was dispossessed, escaping to the camp of an ally until meeting an inevitable death.

The decline was set to continue, as the correspondence reflects – here a letter from Shuwardata, mayor of Qiltu(?):

> 'Be informed, O king, my lord, that all the lands of the king, my
> lord, have been taken away….'

But nothing could be done: by the time the urgency of the situation was pressed home to the king, his troops had other, more serious matters on their hands – propping up an increasingly unpopular regime at home.

THE TERROR

With the death of Amenophis III, the Aten had been elevated to the privileged position of Egypt's principal state god. But Amun's temples had continued to function, if on a reduced scale, and the worship of the traditional pantheon was still tolerated, if not officially encouraged. Pharaoh, perhaps, had been biding his time: now, established and secure in his new city, he could safely contemplate his next move. If, as seems likely, the Amun priesthood had been continuing in their opposition to the new reality, they were set to pay the price in full.

The second half of Akhenaten's reign is, for the historian, shrouded in obscurity. Indeed, after the programme related in such explicit detail on the boundary stelae at el-Amarna, the textual narrative is bitty in the extreme. None the less, at a date between Years 8 and 12, and probably in Year 10 of the reign (following the official occupation of the new city), it is evident that a persecution was instigated by the king specifically against Amun and his divine consort Mut. An order went out from the palace to smash up the divine statues and hack out the names and images of these gods wherever they occurred – on temple walls, on obelisks, on shrines, on the accessible portions of tombs. This was accompanied by a focused attack on the divine birth scenes both of Hatshepsut at Deir el-Bahri and, to a lesser though still discernible extent, on the similar reliefs of his father Amenophis III also, at Luxor; mythological fantasies of this sort were no longer to be tolerated. But it was not only the Theban divinities Akhenaten had in his sights: since there was only one true deity, the Aten, the plural hieroglyphic group for 'gods' was similarly excised wherever it was found. Henceforth there would be recognized but a single power, and that was Akhenaten himself.

This campaign was no academic exercise, but a true persecution which generated a real and tangible fear among the Egyptian people: for it was not only from Egypt's large, public monuments that the offending hieroglyphs were excised. As the archaeological record shows, small, personal items such as pots for eye make-up and commemorative scarabs were dealt with in the same relentless fashion. Fearful of being found in possession of such seditious items, the owners themselves gouged or ground out the three offending signs which articulated the god Amun's name, even in tiny cartouches containing the old king's birth name. Such displays of frightened self-censorship and toadying loyalty are ominous indicators of the paranoia which was beginning to grip the country. Not only were the streets

Large scarab of glazed steatite commemorating a kill of some 102 lions between regnal years 1 and 10 of Amenophis III; from the Egypt Exploration Society's excavations at el-Amarna. The paranoia generated by Akhenaten's persecution of Amun is demonstrated by the erasure here – presumably by the ancient owner himself – of the old king's name.

Small votive stela of limestone, offered to Amun in the name of Tuthmosis IV by a contemporary of this king whose name, 'Nefernefer', is inscribed on the lower edge. The image of Amun, as well as the name, were subsequently hacked out during Akhenaten's persecution of the god around regnal year 10.

filled with pharaoh's soldiers (predominantly Nubian and Asiatic); it seems the population now had to contend with the danger of malicious informers.

A picture painted by Manetho of Hyksos excesses may in fact preserve a garbled memory of these sorry times:

> '... not only did they [pharaoh's men] set towns and villages on fire, pillaging the temples and mutilating images of the gods without restraint, but they also made a practice of using the sanctuaries as kitchens to roast the sacred animals which the people worshipped; and they would compel the priests and prophets to sacrifice and butcher the beasts, afterwards casting the men forth naked.'

ECONOMICS

'At Akhetaten in this place shall I make all revenues that are in the entire land to belong to the Aten, my father.' EXTRACT FROM THE EARLIER PROCLAMATION OF THE EL-AMARNA BOUNDARY STELAE

For all Egypt's much-vaunted wealth, the construction of Akhetaten had placed an enormous strain on the financial resources of both the king and his officials – at a time when, through a combination of regal apathy and unsettled conditions abroad, income in the form of local taxation and foreign tribute was beginning to falter. Pharaoh's latest move – the imposition of a single, official cult – provided a convenient excuse to lay kingly hands on the gods' considerable financial resources. As a result, the strain was temporarily relieved, allowing the regime to limp along for a few years more.

But the temples – and that of Amun in particular, which had over the years insinuated itself into every aspect of the running of the country – were the very motor of the Egyptian economy. Now their doors were closed and corruption increasingly rife thanks to pharaoh's careless delegation in those areas of statecraft – including taxation – which did not interest him. Disaster loomed.

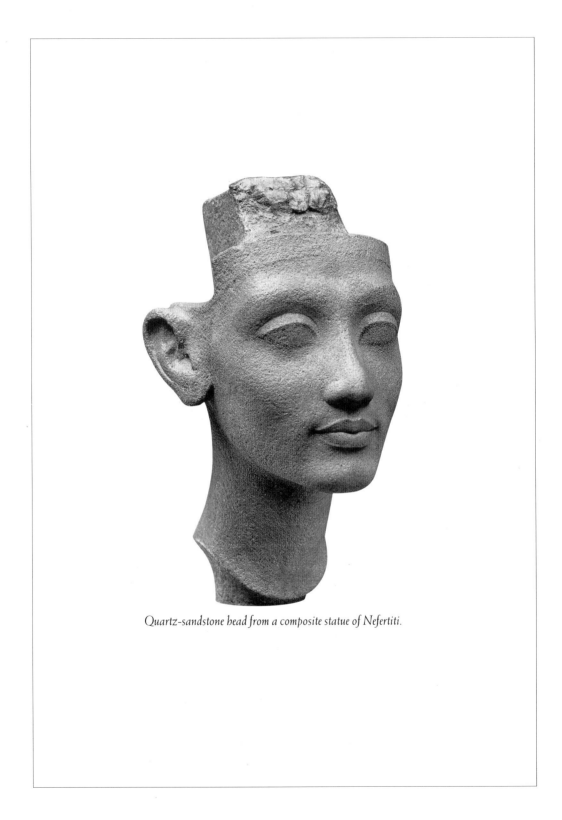

Quartz-sandstone head from a composite statue of Nefertiti.

CHAPTER EIGHT

ROYAL WOMEN

A SCULPTOR'S WORKSHOP

Of several artists known from the reign of Akhenaten – including Bek and queen Tiye's personal sculptor, Iuty – none is more famous today than Thutmose, the owner of a workshop excavated by the Deutsche Orient-Gesellschaft in the South Suburb (house P47.1-3) in 1912. The name of this artist was encountered quite by chance with the discovery, in a nearby rubbish-pit, of an inscribed ivory horse-blinker – which indicated that Thutmose was a man of substance, and sufficiently wealthy to possess his own chariot (no doubt a gift from the king) with fittings made from the costliest materials.

As the excavators found, the rooms of Thutmose's villa had for the most part been swept clean before the complex was finally abandoned and the domestic furniture carried off for reuse. Fortunately for posterity, the intrinsically worthless casts, models and unfinished studies of Thutmose's professional life were sealed away and abandoned. Perhaps, with Akhenaten's death, they were considered redundant; possibly there had been in the sculptor's mind the thought that, one day, he would return. This was a prospect entertained, if reluctantly, by many of the inhabitants of el-Amarna who neatly and carefully bricked up the entrances to their dwellings to keep them free, in the interim, from sand and squatters. And this is the condition in which, more than thirty centuries later, their ruins were eventually dug out.

The most famous art work recovered from Thutmose's studio was the polychrome bust of Nefertiti now in Berlin. But there were other portrait studies, too, of comparable quality – including images in a range of hard and soft stones and in plaster of Amenophis III, Tiye and Akhenaten and his principal consort. Several portraits from the find, however, are of less familiar subjects, and among this anonymous crowd one particular face stands out, by virtue of its undeniable charm. The face in question is that of a young woman characterized by an impudent moue and stylishly large ear ornaments. This woman, as we may be reasonably certain from images in relief sporting these same distinctive items of jewelry, was Kiya, Akhenaten's obscure secondary wife – the source of much trouble to come and the inspiration for at least one literary work circulated in the succeeding dynasty.

THE GREATLY BELOVED: KIYA

'The only surviving copy of the "[Story of] Two Brothers" was
written out by the scribe Inina sometime in the reign of Sethos

II. The tale is made up of at least two stories, originally separate, each with a plot revolving around an unfaithful wife. The first section, relating the unsuccessful attempt by Anubis' wife to seduce the young Bata, her brother-in-law, is simple and straightforward: the second part, describing the exile of Bata, is interwoven with myth and magic. The woman who appears in the latter is the wife of Bata, eventually to become queen of Egypt under the name Ta-Shepset.

The king of Egypt first comes to know of her through a lock of her hair, which he is told belongs to a daughter of [the god] Re-Harakhty. Envoys are sent to search for her in all foreign lands, but especially in the Valley of the Pine Tree – which was presumably somewhere in northern Syria or Asia Minor. When she is brought to the king, he loves her exceedingly and appoints her as [shepset aat – "great noble lady"]. Although created by Re-Harakhty and fashioned by Khnum, the girl is of foreign origin – her lock of hair is described as "tribute from another country" – and up to this point in the story she has been nameless. From now on she is referred to as [ta shepset – "noble lady par excellence"], and this in effect becomes her name, in the combination [hemet nesu ta shepset – "the king's wife and noble lady par excellence"].'

As Danish Egyptologist Lise Manniche (who penned the above summary) brilliantly discerned more than twenty-five years ago, the creator of the extraordinary story of the Two Brothers

'must have had a specific reason for calling the [second woman in the story] [(ta) shepset], in that the word was no longer in ordinary use as a title. His choice of the term may well have been prompted by the knowledge that this part of the story reflected actual happenings, in which the lady involved had held the title, or had been known as [(ta) shepset]. The designation is indeed so exceedingly rare in the New Kingdom that it is tempting to identify the wife of Bata with the only other woman in the not too distant past who seems to have borne it, i.e. Kiya, the "other" wife of Akhenaten.'

One of three closely similar plaster studies from the workshop of the sculptor Thutmose at el-Amarna: a young and pretty member of the royal court – to judge from the earrings which seem to be a characteristic feature of her representations in relief, the 'greatly beloved wife' Kiya, Akhenaten's mysterious 'other woman'.

Among the mass of dismantled temple reliefs brought to light at el-Ashmunein (Hermopolis) in 1939 was this fragment with two conjoint heads in Egyptian profile – that on the left evidently Akhenaten himself, the head on the right, by its peculiar wig, a variant representation of Kiya. The fact that the two are represented at virtually the same scale testifies to Kiya's importance at court – we may guess following the birth of a male heir, Tutankhaten.

Kiya's full, formal title was 'Greatly beloved wife of the king of Upper and Lower Egypt, living on truth, lord of the Two Lands, Neferkheprure-waenre, [who is] the goodly child of the living Aten and who lives for ever and eternity, Kiya' – a standardized formula, as we know from the existence of a number of gypsum models circulated (as doubtless were the plaster masks) to guide pharaoh's sculptors on site. The lady's first, published appearance on the Egyptological scene, in 1959, was a modest one, prompted by the discovery of her name on a small, inscribed cosmetic jar now in the Metropolitan Museum of Art in New York; Kiya has been the talk of Amarna studies ever since, and much additional evidence for her existence has in the interim come to light. Particularly significant has been the discovery that a great deal of the evidence previously assumed to chart a decline in the fortunes of Nefertiti – the erasures and palimpsests on blocks from the North Palace, Maru-Aten and Hermopolis – in fact relates to the rise and subsequent fall not of Akhenaten's great royal wife at all but of this 'other woman'.

What do we know of this creature? The Thutmose studio portraits convey a strong impression of the girl's appeal: pretty and accessible, a complete contrast with the cool, haughty beauty of Nefertiti; the basic meaning of the lady's name – 'Monkey' – speaks for itself. Yet behind this façade, if the character of Bata's wife indeed reflects anything of our subject, Kiya possessed a character which was both cruel and self-seeking; she may even have been regarded, by posterity, as the evil genius behind many of Akhenaten's excesses – the Chiang Ch'ing (Madame Mao) of Egypt's 'Cultural Revolution'.

Lise Manniche's studies originally suggested that Kiya might have been a princess of Mitannian origin, and perhaps none other than Tadukhepa, the daughter of Tushratta, king of Mitanni – about whose marriage arrangements and enormous dowry so much information is preserved in the Amarna letters. Several wine-jar dockets – important markers for reconstructing events at this time – have been recovered from excavations at el-Amarna, and of these a number make mention of this *ta shepset*, or 'noble lady'.

Especially intriguing, however, was Manniche's highlighting of the text on a series of clay 'funerary cones' – stamped elements employed for architectural inlay above the doors of Theban tomb chapels; these had been prepared for a certain Bengay, steward to 'ta shepset of Naharin [Mitanni]'. That Bengay's ta shepset cannot, in fact, be Kiya has recently been argued by Dutch scholar Jacobus van Dijk: he believes the cone in question to be earlier in date than Kiya's lifetime. But it is possible, none the less, that during the 18th Dynasty the term ta shepset was one in general, if restricted, official employ as a desig-nation for certain types of foreign princess, and the association of Kiya and Mitanni cannot necessarily be ruled out.

Kiya's presence at el-Amarna, where she had an estate, may be discerned before the change in the Aten's name just prior to the terror, and continued up to Year 12 when she disappears from view, perhaps a casualty of child-birth. The lady's memory, it is clear, was subsequently persecuted: her images and inscriptions are today found erased and sometimes abused (the eyes poked out), and superimposed by figures and texts of the king's eldest daughter, Meritaten (less frequently by those of the third daughter, Ankhe-senpaaten). Kiya's splendid coffin and canopic jars were discovered by Theodore M. Davis in Tomb 55 in the Valley of the Kings in 1907: they had been adapted and re-employed for the reburial of her husband, a fact first established by the Russian Egyptologist Yuri Perepelkin in 1967. Her mummy is today completely unknown, but an original interment within the royal tomb at el-Amarna may perhaps be assumed.

Kiya's popularity with Akhenaten will clearly have posed a threat Nefer-titi could not afford to ignore – and it is not by chance that, with Kiya's demise, the extraordinary rise in the great royal wife's fortunes begins to gather pace.

INCEST

That Akhenaten was a king with a strong sexual appetite who fathered several children is well established; as we have seen, the old theory that his peculiar physiognomy was the result of an endocrine disorder, 'Froehlich's Syndrome', denying him the joys of fatherhood, is today dismissed as sheer fantasy. Pharaoh's principal wife, Nefertiti, was one of the most beautiful women of her generation; while Kiya, if a lady of lesser rank, was clearly pos-sessed of considerable charm also. And there will have been other conquests, too, members of a constantly replenished royal harem, skilled in a variety of sexual arts, to whom pharaoh could turn as and when the mood might, and evidently did, take him.

Akhenaten's children by Nefertiti were six in number, all daughters, and all, it appears, alive and kicking by Year 10 of the reign: the first three – Meritaten, Meketaten and Ankhesenpaaten – are mentioned in 'official' texts or temple reliefs commissioned during the early part of the occupation of el-Amarna; while representations of the three younger princesses – Nefernefruaten-

Beautifully sculpted head in quartz-sandstone from a composite statue of one of Akhenaten's daughters. The subject is identified by the shaven head and distorted cranium – this last an over-emphasis, it is suggested, of hereditary traits present in the Tomb 55 and Tutankhamun mummies. The eyes and eyebrows are recessed for inlay.

tasherit, Nefernefrure and Setepenre – are encountered only in those el-Amarna nobles' tombs which were quarried in the second half of the reign. After Year 10, Nefertiti's child-bearing days seem to have drawn to a close.

But further children, by other women, would follow – perhaps in a Henry VIII-style quest for an heir. This desire was evidently achieved with the lady Kiya who, probably giving birth to Tutankhaten – the king's only son – seems to have produced at least one daughter also, though the name of this child is now lost to us. Two other 'king's daughters', of unspecified parentage, were Meritaten-tasherit and Ankhesenpaaten-tasherit, at one time recognized as further Kiya offspring. Since the second element in both of these names translates as 'the child' (or, in American parlance, 'junior'), an older theory again holds sway – that the -tasherit girls were in fact daughters of Akhenaten's first and third offspring by queen Nefertiti, Meritaten and Ankhesenpaaten. The implications of this are serious, however, since the father of these children can have been none other than Akhenaten himself. This unhealthy sexual interest in his children appears to have resulted in at least one tragedy: the decoration of his second daughter's tomb-chamber incorporates the scene of a nurse holding a newly born child of high rank (denoted by the presence of two fan-bearers), from which it is assumed that Meketaten, like Kiya, died giving birth – and, we may guess, to another of her father's incestuous offspring.

A possible precedent for such father-daughter relationships has already been mentioned – that which may have underlain the ritualistic role of princess Sitamun as great royal wife to her father, Amenophis III. Such associations were very far from the Egyptian norm; while marriage between brothers and sisters was not infrequently practised within the royal family – particularly at periods of dynastic vulnerability – father-daughter relationships are rarely attested. Since no divine precedent could be cited for the practice, there is little doubt that Egyptian society as a whole would have found it profoundly unsettling. But Akhenaten, like his father, had by the end of his reign achieved divinity in his own right. What need had he for the sanction of gods whose very existence he denied? For such couplings – undertaken, we may suppose, with the desire of keeping ultimate power within his closed family circle – he would doubtless have been able to muster his own theological justification.

PHARAOH JOINS THE GODS

'There is an incongruity about the reliefs found upon the El-'Amârna site ... Akhenaten's own portrait was always very much in the centre of the picture, and the manner in which his cartouches are set side by side with those of the Aten show that he was by no means disinclined to claim a share in his divine father's divinity; indeed, one has sometimes the impression that this share approached complete identity ...' ALAN GARDINER

As the Aten's *alter ego* and 'co-regent' on earth, Akhenaten had enjoyed an ambiguous divinity from the very start of his sole reign, and there are hints that this status was perhaps formalized (in the same way as his father's late promotion to the ranks of the gods) before its end. The precise circumstances of this supposed elevation remain obscure; as with Amenophis III, the records preserve only the most tantalizing of hints.

One of the principal clues occurs in the famous scenes showing the 'reception of foreign tribute' in the tombs of Meryre II and Huya at el-Amarna. In the former tomb, the event is dated to Year 12 of Akhenaten; in the latter, significantly, it is dated to Year 12 *of the Aten* – which may indicate that the king and his god were now regarded as one and the same. What is more, we discern but a short time after this date the existence of a new co-regent, Ankhkheprure Nefernefruaten – of whom more presently. Were these two events perhaps connected? Did the induction of this co-regent complement on earth Akhenaten's newly assumed role in heaven? It seems a more than distinct possibility.

The logistics of the co-regency system, as considered earlier, are quite uncertain. What we learn from the apparent period of joint rule between Amenophis III and Amenophis IV, and the revolutionary changes which followed on from the former's death, is that the junior king's powers were in that instance very much prescribed. Was this the case with Nefernefruaten? It may be doubted; but before suggesting why, let us first take a closer look at the evidence for this period.

THE PAWAH GRAFFITO

Akhenaten was clearly not a man open to reasoned argument: far above the sphere of ordinary mortals, he demanded from his subjects complete and utter subservience. The tomb and temple reliefs show him and his family

Facsimile copy (right) and hieroglyphic transcription (left) of part of a long hieratic graffito from the reign of Akhenaten's co-regent – Ankhkheprure Nefernefruaten – in the tomb of Pere (TT139) at Thebes. The date, 'Year 3', presumably indicates the co-regent's employment of an independent system of dating which would equate to around Year 14 of Akhenaten himself.

adored by a grovelling populace, but the adoration is far from spontaneous: closer inspection reveals that the people are kept in check by large numbers of troops with batons; and *their* loyalty has been bought by the favours bestowed from the 'Window of Appearance' upon their commanders and those charged with the execution of the royal will. For ordinary folk, there is little doubt that Akhenaten's actions as king over time inflicted the greatest misery: the people were confused by the man's religious vision, frightened by the ruthless manner in which it was imposed, and quite likely appalled by his personal behaviour. Denied the celebration of the traditional religious festivals which gave form to their year, and brought to the very verge of bankruptcy by their king's over-ambitious schemes and administrative incompetence, disillusionment was clearly widespread.

The following text imparts a flavour of the despondency which had settled on the country towards the reign's end:

'Year 3, 3rd month of inundation, day 10. The king of Upper and Lower Egypt, lord of the Two Lands, Ankhkheprure-beloved of Aten(?), son of Re Nefernefruaten-beloved of Waenre(?).

Giving praise to Amun, kissing the ground before Onnophris by the *wab*-priest and scribe of divine offerings of Amun in the temple of Ankhkheprure in Thebes, Pawah, born to Itefseneb.

He says:

My wish is to see you, O lord of persea trees! May your throat take the north wind, that you may give fullness without eating and drunkenness without drinking.

My wish is to look at you, that my heart might rejoice, O Amun, protector of the poor man: you are the father of the one who has no mother and the husband of the widow.

Pleasant is the utterance of your name: it is like the taste of life; it is like the taste of bread to a child, a loincloth to the naked, like the taste of [cucumber?] in the hot season.

You are like [...] with one who bears [...] when his father was [...]. You are like the taste of favour from the ruler, the breeze [of freedom] to him who was in prison, peace [to the troubled man(?) who] invokes a possessor of good character when he has returned.

Come back to us, O lord of continuity! You were here before anything had come into being, and you will be here when they are gone. As you have caused me to see the darkness that is yours to give, make light for me so that I can see you. As your *ka* endures and as your handsome, beloved face endures, may you come from afar and allow this servant, the scribe Pawah, to see you! Grant him the condition of "Re awaits him!", for indeed the following of you is good.

O Amun, O great lord who can be found by seeking him, may you drive off fear! Set rejoicing in people's hearts. Joyful is the one who sees you, O Amun: he is in festival every day....'

This heart-rending appeal to Amun to return to his abandoned flock was first discovered in 1893 tucked away above the inner doorway of a deserted tomb chapel in the Theban hills (TT139). The beneficiary of the prayer, penned by his brother, was Pawah, a *wab* ('pure')-priest and scribe attached, as the text states, to the temple of Amun in the temple of Ankhkheprure – Akhenaten's co-regent – in Thebes. Written in the co-regent's third regnal year, only a short time before the senior king's death, it represents the first shaft of light to be thrown on events at Thebes for more than a decade – and it is a curious one.

What we glimpse in the Pawah graffito is a demoralized Amun priesthood, but one which, following the recent persecution, is again operating officially and, more surprisingly, within the mortuary temple of the heretic's co-ruler. The Amarna revolution had clearly entered a new phase – perhaps because earthly power was now vested in the hands not of Akhenaten himself but of this same mysterious co-regent, Ankhkheprure Nefernefruaten, who was taking a decidedly softer line. It now remains to consider who this co-ruler actually was.

THE 'SEXLESS' PHARAOH

One of the more intriguing results of the work of the Akhenaten Temple Project at Karnak has been the light shone on the elevated status enjoyed by the great royal wife Nefertiti from the beginning of the reign, maintaining and even extending the high profile initiated by the chief queen of Amenophis III, Tiye. Not only is Nefertiti shown worshipping alone in the decoration of the *Hutbenben* temple, but the frequency of her depictions elsewhere among the *talatat* is roughly twice that of pharaoh himself.

Even more extraordinary are the types of scenes in which the queen is shown taking part – most significantly, smiting the heads of enemies, an iconography hitherto restricted to pharaoh himself. Nefertiti, from the start, was no ordinary great royal wife, but a key player in the life and more particularly the cult of the new regime. And this status was to evolve as the reign progressed.

The first obvious indication we have of the queen's rise seems relatively innocuous – the adoption (not far distant in time from her husband's switch from 'Amenophis' to 'Akhenaten') of an elaborated name-form: Nefernefruaten-Nefertiti. This name change was of fundamental importance, brought about by the death of Amenophis III and his full translation to the divine sphere. As already described, in Akhenaten's new theological scheme the old divine 'families' at Thebes (Amun-Mut-Khonsu), Memphis (Ptah-Sekhmet-Nefertem), and elsewhere were displaced by a new 'earthly' trinity comprising Aten-king-queen; and this trinity was equated directly with the ancient Heliopolitan triad consisting of the creator-god Atum, his self-seeded offspring Shu and his twin sister Tefnut. A little-known representation of Akhenaten and Nefertiti in

The so-called 'sexless colossus' – one of the series of architectural sculptures excavated at Karnak by Henri Chevrier in and after 1925. The old assumption that the subject of the entire series was Akhenaten himself, and that the absence of genitalia here mirrors a royal and horrible reality, is now discarded; the most likely explanation is that this particular sculpture represents queen Nefertiti.

165

Whip-stock knob of brilliant blue faience. This fine object, inscribed with the names of Akhenaten and Nefertiti, is decorated with representations of the royal couple as Shu and Tefnut, self-seeded twins of the creator-god Atum, seated within a barque and with hands raised in adoration of the solar-disc.

their roles as creator gods is on a beautiful terminal of brilliant blue faience now in Copenhagen, plausibly identified as the counterweight for a riding-whip stock and doubtless once a gift from the king to some now forgotten official.

A far more dramatic illustration of the new reality is the extraordinary series of colossal statues brought to light by Henri Chevrier at Karnak in the 1920s, which are among the most startling sculptures ever produced in Egypt. They have also proved among the more misleading – the problem originating in the assumption, when they were first dug up, that all, without exception, were representations of the king himself. It was a legitimate preliminary conclusion: the significance of Nefertiti's role had not at that time been recognized, the statues were in fragments, and the style of none of the works made much concession to femininity. Unfortunately, however, this tentative identification was not seriously reassessed for half a century – a delay which would have far-reaching consequences for the study of the period. For one of the statues was so notably lacking in any masculine characteristics that Amenophis IV-Akhenaten's physical status was slowly but surely called into question. Perhaps, it was argued, he was a eunuch – an old, 19th-century delusion again trotted out to explain the apparent lack of genitals and the general oddity of the king's appearance; or perhaps he had suffered from some appalling illness which had withered his sexual equipment away to nothing. Certainly, it was agreed, he could not have had children. Which was all well and good – had it not been for the fact that the king most certainly *did* have children, and an interest in women which, if not quite the equal of his father's and in certain respects somewhat peculiar, was evidently active enough.

But how to explain the absence of the royal genitalia? For some, sceptical about taking appearances too literally, the statue was nothing more than an artistic affectation appropriate to pharaoh-Shu's role as father and mother of mankind. In fact, the answer is far more straightforward, as John R. Harris pointed out some years ago: the sculpture represents not the king himself but his queen, who was built along rather different lines from her spouse. As most scholars now recognize, the so-called 'sexless colossus' is in fact a representation of Nefertiti as Tefnut; and it is one of a number set up at Karnak in company with images of pharaoh as Shu. The sexually challenged king has proved, in short, to be a figment of the scholar's fervid imagination.

THE FANTASY OF THE HOMOSEXUAL KING

This imagination has indeed, over the years, proved to be an active one. For, once Egyptologists' doubts about Akhenaten's sexuality had been raised, further intimate questions began to be asked. If the king was a eunuch, as some supposed, then he was obviously peculiar and there must be other skeletons tucked away in his closet also.

It seemed that these suspicions had found confirmation with the publication by British Egyptologist Percy E. Newberry, in 1928, of a small private stela in the Berlin Museum. On this stela, which was made for a military officer by the name of Pase, we encounter a representation of two kings (identified by their crowns) seated side by side, the first with one arm thrown casually around the second who turns affectionately to tickle the other under the chin. The carving, however, is unfinished: although several sets of cartouches were outlined, they have all been left empty. According to Newberry, here, indubitably, was a representation of Akhenaten and his co-regent and successor (referred to as 'Smenkhkare'), executed while the senior king was still alive. Since the male sex of Smenkhkare was taken for granted – was he not shown in a relief in the tomb of Meryre II at el-Amarna standing beside his chief queen, Akhenaten's daughter Meritaten? – the affectionate relationship between the two figures on the Pase stela aroused obvious Egyptological unease.

The conclusion might have been distasteful in 1920s Britain, but had to be faced: Akhenaten was a homosexual. And, as the splintered records of the era were ransacked for further proof of this 'unwholesome' relationship between Akhenaten and his co-regent, it was found in several other scenes of touching intimacy.

Small limestone stela offered by Pase, a soldier attached to the boat or regiment Khaemmaat ('Appearing in Truth'). On this stela, two kings are represented in affectionate pose – a further indication, it was once thought, that Akhenaten was not 'as other men'. The cartouches, though never filled in, tell a different story: the figures are identified not by the two pairs which flank and indeed were intended to identify the rayed disc, but by the block of three ovals above the table of offerings. Despite the kingly crowns sported by the two figures, three ovals identify a single king and his queen – Akhenaten and Nefertiti.

Pharaoh Ankhkheprure Smenkhkare and the great royal wife Meritaten beneath the rays of the solar disc – the only named representation of the royal couple extant, in a scene sketched out in ink on a wall in the tomb of Meryre II (no. 2). A box-fragment discovered by Carter outside the tomb of Tutankhamun reveals that Meritaten had previously functioned as great royal wife to Akhenaten's co-regent, Ankhkheprure Nefernefruaten.

For 50 years this was the given of Amarna studies, and much confusion and additional fantasy did it spawn. Only in 1973 was the falseness of Newberry's premise finally revealed, in a ground-breaking article published in the Danish journal *Acta Orientalia*, again by John R. Harris. Counting up the number of empty cartouches on the Pase stela, Harris realized that here was a problem: there were seven in total. Two pairs of ovals, flanking the solar disc, had clearly been meant to contain the name of the Aten – which left a block of three blank cartouches, clearly, from their positioning, intended to identify the senior and junior kings. Two kings, however, require *two* sets of *two* cartouches; three can refer only to a king and his queen – despite the kingly crowns. And this conclusion is confirmed by certain artistic conventions displayed in the composition – the convex, male curve of the neck on the figure to the left, and the concave, female curve of that positioned to the right. The images on the Pase stela were not, therefore, representations of Akhenaten and his boyfriend Smenkhkare, but of Akhenaten and a queen.

Unfinished statuette from Ludwig Borchardt's excavations of 1912: a seated king kisses a second, smaller figure seated upon his lap. The identification is uncertain – Kiya or Nefertiti? – but the old interpretation of Akhenaten in a homosexual embrace with his mythic male co-regent is today considered very wide of the mark.

Nefertiti's evolving status is confirmed in the representation and cartouches of this second stela from Berlin. The two figures are Akhenaten and, from the crown, his principal queen; in its final form, however, the number of cartouches has been increased from three to four – to reflect Nefertiti's elevation from queen to co-regent.

But who was this queenly co-regent? Another object in Berlin – the crucial significance of which has gone unnoticed for almost a century – confirms, without the slightest shadow of a doubt, that the lady in question was Nefertiti. The small, round-topped limestone stela, Berlin 25574, is a modest monument, uninscribed and unfinished. Even completed, it would have had little visual impact. Historically, however, it is priceless because it represents one of the missing links of Amarna studies.

The stela is incised with two figures standing before a table of offerings, the solar disc in the sky above. Three cartouches, left blank, were clearly intended to identify the two figures: the first, wearing a bag wig, is presumably Akhenaten himself; the second figure, wearing her unique, flat-topped crown, can be none other than Nefertiti.

A common enough scene – until one looks more closely. For in front of the three blank cartouches, a *fourth* blank cartouche has been squeezed in, evidently later since it is smaller, cut differently and sits at a peculiar angle. This extra cartouche indicates clearly that the status of the figures had changed while the stela was in process of manufacture. Three cartouches, as we have seen, identify a king and his queen; four cartouches identify a pharaoh and his co-regent. Nefertiti, demonstrably, had become a king.

Where all of this is leading, we may now begin to consider.

NEFERTITI'S 'DISGRACE'

The traditional view of Nefertiti's fate was neatly summarized by E. F. Campbell in 1964:

> '... the excavations at Amarna have established conclusively that Nefertiti was eclipsed as the dominant figure beside her husband at a time after the twelfth year of his reign. The twelfth year is the last to which a dated depiction can be assigned of the royal family as a unity. The date appears on the scene of the receipt of foreign tribute found in the tomb of Huya. A scene of the event presented in a different way, and with the inscription broken in such a way as to make the date uncertain ... occurs in the tomb of Meryre II. Presumably some time after the twelfth

year the events occurred which led to the erasure of the name of
Nefertiti from a great many of the reliefs and monuments in the
Maru-Aten precinct of Akhetaten, to the south of the main
complex. Surcharged over the name of Nefertiti is the name of
Meritaten; in some cases the surcharge includes the specific
information that Meritaten was the king's daughter, and under
no circumstances is she said to be his wife....

Nefertiti's eclipse, however, does not seem to have meant her
death, but rather her banishment to a precinct of her own to the
north of the main complex. There is evidence that she
continued to live there in more or less seclusion, although how
long she lived is unknown.'

The assumed 'disgrace' of Nefertiti is now recognized as yet another of
the great fallacies of Amarna historiography. For, as a close scrutiny of the
inscriptions now reveals – from the North Palace and Maru-Aten, and
particularly from Hermopolis – the queen who fell from favour was not
the great royal wife at all, but Kiya, Akhenaten's 'other' woman; and with
the disappearance of her rival, Nefertiti's influence at court was in fact set
to increase. Of the principal queen's survival there can now be no doubt –
though some scholars have attempted to breathe new life into the old
story from the existence of two fragments of funerary statuettes prepared
for Nefertiti as queen. These two fragments (which in fact turn out not
to belong to the same figure, as was once thought) are certainly interesting,
but they are not true *shabti*, or servant, statuettes, produced after death.
Like similar images of queen Tiye discovered in the burial of her husband,
Amenophis III, they were votive offerings prepared during the donor's
life. Nefertiti was very much alive when her alabaster statuettes were
created during the first half of her husband's reign, and the queenly
titulary the pieces carry is of no relevance whatsoever to her rank at
death.

As an increasing number of Egyptologists now acknowledge, the 'disappearance' of the great royal wife Nefertiti was the result not of death or
disgrace but of a change of name, itself the result of an enhancement in
status – from that of queen to co-regent. In this new guise Nefertiti adopted
a royal, cartouched titulary with new throne name and a nomen which
incorporated the epithet which had been bestowed upon her earlier in the
reign: Ankhkheprure *Nefernefruaten*. That this new 'king' might be queen
Nefertiti in disguise had first been proposed in 1912 by Henri Gauthier; but
the idea was soon dropped in favour of seeing this kingly reference as a later,
variant name-form of Akhenaten's successor, Smenkhkare – and everyone
assumed 'him' to be a young man. Again, John R. Harris re-examined the evidence in 1973. And, already alerted by the indisputable trappings of
kingship Nefertiti so confidently displayed as great royal wife – including
the kingly crowns depicted on the Pase stela and elsewhere – he was led

independently to concur with Gauthier's original, extraordinary conclusion. Digging a little deeper, Harris was able to resolve the misconception which had caused Gauthier to abandon his thesis: contrary to what had hitherto been assumed, 'the first and original name of the co-regent of Akhenaten was Nefernefruaten, and … the adoption of the alternative nomen Smenkhkare was a subsequent modification'.

Harris summarized his initial results in a modest article entitled simply 'Nefernefruaten', which appeared in 1973 in the German periodical *Göttinger Miszellen*. Its two-and-a-half pages were to change the course of Amarna studies for good, and inspire a generation of students:

> 'In the 13th year of the reign of Akhenaten (or at some time not far removed), queen Nefernefruaten-Nefertiti, having assumed the crown of kingship but not the full titulary, seems suddenly to dissolve from sight. At about the same time, there appears as co-regent an otherwise unknown person, bearing the nomen Nefernefruaten but with a different epithet, and having the given prenomen Ankhkheprure. Under the co-regency, the position of [*ḥemet nesu weret* – "great royal wife"] devolves upon Meritaten, who continues in this capacity in association with Nefernefruaten alone, and when the latter adopts the name Smenkhkare – possibly as sole ruler….
>
> Two kingly persons of similar name, and not clearly distinguishable in any respect, may thus be seen to succeed each other with no perceptible interval, though without any overlap. The case for a simple identification is sufficiently obvious, and, in that it can be supported as circumstantially as the accepted position (which rests on tacit assumptions rather than any proof), the overall implications merit objective assessment.'

Further research, by Harris, Julia Samson and others, has indeed demonstrated the basic reliability of this hypothesis, which would find unambiguous confirmation quite by chance. Sorting through a collection of faience ring bezels found by Petrie at el-Amarna in 1891–92, it was discovered that several among their number were inscribed not in the normal, masculine form 'Ankhkheprure' but in an emphatically feminine manner: 'Ankhetkheprure'. As further examples turned up, there could be no doubt about it: the 18th Dynasty had produced another ruling woman – a second Hatshepsut.

One of the proofs that Akhenaten's co-regent was not a man but a woman is a series of faience ring bezels (one shown here). These rings, perhaps prepared for the regnal year 12 coronation, are inscribed with the junior pharaoh's prenomen, 'Ankhkheprure', written with a feminine t and elaborated with an epithet expressing dependence on the senior king (here, 'beloved [with feminine t] of Waenre' – i.e. Akhenaten).

Nefertiti as Co-regent and Successor

As Harris observed in 1973, there is a clear developmental sequence in the names employed by queen Nefertiti, by Akhenaten's co-regent, and finally by Akhenaten's successor. The progression, since developed, is demonstrated in the following table, where these links are in italics:

- queen *Nefertiti* becomes queen Nefernefruaten-*Nefertiti*
- queen *Nefernefruaten*-Nefertiti becomes co-regent Ankhkheprure + epithet *Nefernefruaten*+epithet (in two cartouches)
- co-regent *Ankhkheprure*+epithet Nefernefruaten+epithet (in two cartouches) becomes co-regent, then ruler *Ankhkheprure* Smenkhkare (in two cartouches)

When might this co-regency have begun? Again, more evidence.

The well-known images of celebration in Year 12 in the tombs of Huya and Meryre II at el-Amarna have for long years been interpreted as depicting no more than a formal reception of tribute from Hatti, Mitanni, Syria, Palestine, Punt and the Mediterranean. It now seems likely, however, that they – as others depicting the supposed 'visit' of Tiye to el-Amarna – in fact represent scenes within a larger and more significant drama at that time being enacted. These scenes, I would suggest, document an early stage in the formal process of the queen's promotion to the status of co-ruler.

The interpretation is suggested by an almost unique, virtual superimposition in these representations of the images of the king and his queen, as if to emphasize the coming 'oneness' of their rule. And it is perhaps not without significance that the two tomb owners in which the Year 12 celebrations are documented 'are here lifted to prominence as stewards of the harem, an elevation', as E. F. Campbell has perceptively observed, 'which corresponds naturally to the time when the harem … is transferred to the new king after the death of the old king'. In this interpretation, the new 'king' would have been Nefernefruaten, the old king Akhenaten himself; the fact that, as a woman, Nefertiti will have had little practical use for the facility, is neither here nor there.

The idea that Nefertiti and Akhenaten's co-regent were one and the same is now accepted by most informed scholars. The identity of Ankhkheprure Smenkhkare, however, is a quite different matter. Though the equation of co-regent and successor was followed as a matter of course when the two were believed to be male, the suggestion that Nefertiti might have further developed her name to 'Smenkhkare' and gone on to rule independently has met with fierce resistance. The reason? The body in much-discussed tomb KV55 in the Valley of the Kings, which is held up again and again as proof positive that Akhenaten's successor was male, anatomically close to that of Tutankhamun and in all probability an elder brother of this king. The Tomb 55 body has been the proverbial red herring of Amarna studies for many years now. Earlier in this discussion, it was emphasized that not a scrap of

Akhenaten and Nefertiti share virtually the same physical outline in this relief of Year 12 in the tomb of Meryre II at el-Amarna. It conceivably depicts an early stage in the promotion of Nefertiti to co-ruler.

evidence may be cited from the tomb to link any one or any thing in it with Akhenaten's successor; on the contrary, the inscriptions and their context offer as good a proof as may reasonably be hoped for that the burial was of Akhenaten himself – and this is a conclusion with which the most recent anatomical and dental estimates of the occupant's age at death now concur.

Close and detailed study of the art, the inscriptions, the archaeology and the history of the period produces *nothing* to contradict the conclusion that Nefernefruaten and Smenkhkare were one and the same person. And there is, as we shall see, much to support the theory – not least the fact that both shared the same 'great royal wife', Akhenaten's eldest daughter Meritaten.

THE DEATH OF AKHENATEN

About Akhenaten himself during these final years we know virtually nothing. His paunch grows noticeably larger, perhaps reflecting a growing indolence, while there are signs in the king's actions that the mental wear and tear of the first few years had been severe. Hints of mockery may be detected in a series of theriomorphic caricatures in limestone depicting, most famously, monkeys acting out roles previously the preserve of the king

The general disillusionment felt by the end of Akhenaten's reign is reflected in this satirical limestone relief recovered from the ruins of el-Amarna. A prestige vehicle, customarily driven by the king, the chariot symbolized the daily course of the sun through the sky. Here, however, the place of pharaoh is occupied by a monkey.

himself. Was he in serious physical decline? Had he finally gone mad? Was he now a virtual prisoner in his el-Amarna folly, while Nefertiti attempted to guide the state back to some semblance of normality? Possibly and perhaps. We simply do not know.

Akhenaten appears to have passed from this life following the wine vintage of his 17th regnal year. Again, we know nothing of the circumstances, and the king's body from KV55 has so far revealed little which might elucidate the situation. Had his heart given way, the inevitable end of the Marfan's sufferer? Or are we to seek a more sinister explanation? If his death had been 'assisted', given the potentially ruthless nature of Egyptian court life it would be less than surprising. Pharaoh's dreams had brought Egypt to its knees, and there were doubtless many prepared to risk his removal while there was still time for the country to recover. Whatever the truth of the matter, with the disappearance of Akhenaten's charismatic presence it would not be long before the whole Amarna edifice came tumbling down for good.

Of Akhenaten's burial arrangements there can be little doubt: his eternal home was to be the great, if unfinished, royal tomb in the eastern hills at Akhetaten, where his mother already lay in funereal splendour. Many fragments of the king's funerary equipment have been recovered, for the most part dating from the early Amarna years, and in their textual coverage these items remain defiantly 'un-funereal'. The prospect of a world beyond this had played but little part in high Amarna theology, and for John Pendlebury it seemed 'that death was a thing which [Akhenaten] ended by refusing to recognize'. Other items – including two of the four magical bricks from Tomb 55 – tell another story: inscribed as they are with the epithet 'the Osiris', they may hint at the impossible – that, by the time of his death, Akhenaten had returned to the traditionalist fold.

THE MYSTERIOUS DAHAMUNZU

The site of the ancient Hittite capital, Hattusa, was first identified in 1906 by the German archaeologist Hugo Winkler not far from the modern village of Bogazkale (formerly Boghazköy) in central Anatolia. It was an exciting discovery, made all the more so by the excavation over the course of the following six years of more than 10,000 cuneiform tablets not dissimilar in appearance and date to those which had been brought to light at el-Amarna a quarter of a century before. Many of these Hittite texts proved to be of great historical interest, the most extraordinary being the annals document known today as 'The Deeds of Suppiluliuma'. These records had been copied, presumably from original masters, for subsequent transfer to, and public display on, tablets of bronze – tablets which have long since gone the way of all scrap metal.

The annals were compiled not by Suppiluliuma himself but by his son, Mursili II, and the light they have shed on events during the second half of the 14th century BC is as astounding as it is unexpected. Western Asia, as will be recalled, was at the time in the grip of a three-cornered struggle between the old rivals Egypt and Mitanni, both in decline, and the newly emergent Hittite state, Hatti, which was to so upset the balance of power. Egypt, it appears, had attacked Hatti following the seizure from Mitanni of the Syrian town of Qadesh, while the Mitannian forces were under Hittite siege at Carchemish. In retaliation for this Egyptian aggression, Hatti had attacked the vassal town of Amqi.

And then, out of the blue, the 'Deeds' inform us, news was received by messenger: pharaoh, 'Niphururiya', was dead. The offer of peace which followed, from a queen of Egypt referred to in the letter as 'Dahamunzu', would astonish not only the Hittites but, in due course, the Egyptians themselves:

> 'My husband died. A son I have not. But to you, they say, the
> sons are many. If you were to give me a son of yours, he would
> become my husband. Never shall I pick out a servant of mine
> and make him my husband! … I am afraid!'

Suppiluliuma was naturally suspicious. 'Such a thing has never happened to me in my entire life!'. The offer of marriage to a female member of the Egyptian royal family was quite unprecedented – such unions were inconceivable, as Amenophis III had once stressed. Curious, none the less, the Hittite king sent his messenger to Egypt to investigate further before concluding the siege and returning to Hattusa for the winter.

This was the reply brought back by messenger from the Egyptian queen:

> 'Why did you say "they deceive me" in that way? Had I a son,
> would I have written about my own and my country's shame to a
> foreign land? You did not believe me and you have said as much
> to me! He who was my husband has died. A son I have not!
> Never shall I take a servant of mine and make him my husband!
> I have written to no other country; only to you have I written!
> They say your sons are many: so give me one of your sons! To
> me he will be husband, but in Egypt he will be king!'

The dowry this woman would bring to such a match was beyond belief – an expansion of Hittite power and influence from Asia Minor in the north to deepest Nubia in the south. It was an offer too tempting to ignore, and so a son, Zannanza, was duly despatched – only to be assassinated en route, presumably by forces in Egypt inimical to the queen's plans. Dahamunzu's plot was foiled.

The treacherous queen

Who was this Dahamunzu? No Egyptian queen on record bore such a name, and the initial inclination was to 'correct' the reading to 'Sankhamun' – a supposed version of the name of Ankhesenamun, the widow of Tutankhamun. Such emendation was unjustified, however, as T. O. Lambdin and Walter Federn were (independently) to demonstrate forty years ago. As these two scholars saw, the designation 'Dahamunzu' is not a proper *name* at all, but the Hittite vocalization of an Egyptian title: *ta hemet nesu*, 'the king's wife'. But which 'king's wife'? Ankhesenamun was clearly one possibility; another is Nefertiti as widow of Akhenaten.

The king's name as recorded in these Hittite annals does not permit of an easy decision in the matter. Despite interminable discussion on the point, it seems that 'Niphururiya', the name given to Dahamunzu's deceased husband, might with equal facility conceal the prenomen of either Akhenaten (Neferkheprure) or Tutankhamun (Nebkheprure). Opinion has tended to favour Tutankhamun – who for Trevor R. Bryce, one recent commentator, is the *only* viable candidate. John R. Harris, however, in a public lecture delivered in Copenhagen in 1993, has argued strongly – and convincingly – for the opposite view: namely, that the Niphururiya of the Hittite annals was Akhenaten, and Dahamunzu his principal queen and co-regent Nefertiti.

In his lecture, Harris reminded his listeners of the observation made some years ago now by Belgian Egyptologist Claude Vandersleyen that the Hittite Dahamunzu conceals reference not to *a* king's wife but, in view of the definite article *ta*, to '*the* king's wife *par excellence*' – which from the start appears a less than appropriate designation for the young and inconsequential widow of Tutankhamun. Harris's elimination of Ankhesenamun continued in a coolly logical manner: the date of the boy-king's death, he observed, may be assigned to the December prior to his burial – which, on the basis of the floral and faunal evidence buried with him, took place between the end of February and the middle of March. As the Hittite annals indicate, however, the Egyptian queen's letter was received by Suppiluliuma in late autumn. If the Egyptian queen was Ankhesenamun, Harris argues that there must, then, have been a hiatus of some nine to ten months following her husband's death before she determined to enlist Hittite aid – and the negotiations for this aid, up to and including the death of Zannanza, will themselves have extended over at least six further months. If Dahamunzu had been the widow of Tutankhamun, the unavoidable conclusion must be that Ankhesenamun was conducting negotiations in secret while Tutankhamun's successor, Ay, already occupied the throne. This, for Harris, is 'beyond belief'; if the Hittite envoy had reported a situation of this sort, it is virtually certain that Zan-nanza would never have set out, for the chances of success would have been virtually nil.

The months immediately following the death of Akhenaten, on the other hand, offer a far more credible background for the Egypto-Hittite negotiations. To judge from the evidence of wine-jar dockets, Akhenaten died close to the end of his 17th regnal year and after the vintaging of that summer's wine at the end of September or beginning of October. This is precisely the time of year at which Dahamunzu made her approach to the Hittite king and, given the relative stability which seems to have existed (Nefertiti had already ruled as co-regent with Akhenaten for some years, and, it seems, continued to exercise control following his death), there will have been ample opportunity for talks to take place.

But the final nail in the coffin of Ankhesenamun's claims to involvement in the Suppululiuma affair is to be found in one of the 'vassal letters' from el-Amarna (EA 170): there can be but little doubt that this text refers to the same military action against Amqi as that mentioned in the Hittite annals as being already in progress at the time of Dahamunzu's first approach to their king. Since Akhetaten seems to have been abandoned as Egypt's administrative centre by the end of Tutankhamun's reign, by the time Ankhesenamun was widowed the Amarna archive was already closed.

If Harris's argument is to be believed, Dahamunzu was none other than Nefertiti herself: 'the king's wife par excellence' – which is how, to an outside world unfamiliar with the Egyptian co-regency system and the niceties of Egypt's internal politics, the lady will perhaps have continued to be known. The explanation for her treason remains unclear – perhaps her ultimate, if naive, aim was to prop up Egypt's economy with funds from abroad. What-ever, it was an extraordinary act for which she would pay dearly – as indeed would others. If Dahamunzu's actions pro-voked the anti-foreigner backlash one might expect, the fate of Egypt's alien population not improbably provided an important strand to the biblical tradition of Exodus.

Limestone statuette of a middle-aged Nefertiti, beautiful and determined, from the workshop of Thutmose at el-Amarna. The queen wears the close-fitting cap-crown favoured during her co-regency with Akhenaten, which began in regnal year 12. Her hold on power evidently continued, as Ankhkheprure Smenkhkare, into the reign of Tutankhamun.

Tutankhamun and Ankhesenamun on the back panel of the king's golden throne.

CHAPTER NINE

RESTORATION AND OBLIVION

THE DEATH AND BURIAL OF NEFERTITI

The fate of Nefertiti-Smenkhkare, in consequence of her failed parley with the Hittite king, is not at all clear: the only thing we know for certain is that Akhenaten's co-regent and successor drops totally from view, and most probably because of death. It was a death, we may guess, in which natural causes played but little part.

Precisely where Akhenaten's widow was interred is unclear – perhaps the 'royal annexe' within the great tomb at el-Amarna, a suite which had probably been cut with this eventuality in mind; the heretic's city was still the notional capital, and would continue as such for a little time to come. The form this burial took remains obscure. Parts of the burial equipment prepared for the use of Akhenaten's co-regent and successor were identified by Howard Carter during his clearance of the tomb of Tutankhamun – most memorably the second coffin and the exquisite canopic coffinettes of inlaid gold, all of which carried the portrait of their original owner. Nefertiti's burial was clearly intended to have been an impressive one; more than that, in character it was purely Osirian, testifying to the rapid collapse of the Aten's dominance following, if not before, Akhenaten's death.

COMPROMISE AND CO-EXISTENCE

Akhenaten's true heir had been a child, Tutankhaten, not yet ten years of age. His origins are as obscure as those of any among the Amarna crew: identified as a 'king's bodily son' on a stray block found at Hermopolis in association with others originally depicting Kiya, he was most probably the child of this

One of the four gold coffinettes inscribed and employed for Tutankhamun's embalmed viscera. As the interior inscriptions reveal, the containers had initially been prepared for Ankhkheprure Nefernefruaten (with one cartouche subsequently altered, it is claimed, for Ankhkheprure Smenkhkare).

A new and unexpected piece of the Amarna jigsaw puzzle – the tomb of Tutankhamun's wet-nurse, Maia; the lady is shown here wearing a heavy festal wig and balancing the young king on her knee. Before the discovery of her Saqqara tomb by French Egyptologist Alain-Pierre Zivie in 1997, the lady was quite unknown to history.

same woman. Of his early life we know little, but a small piece of the puzzle has recently been supplied by the discovery at Saqqara, by French Egyptologist Alain-Pierre Zivie, of the tomb of the king's nurse, Maia – a tomb particularly memorable for its depiction of the child-king seated upon the lady's lap. For a time, clearly, because of his age, power will have been retained by Nefertiti-Smenkhkare, with their reigns – like those of Hatshepsut and Tuthmosis III – running concurrently.

On the successor's well-known restoration decree (preserved in two copies on stelae dug up at Karnak in 1905 and 1907) we encounter the name of the boy-king in the new and more familiar form adopted in Year 3 or 4 of his reign: 'Tutankhamun', which translates as 'Living image of Amun'. The name of Ankhesen-paaten – the half-sister to whom he had

Head of the young king Tutankhamun in indurated limestone: part of a larger composition which showed the blue crown being set in place by the god Amun.

been married, doubtless in an attempt to reconcile the various factions within the royal family – was similarly modified, to 'Ankhesenamun'. If we are to believe the propaganda of the Amun priests, the adoption of these names signalled the monarchy's full-blown return to the traditionalist fold. It seems the kingship had experienced too many setbacks of late for the Atenist dream to survive – at least in a pure form.

Contrary to general belief, however, the indications are that the young king's accommodation with the old regime did not involve a *total* repudiation of his father's religious views. The clearest evidence for this is the magnificent gold throne (a heavily adapted piece, initially made for Akhenaten himself), which not only retains the Atenist iconography of the multi-rayed disc, but in the balance of its final design gives equal weight to both the 'Tutankhaten' and 'Tutankhamun' name-forms. Similar compromise is seen in a modest private stela (now in Berlin Museum) in which Tutankh*aten* makes offerings to Amun.

Full rejection of the Amarna philosophy would not, in fact, occur for some years to come: el-Amarna and its divinity continued to function, as did Aten's temples up and down the country, retaining personnel like the treasury scribe Penbuy whose continuing Atenist affiliation is recorded on a box lid taken from his tomb. This reluctance to ditch the Aten as an independent divine power was doubtless a principal reason for the condemnation by posterity not only of Akhenaten, but of his successors also –

The splendid golden throne from Tutankhamun's Valley of the Kings tomb (KV62) had been heavily altered in antiquity. In its final form, however, it sported both the 'Tutankhaten' (above) and 'Tutankhamun' forms of the name in equal balance – reflecting the political tightrope the young king and his advisers were attempting to walk.

181

Smenkhkare, Tutankhamun and Ay. They had kept alight the heretical flame, which would not be extinguished completely until after Ay's death and the advent of Horemheb and his successors.

This hope for a happy co-existence between Aten and Amun may have been a strategy originating with Ay. But it proved vain: too much hatred had been stoked up among all classes of society for the accord to stand any real chance of success. And, besides, without the driving force of Akhenaten himself, his cult of kingship was destined quickly to wither and die. By the time of Tutankhamun's death, as the wholly orthodox nature of the boy-king's burial arrangements signals, the pre-eminence of the traditional gods was again effectively secure.

RESTORING THE OLD GODS

The situation inherited by Tutankhamun following the wanton destruction and deliberate neglect of Akhenaten's reign was dire, as the words of his restoration decree issued from the ancient Memphite capital record:

'… the temples and the cities of the gods and goddesses, starting from Elephantine as far as the Delta marshes … were fallen into decay and their shrines were fallen into ruin, having become mere mounds overgrown with grass. Their sanctuaries were like something which had not yet come into being and their buildings were a footpath [i.e. public] – for the land was in rack and ruin. The gods were ignoring this land. When an army was sent to Djahy [Palestine] to broaden the boundaries of Egypt, it was unsuccessful; if one prayed to a god, to ask something from him, he did not come at all; and if one beseeched any goddess in the same way, she did not come at all….'

Pressing on with the work of restoration already set in train by Nefertiti before Akhenaten's death, Tutankhamun offered the hope at last of a return to some semblance of normality.

The text of the 'Restoration Stela' of Tutankhamun is today found in two copies; both of these were usurped by Horemheb who wished to take credit for restoring the old regime following the disruption of the Amarna years. The crude chisel slots which disfigure this fine monument were cut later in an attempt to split the block into two equal halves for reuse.

Tutankhamun's rapprochement with the Amun priesthood manifested itself in a mass renewal of the god's sculptural images, a good number of which had been destroyed during Akhenaten's terror. The greater proportion of the god's statues and statuettes extant today, like the colossal sculpture shown here still in place at Karnak, carry the features of the young king.

The task facing the new regime was enormous, and would deplete still further Egypt's now rattling coffers, as the following extract from the king's restoration text suggests:

> 'After some time had passed over this, his majesty [Tutankhamun] appeared upon the throne of his father and he ruled over the shores of Horus [i.e. Egypt].... His majesty took counsel with his heart, investigating every excellent deed, seeking benefactions for his father Amun and fashioning his noble image out of genuine electrum.
>
> He gave more than what had been done previously:
> – he fashioned his father Amun ...;
> – he fashioned Ptah-South-of-his-Wall ...;
> – and his majesty made monuments for the gods ... building their shrines anew as monuments of eternity endowed with possessions forever; instituting divine offerings for them, consisting of regular daily sacrifices; and providing their food offerings on earth.
>
> He gave more than what had existed before, surpassing what had been done since the time of the ancestors: he installed lay priests and higher clergy from among the children of the officials of their cities, each one being the son of a man whose name was known....
>
> As for the gods and goddesses who are in this land, their hearts are joyful: the lords of shrines are rejoicing, the shores are shouting praise, and exultation pervades the entire land now that good plans have come to pass....'

It was an impressive achievement, as the epithet attached to the king's name on one of the seals of his tomb acknowledged: 'Nebkheprure [Tutankhamun], who spent his life fashioning images of the gods ...'. The extent of Egypt's debt is indicated today by a single, striking irony: of those large-scale images of the god Amun which have come down to us, the greatest number by far carry the features of Akhenaten's son.

A RETURN TO NORMALITY

'Year 8, third month of *peret*-season, day 21 under the majesty of
... the son of Re, Tutankhamun, who gives life. On this day his
majesty ordained the hereditary prince and count, fanbearer on
the king's right hand, the royal scribe and overseer of the
treasury, Maya, to tax the entire land and institute divine

*The god's father Ay, now become king, performs the ritual of 'opening the mouth' on the mummy of
his young ward, Tutankhamun. With Ay in control before the tomb of his predecessor had even
been closed, there would have been no opportunity for Tutankhamun's widow to approach the
Hittites for a son to rule Egypt by her side.*

offerings for all the gods of the tilled land [Egypt], starting from
Elephantine and ending at Smanebbehdet [in the Delta] ...'

Amun was well on the way to being restored to the position of Egypt's
supreme deity, his glory reflected in the renewed and improved trappings
now bestowed upon him, upon his temples and upon the god's priests. As the
old system was reinstated, construction again got under way – most notably
on the west bank at Thebes, with the erection of a mortuary temple later
usurped by Ay and Horemheb; at Luxor temple, where Tutankhamun completed Amenophis III's Opet Festival scenes; and at Karnak, where he lined
with converted Akhenaten/Nefertiti andro-sphinxes the avenue between
the tenth pylon and the Mut temple. For areas beyond Thebes we know
little, but Tutankhamun was clearly active at Memphis, the ancient capital,
where his efforts included the resumption of the Apis burials first set in train
by Amenophis III – the king, his grandfather, with whom he chooses repeatedly to associate himself here, at Thebes and elsewhere. Outside Egypt, in
Nubia, temple construction was undertaken at Soleb, Kawa and Faras; while
in the north active campaigning resumed under general Horemheb in
pharaoh's name and perhaps even in his physical presence. And, most important of all, as Horemheb records in his famous 'Decree', the administration
was overhauled and the curse of widespread corruption at long last
addressed.

THE GOD'S FATHER AY

Although the new Amun clergy was drawn from the old, pre-Amarna ranks,
the inner circle of pharaoh continued to include a number of survivors from
Akhenaten's time. One of the more intriguing was Pentju, pharaoh's chief
physician, 'one who approaches the god's flesh'. Why was a man such as this
given a second chance? We cannot know. Another familiar, and much more
significant, face is that of the god's father Ay, scion of the powerful Yuya-
Tjuyu clan and probable great-uncle of the new king. As principal adviser to
Tutankhamun, Ay controlled access to the boy and exercised the affairs of
state in his name.

Ay's commitment to the Atenist ideal has generally been assumed, both
from his supposed position as father-in-law to Akhenaten and from the
fulsome articulation, in his el-Amarna tomb, of the Great Hymn to the Aten;
but actually it seems clear that the man's role at Akhetaten was that of a
favoured executive of the regime rather than an intellectual driving force.
Compromise was clearly Ay's forte, and it is probable that his is to be recognized, from the start, as the guiding hand behind the reconciliation with
Amun. Ay's survival of the Zannanza incident – if he was indeed the father of
Nefertiti – is more difficult to understand; the queen's traitorous, last-ditch
attempt at holding on to power ought to have compromised him also. In the
absence of firm evidence, we can again only speculate. Perhaps the key point

is that Nefertiti, despite her final political error – and conceivably under Ay's influence – had initiated the return to normality which Tutankhamun would later formalize in stone in his restoration decree. The ultimate proof of Ay's influence and power at court was, of course, yet to come – with his elevation to the throne following the unexpectedly early death of his own kingly charge, the last in the direct line of succession of the 18th Dynasty.

THE TOMB OF TUTANKHAMUN

As the dried plant remains from the burial of Tutankhamun allow us to establish from the date of their flowering, the burial of the boy-king took place between the end of February and the middle of March; the year is usually calculated as 1323 BC. He had died, therefore, some 70 days previously – the length of time required by the Egyptian embalmers to transform, physically and ritually, the corpse into a mummy. And this mummy, by a miracle, was discovered undisturbed within its tomb (KV62) in the Valley of the Kings in November 1922. The story of Howard Carter's discovery of Tutankhamun today reads more like a fairy-tale fiction than the work of sober science it actually was. As the excavator describes in his 1923 publication:

'Slowly, desperately slowly it seemed to us as we watched, the remains of passage debris that encumbered the lower part of the

Howard Carter brushes the dust of centuries from the innermost of Tutankhamun's three anthropoid coffins – a masterpiece of the metal-worker's art, beaten from solid gold, measuring an average of 3 mm (0.2 in) in thickness and weighing in at over 110 kg (296lb troy).

doorway were removed, until at last we had the whole door clear before us. The decisive moment had arrived. With trembling hands I made a tiny breach in the upper left hand corner. Darkness and blank space, as far as an iron testing-rod could reach, showed that whatever lay beyond was empty, and not filled like the passage we had just cleared. Candle tests were applied as a precaution against possible foul gases, and then, widening the hole a little, I inserted the candle and peered in, Lord Carnarvon, Lady Evelyn and Callender standing anxiously beside me to hear the verdict. At first I could see nothing, the hot air escaping from the chamber causing the candle flame to flicker, but presently, as my eyes grew accustomed to the light, details of the room within emerged slowly from the mist, strange animals, statues, and gold – everywhere the glint of gold. For the moment – an eternity it must have seemed to the others standing by – I was struck dumb with amazement, and when Lord Carnarvon, unable to stand the suspense any longer, inquired anxiously, "Can you see anything?" it was all I could do to get out the words, "Yes, wonderful things".'

Although the tomb consisted of no more than four small chambers, they were chambers packed to the roof with the most magnificent array of Egyptian burial equipment seen in modern times. Entered at least twice by petty criminals within a matter of months of the original closing, the sepulchre yet preserved its main contents virtually intact. The mummy of the king lay untouched, just as the burial party had left it under Ay's command as successor more than three thousand years before – packed away safe and sound within a solid gold coffin, two further coffins of gilded and inlaid wood, a quartz-sandstone sarcophagus, four gilded wooden shrines and a sequin-bedecked linen pall. And with the discovery of Tutankhamun's corpse, details of the final act in the Atenist drama would at last be revealed.

MURDER?

The autopsy on Tutankhamun's mummy began on 11 November 1925, the work of dissection being undertaken by anatomist Douglas Derry under the supervision of Howard Carter; Lord Carnarvon, by this time, was dead, supposed victim of 'pharaoh's curse' invented by Egyptologist-journalist Arthur Weigall. Extracting the mummy from its resinous carapace proved an onerous task, which the king's fragile remains barely survived; the poor state of preservation of the mummy had been caused by an over-generous application of unguents, soaking into and rotting the wrappings. Nor was the condition helped by Carter's attempts to soften the fixative by means of a blow lamp.

Not surprisingly, perhaps, the mummy's flesh, instead of being dry and leathery, when eventually revealed looked as if it had been burnt. The king's

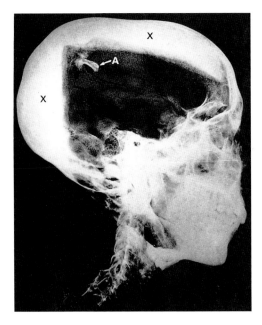

Radiograph of Tutankhamun's skull. The two radiopaque areas at 'X' indicate that resin was introduced into the king's skull on two separate occasions during the embalming process – once while the body was hung upside down, and again while it lay flat on the embalming slab. The fragment of bone at 'A' appears to have been displaced during the removal of the brain by insertion of a copper hook through the nasal cavity.

features were thus poorly defined, though a curious blemish 'resembling a scab' was noted on the king's left cheek, just in front of the ear-lobe; this, the superstitious would have us believe, was the very place Lord Carnarvon had been bitten by pharaoh's vengeful mosquito. It cannot wholly be ruled out that the king died of natural causes – perhaps (as the scab might suggest) from the plague which we know from texts to have been endemic in the Near East at this time, or from massive cardiovascular failure as a consequence of Marfan's Syndrome (with which might be connected the curiously absent sternum and ribs). X-rays of the skull, on the other hand, prepared in 1968, have suggested a rather more dramatic possibility – that Tutankhamun was, in fact, murdered.

The first to voice this idea was R. G. Harrison, Professor of Anatomy at Liverpool University, in a BBC television documentary screened shortly after the X-rays had been taken. Harrison himself died before he was able to pronounce formally on the findings, but a recent re-examination of the radiographs claims to support his view. A density at the base of Tutankhamun's skull is thought to represent a haemorrhage beneath the membranes overlying the brain (a 'chronic subdural hematoma'), a clot over which, significantly, there was time for a calcified layer to develop before death ended the process.

If this interpretation is correct (and it has inevitably been challenged), the implication would be that Tutankhamun suffered a blow to the head, and lingered, drifting in and out of consciousness, for some weeks. What is interesting is that the position of this supposed blow would indicate that the damage had been sustained intentionally rather than by accident – at a time when political manipulation of the god-king was the norm, and regicide a rather more common occurrence than the Egyptian state cared formally to acknowledge. With his charge in a coma, it is proposed, Ay moved swiftly to formalize his position as co-regent – evidenced in his adoption of a new title, 'eldest king's son', or heir apparent, and by the carving of a series of architrave blocks brought to light at Karnak in which the titularies of himself and his dying ward are juxtaposed. Before Tutankhamun finally slipped into the void, it would appear that Ay was already formally in control, and arrangements were well in hand to abandon el-Amarna for good.

BEHIND THE GOLDEN MASK

The scholarly assessment of Tutankhamun's reign has changed over the years: initially seen as an inconsequential, minor pharaoh distinguished by the chance preservation of a magnificent burial equipment, he is now widely regarded as the saviour of Egyptian traditions, the king responsible for righting an upturned country and for re-establishing the rule of law. On one thing there has been general and consistent agreement since the discovery of his tomb: that the young pharaoh's death was a tragedy, an innocent life cut woefully short.

This sense of sadness is compounded by the suspicion of foul play, which proves difficult to shake off. There was, indisputably, one man with much to gain from the boy's passing – and that was the god's father Ay, Tutankhamun's guardian and the one responsible for reimposing normality on pharaoh's realm. An old man with few years left, Ay had become accustomed to the exercise of power during his charge's minority; and it was a power he may have proved reluctant to surrender as and when the boy came of age.

But Ay's presumed guilt may conceal an even grimmer reality. For, captivated by that sweet young face, we tend to forget whose son Tutankhamun was. Inculcated in the Atenist dream from his earliest years, who knows what resentments he may have harboured at the dismantling of Akhenaten's achievement, and at his father's ultimate fate? Perhaps Ay feared, and with reason, that behind the boy's smile lurked an all too familiar ruthless ambition to reimpose the regime Akhenaten's death had allowed to collapse. If so, it was a risk Ay declined to run, as the sins of the father, his excesses familiar to all, were visited mercilessly upon the son, a potential monster in waiting.

HOREMHEB: THE END OF THE NIGHTMARE

Ay's four-year reign was an inconsequential one, perhaps formalized in some manner by marriage to Tutankhamun's widow – as suggested by the couple's conjoined cartouches on a small, glass ring bezel in Berlin Museum. The successor buried his ward in style, as he was obliged – but after that

Did Ay seek to reconcile opposing factions within the royal household by marriage to Tutankhamun's widow, Ankhesenamun – Akhenaten's third daughter, Ankhesenpaaten? This would seem to be the implication of a fingerring of discoloured blue glass, now in Berlin, in which the names of the two are arranged side by side.

A list of his pharaonic predecessors carved on the wall of Sethos I's famous mortuary temple at Abydos. Only legitimate rulers are included – the Amarna kings being completely ignored, with the throne shown to pass directly from Amenophis III to Horemheb.

the situation becomes hazy in the extreme. Ay's own nominated heir is thought to have been a son, the military officer Nakhtmin; in the period of unrest which followed Ay's death, however, Nakhtmin appears to have been soundly defeated by Tutankhamun's general, Horemheb, who seized the throne for himself.

Horemheb's queen was a lady by the name of Mutnedjmet, whom some scholars identify as Nefertiti's sister and thus perhaps Ay's daughter, taken in marriage to compensate for the victor's commoner status. The new king's priorities were clear: no compromise, no middle way – simply an unambiguous return to the days of old. The administration was set on a fresh footing, and the army, which had early fallen under Akhenaten's spell, was completely reor-

Nakhtmin: head from a dyad representing the man – presumed to be a son of the god's father Ay – and his unnamed, beautiful wife. The inscription on the rear of the sculpture records Nakhtmin's principal title: 'king's son of . . .' – which is perhaps to be completed as 'king's son of [his body]', or heir. However, it was not Nakhtmin who would succeed, but the military officer Horemheb.

ganized and purged. More importantly, the primacy of the Aten was brought to a full and final end (though the cult itself would continue into and beyond the reign of Sethos I), with Amun reinstated as undisputed king of the gods. The monuments of Akhenaten's years were dismantled, and under Ramesses II the foundations of the Great Aten Temple at el-Amarna finally cemented over 'to seal in as it were the infection of the accursed spot'. Further occupation of 'Horizon of the Aten' may have been prohibited; or else, regarded by many as cursed, the site was simply shunned.

Along with his successors, Akhenaten was consigned to oblivion; he, Smenkhkare, Ay and Tutankhamun were struck from the records, and on more than one occasion their monuments usurped. History, as proclaimed in the king-lists at Abydos and elsewhere, was rewritten to show that the throne had passed directly from the pre-deification days of Amenophis III to Horemheb. References thereafter to Akhenaten and his reign were rare, oblique and always unfavourable. 'The beautiful child of the living Aten' lived on only as the bogeyman of oral tradition – Akhenaten, 'the enemy of Akhetaten' responsible for the time 'of the rebellion'.

Horemheb alone escaped the ire of the Ramessid pharaohs – and for the simple reason that he, by the nomination of his successor, the general Paramessu, had put them on the throne. Under the last of their number, Ramesses XI, the fear which had driven the Amarna revolution became a reality: around 1100 BC the militaristic high-priest of Amun's pampered cult, Herihor, declared himself ruler. By the following, 21st Dynasty, the only real king of Egypt was Amun himself.

Akhenaten's nightmare had become a reality.

Horemheb, Tutankhamun's general and Ay's successor as king of Egypt, seen here in a life-sized statue as scribe. Since Horemheb would die without issue, the throne subsequently passed to his general, Paramessu – who ascended the throne as Ramesses I, ushering in the 19th Dynasty and the final obliteration of the Amarna regime.

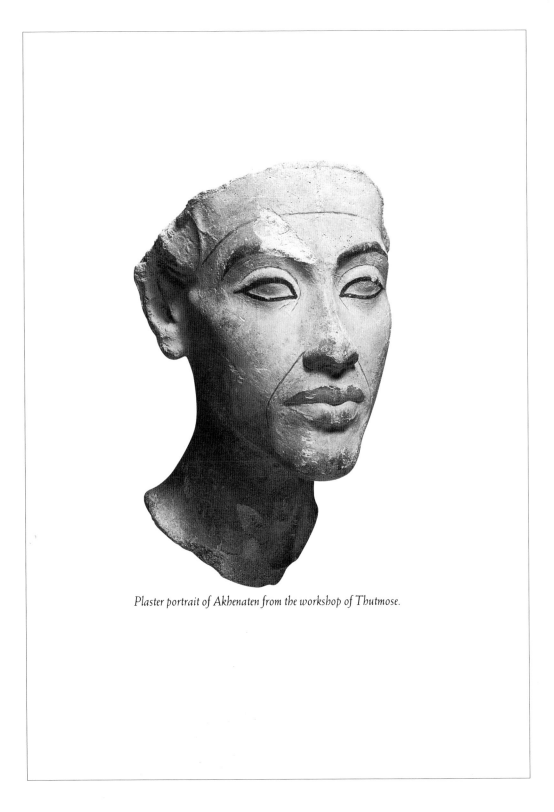

Plaster portrait of Akhenaten from the workshop of Thutmose.

EPILOGUE

'For you, [O Aten, pharaoh] has made Akhetaten.... One
rejoices at seeing its beauty, fair and lovely. One sees it as if
looking at the sky – its limits unreachable – with the Aten rising
in it to fill it with his rays ...' INSCRIPTION FROM THE TOMB OF
MAYA, EL-AMARNA

More than three millennia have passed since the day Akhenaten, standing in
his chariot of gold, read out his proclamation of revelation and hope to an
inspired and enthusiastic audience gathered on the site of his new city at el-
Amarna. Little could the people have imagined the depths the regime would
soon plumb, and the revulsion and loathing with which the architect of this
grand scheme would be regarded by succeeding generations. In 17 years of
dictatorial rule, dominated by the paranoia of an Amunist conspiracy, the
heretic king had brought the country and its people to the very brink of disaster.

Akhenaten's city vanished as quickly as it had risen, robbed of its people
and plundered of its materials by more than one fearful successor. Untended,
it quickly fell prey to the site's prevailing north wind – the same breeze
whose sweetness had once brought life to the faces of pharaoh and his
queen; a wind which now wore down the walls and sanded over their forms.

Though bathed in the same heat and light of the sun once known as Aten,
the heretic's capital was lost, forgotten, and fell into silence. It was a silence
not truly broken until, a hundred and
more years ago, a chance discovery
of peculiar clay tablets by a local
peasant woman returned to this
distant place and period a voice ...

Worthless! Pah!

Not gold, to be sure: a thing
more precious by far.

*Adoration made and offerings piled before
pharaoh's empty throne, still blessed by the
rays of his god, the Aten – a limestone block
from Hermopolis (el-Ashmunein).*

ACKNOWLEDGMENTS

Any merits this book may have are a direct result of the teaching and friendship of John R. Harris, a constant and selfless source of Egyptological and other counsel and inspiration over many years. I owe him much, and am pleased to acknowledge it. For new information and illuminating discussion on matters architectural both at Thebes and el-Amarna I am most grateful to Michael Mallinson; while for time taken from their own pressing schedules to read through and comment upon the completed text, or extracts from it, I should like to thank George Hart, W. Raymond Johnson, Piers Litherland, Geoffrey T. Martin, Stephen Quirke, Ian Shaw, Helen and Nigel Strudwick, and John Taylor. For valuable discussion on several points, and much common-sense advice, I am, as ever, indebted to Yumiko Ueno; others from whose comments and opinions I have benefited are Tom Blackmore, Paul Sussman and Stephen Ulph. For views expressed – and errors – the responsibility is mine alone.

FURTHER READING

The number of works written about or touching upon Akhenaten and the Amarna period is enormous, and for this reason this list has been restricted almost entirely to books in English. Specialist studies have appeared in other languages, both as monographs and in periodicals such as *Acta Orientalia, Amarna Letters, Annales du Service des Antiquités de l'Égypte, Bulletin de l'Institut français d'archéologie orientale, Bulletin de la Société d'Égyptologie, Genève, Chronique d'Égypte, Discussions in Egyptology, Göttinger Miszellen, Journal of the American Research Center in Egypt, Journal of Cuneiform Studies, Journal of Egyptian Archaeology, Journal of Near Eastern Studies, Mitteilungen des Deutschen Archäologischen Instituts Abteilung Kairo, Mitteilungen des Deutschen Orient-Gesellschaft, Orient, Revue d'Égyptologie, Studien zur altägyptischen Kultur* and *Zeitschrift für ägyptische Sprache und Altertumskunde.* In addition to those authors cited independently below, works by the following have proved particularly helpful in the writing of this book: James P. Allen, Martha R. Bell, Ludwig Borchardt, Trevor R. Bryce, Alwyn L. Burridge, Henri Chevrier, R. C. Connolly, Jacobus van Dijk, Walter Fritz, Renate Germer, Hans G. Güterbock, Robert Hari, James E. Harris, John R. Harris, R. G. Harrison, Wolfgang Helck, Erik Hornung, W. Raymond Johnson, Jiro Kondo, Marianne Eaton-Krauss, Peter Lacovara, Ronald J. Leprohon, Christian Loeben, Beatrix Löhr, Michael Mallinson, Lise Manniche, Edmund S. Meltzer, Robert Morkot, Maya Müller, Maarten J. Raven, John D. Ray, Gay Robins, Otto J. Schaden, Heinrich Schäfer, Hermann A. Schlögl, Ian Shaw, Sayed Tawfik, Claude Traunecker, Eric P. Uphill, Claude Vandersleyen, Robert Vergnieux, Dietrich Wildung and Alain-Pierre Zivie. Those requiring a comprehensive guide to the published work of these and other scholars are referred to Geoffrey T. Martin, *A Bibliography of the Amarna Period and its Aftermath* (London, 1991), and now Marc Gabolde's *D'Akhenaton à Toutânkhamon* (Lyon, 1998), pp. xvii-lxx – an important assemblage of data to which I had access only after the present text had been submitted for publication.

Further and more specific bibliographical references will be found in Sources of Quotations.

General works

Baines, J. & J. Málek, *Atlas of Ancient Egypt* (Oxford & New York, 1980)

Breasted, James Henry, *A History of Egypt* (2nd ed., New York, 1910)

Edwards, I. E. S., C. J. Gadd, N. G. L. Hammond & E. Sollberger, *The Cambridge Ancient History*, II, parts 1–2 (Cambridge, 1973)

Gardiner, Alan H., *Egypt of the Pharaohs* (Oxford, 1961)

Hari, Robert, *Répertoire onomastique amarnienne* (Geneva, 1976)

Helck, Wolfgang, Eberhard Otto & Wolfhart Westendorff, *Lexikon der Ägyptologie* (Wiesbaden, 1975–92)

Kemp, Barry J., *Ancient Egypt. Anatomy of a Civilization* (London & New York, 1989)

Lichtheim, Miriam, *Ancient Egyptian Literature*, II. *The New Kingdom* (Berkeley, 1976)

Porter, B., R. L. B. Moss, E. Burney & J. Málek, *Topographical Bibliography of Ancient Egyptian Hieroglyphic Texts, Reliefs, and Paintings*, I–VIII (Oxford, 1927–2000)

Excavations, epigraphy

Carter, Howard (& Arthur C. Mace), *The Tomb of Tut.ankh.Amen*, I–III (London, 1923–33)

Chubb, Mary A., *Nefertiti Lived Here* (2nd ed., London, 1998)

Davies, Norman de Garis, *The Rock Tombs of El-Amarna*, I–VI (London, 1903–08)

Davies, Norman de Garis, *The Tomb of the Vizier Ramose* (London, 1941)

Davis, Theodore M., *The Tomb of Iouiya and Touiyou* (London, 1907)

Davis, Theodore M., *The Tomb of Queen Tîyi* (London, 1910; 2nd ed., San Francisco, 1990)

Davis, Theodore M., *The Tombs of Harmhabi and Touatânkhamanou* (London, 1912)

Epigraphic Survey of the University of Chicago, *The Tomb of Kheruef: Theban Tomb 192* (Chicago, 1980)

Frankfort, Henri & John D. S. Pendlebury, *The City of Akhenaten*, II (London, 1933)

Gohary, Jocelyn, *Akhenaten's Sed-festival at Karnak* (London & New York, 1992)

Hanke, Rainer, *Amarna-Reliefs aus Hermopolis* (Hildesheim, 1978)

Kemp, Barry J. (ed.), *Amarna Reports*, I– (London, 1984–)

Kemp, Barry J. & Salvatore Garfi, *A Survey of the Ancient City of El-'Amarna* (London, 1993)

el-Khouly, Aly & Geoffrey T. Martin, *Excavations in the Royal Necropolis at El-'Amarna 1984* (Cairo, 1987)

Martin, Geoffrey T., *The Royal Tomb at El-'Amarna*, I-II (London, 1974–89)

Peet, Thomas Eric & Charles Leonard Woolley, *The City of Akhenaten*, I (London, 1923)

Pendlebury, John D. S., *Tell el-Amarna* (London, 1935)

Pendlebury, John D. S. et al., *The City of Akhenaten*, III (London, 1951)

Perepelkin, G., *The Secret of the Gold Coffin* (Moscow, 1978)

Petrie, W. M. Flinders, *Tell el-Amarna* (London, 1894)

Quibell, James Edward, *The Tomb of Yuaa and Thuiu* (Cairo, 1908)

Reeves, C. Nicholas, *Valley of the Kings. The Decline of a Royal Necropolis* (London, 1990)

Reeves, Nicholas, *The Complete Tutankhamun* (London & New York, 1990)

Reeves, C. Nicholas (ed.), *After Tut'ankhamun. Research and Excavations in the Royal Necropolis at Thebes* (London, 1992)

Reeves, Nicholas & Richard H. Wilkinson, *The Complete Valley of the Kings* (London & New York, 1996)

Roeder, G., *Amarna-Reliefs aus Hermopolis* (Hildesheim, 1969)

Smith, Ray Winfield & Donald B. Redford, *The Akhenaten Temple Project*, I (Warminster, 1976)

History, chronology, texts

Aldred, Cyril, *Akhenaten, Pharaoh of Egypt. A New Study* (London, 1968)

Aldred, Cyril, *Akhenaten, King of Egypt* (London & New York, 1988)

Blankenberg-van Delden, C., *The Large Commemorative Scarabs of Amenhotep III*

(Leiden, 1969)

Breasted, James Henry, *Ancient Records of Egypt*, II. *The Eighteenth Dynasty* (London, 1988)

Brier, Bob, *The Murder of Tutankhamen* (New York & London, 1998)

Bryan, Betsy M., *The Reign of Thutmose IV* (Baltimore, 1991)

Campbell, Edward Fay, Jr., *The Chronology of the Amarna Letters* (Baltimore, 1964)

Cumming, Barbara/Benedict G. Davies, *Egyptian Historical Records of the Later Eighteenth Dynasty*, I–VI (Warminster, 1982–1995)

Desroches-Noblecourt, Christiane, *Tutankhamen: Life and Death of a Pharaoh* (London & New York, 1963)

El Mahdy, Christine, *Tutankhamen. The Life and Death of a Boy King* (London, 1999)

Gabolde, Marc, *D'Akhenaton à Toutânkhamon* (Lyon, 1998)

Giles, Frederick J., *Ikhnaton, Legend and History* (London, 1970)

Giles, Frederick J., *The Amarna Age: Western Asia* (Warminster, 1997)

Hornung, Erik, *Akhenaten and the Religion of Light* (Ithaca, 1999)

Krauss, Rolf, *Das Ende der Amarnazeit* (Hildesheim, 1978)

Montserrat, Dominic, *Akhenaten. History, Fantasy and Ancient Egypt* (London & New York, 2000)

Moran, William L., *The Amarna Letters* (Baltimore, 1992)

Murnane, William J., *Ancient Egyptian Coregencies* (Chicago, 1977)

Murnane, William J., *The Road to Kadesh* (2nd ed., Chicago, 1990)

Murnane, William J., *Texts from the Amarna Period in Egypt* (Atlanta, 1995)

Murnane, William J. & Charles C. van Siclen III, *The Boundary Stelae of Akhenaten* (London & New York, 1993)

O'Connor, David & Eric H. Cline (eds), *Amenhotep III. Perspectives on his Reign* (Ann Arbor, 1998)

Perepelkin, Y. Y., *Perevorot Amen-khotpa IV*, I–II (Moscow, 1967–84)

Redford, Donald B., *History and Chronology of the Eighteenth Dynasty. Seven Studies* (Toronto, 1967)

Redford, Donald B., *Akhenaten, the Heretic King* (Princeton, 1984)

Samson, Julia, *Amarna, City of Akhenaten and Nefertiti. Nefertiti as Pharaoh* (Warminster, 1978)

Samson, Julia, *Nefertiti and Cleopatra* (London, 1990)

Tyldesley, Joyce, *Hatchepsut, the Female Pharaoh* (London, 1996)

Tyldesley, Joyce, *Nefertiti, Egypt's Sun Queen* (London, 1998)

Waddell, W. G., *Manetho* (Cambridge, Ma., 1997)

Watterson, Barbara, *Amarna, Ancient Egypt's Age of Revolution* (Stroud, 1999)

Weigall, Arthur, *The Life and Times of Akhnaton, Pharaoh of Egypt* (Edinburgh, 1910; new ed., London, 1922)

Religion, art and culture

Aldred, Cyril, *Akhenaten and Nefertiti* (New York & London, 1973)

Anthes, Rudolf, *The Head of Queen Nofretete* (Berlin, 1958)

Arnold, Dorothea, *The Royal Women of Amarna* (New York, 1996)

Assmann, Jan, *Egyptian Solar Religion in the New Kingdom: Re, Amun and the Crisis of Polytheism* (London & New York, 1995)

Berman, Lawrence M. (ed.), *The Art of Amenhotep III: Art Historical Analysis* (Cleveland, 1990)

Cooney, John D., *Amarna Reliefs from Hermopolis in American Collections* (Brooklyn, 1965)

Freed, Rita E., Yvonne J. Markowitz & Sue D'Auria, *Pharaohs of the Sun: Akhenaten, Nefertiti, Tutankhamen* (Boston & London, 1999)

Hayes, William C., *The Scepter of Egypt*, II. *The Hyksos Period and the New Kingdom* (1675–1080 BC) (New York, 1990)

Hornung, Erik, *Conceptions of God in Ancient Egypt. The One and the Many* (Ithaca, 1982)

Kozloff, Arielle P. & Betsy M. Bryan (eds), *Egypt's Dazzling Sun. Amenhotep III and his World* (Cleveland, 1992)

Nims, Charles F., *Thebes of the Pharaohs* (London, 1965)

Riefstahl, Elizabeth, *Thebes in the Time of Amunhotep III* (Norman, 1964)

Simpson, William Kelly (ed.), *Religion and Philosophy in Ancient Egypt* (New Haven, 1989)

SOURCES OF QUOTATIONS

p. 8 '... at the name Akhnaton ... of its workings ...' A. Weigall, *The Life and Times of Akhnaton, Pharaoh of Egypt* (Edinburgh, 1910), p. 2. p. 9 'Only where one ... imagination free rein' L. A. White, *Journal of the American Oriental Society* 68 (1948), p. 109. p. 9 'highly theoretical ... by future discoveries....' J. D. S. Pendlebury, *Tell el-Amarna* (London, 1935), p. xvi. p. 11 'May my brother ... me no distress....' Amarna letter EA 19: after W. L. Moran, *The Amarna Letters* (Baltimore, 1992. All extracts reprinted with permission of The Johns Hopkins University Press), p. 44. p. 13 '... a trickle of ... name was Akhenaten ...' M. A. Chubb, *Nefertiti Lived Here* (2nd ed., London, 1998), pp. 13–14. p. 13 'cut with his own hand' after H. Carter, *The Tomb of Tut.ankh.Amen*, II (London, 1927), p. 36. p. 13 'evil reputation' N. de G. Davies, *The Rock Tombs of El-Amarna*, I (London, 1903), p. 3. pp. 14–15 'I was surprised ... forty-eight metres wide....' E. Jomard, *Description de l'Égypte. Antiquités, Descriptions*, II, chapter XVI: quoted in B. J. Kemp & S. Garfi, *A Survey of the Ancient City of El-'Amarna* (London, 1993), pp. 10–11. p. 16 'the best-equipped ... among the members' W. R. Dawson, E. P. Uphill & M. L. Bierbrier, *Who Was Who in Egyptology* (3rd ed., London, 1995), p. 249. p. 17 'Through the monuments ... the Sun's disk" ...' K. R. Lepsius, *Letters from Egypt, Ethiopia, and the Peninsula of Sinai* (London, 1853), p. 27. p. 20 'You lived on ... ate the tin' M. A. Murray, *My First Hundred Years* (London, 1963), p. 112. p. 21 '... O Living Aten ... adoring your *ka* ...' Great Hymn to the Aten, tomb of Ay, el-Amarna: after W. J. Murnane, *Texts from the Amarna Period in Egypt* SBL Writings from the Ancient World, 5 (Atlanta, Scholars Press, 1995), pp. 112, 113. All extracts reprinted by permission of the Society of Biblical Literature. p. 22 'Though so much ... we yet know.' W. M. F. Petrie, *Seventy Years in Archaeology* (London, 1931), p. 141. p. 22 'cocky little Ludwig Borchardt' J. A. Wilson, *Thousands of Years* (New York,

1972), p. 58. p. 24 'What the German ... they keep!' Reported in a lecture by Hans G. Güterbock at the University of Chicago, February, 1987; information courtesy of Peter Lacovara. p. 25 'The English staff ... he has removed ...' J. D. S. Pendlebury, *Tell el-Amarna* (London, 1935), p. xxiv. p. 25 'the Cretan Lawrence' H. Hünger & E. E. Strassl, *Kampf und Intrigue im Griechenland* (Munich, 1942), p. 272. p. 25 'Behind his normal ... of the present' M. A. Chubb, *Nefertiti Lived Here* (2nd ed., London, 1998), p. 51. p. 30 'Tutimaeus. In his ... striking a blow....' Manetho, fr. 42, from Josephus, *Contra Apionem*, I.14, paras 73–92: after W. G. Waddell, *Manetho* (Cambridge, Ma., 1997), p. 79. p. 32 'to slake his ... foreign lands' Biography of Ahmose son of Ibana: after D. B. Redford, *Akhenaten, the Heretic King* (Princeton, 1984), p. 17. p. 33 'a great sacerdotal ... the whole land' J. H. Breasted, *A History of Egypt* (2nd ed., New York, 1910), p. 247. p. 37 'I did this ... *who gives instructions.*' Karnak obelisk (N) of Hatshepsut: after B. M. Bryan, in D. O'Connor & E. H. Cline (eds), *Amenhotep III. Perspectives on his Reign* (Ann Arbor, 1998), p. 29. p. 38 'Every king of ... guidance men live' Inscription in the tomb of Rekhmire, vizier of Tuthmosis III, after C. Aldred, *Akhenaten and Nefertiti* (New York & London, 1973), p. 14. p. 41 '*maryannu* [chariot-warriors], ... weapons of warfare' Stela of Amenophis II, Memphis: after A. H. Gardiner, *Egypt of the Pharaohs* (London, 1961), p. 202. p. 41 'Tally of those ... this tribute: 2657.' Inscription of Usersatet: after D. B. Redford, *Akhenaten, the Heretic King* (Princeton, 1984), p. 27. p. 43 'Egypt had enlarged ... what they had.' J. D. S. Pendlebury, *Tell el-Amarna* (London, 1935), p. 4. p. 46 'a puppy' W. J. Murnane, *Ancient Egyptian Coregencies* (Chicago, 1977), p. 254. p. 46 'One of these ... and my protector"' Dream Stela of Tuthmosis IV: after B. M. Bryan, *The Reign of Thutmose IV* (Baltimore, 1991), p. 146. p. 47 'I am your ... and my protector' ibid. **p. 49** 'subjects to the rule of Aten forever' British Museum scarab EA 65800: after A. W. Shorter, *Journal of Egyptian Archaeology* 17 (1931), p. 23. **p. 50** 'The princes of ... of Aten forever.' ibid. **p. 53** 'But soon ... purple overcame him.' J. D. S. Pendlebury, *Tell el-Amarna* (London, 1935), p. 6. **p. 53** 'When he had ... like Re forever."' Divine birth scenes of Amenophis III, Luxor: after A. P. Kozloff & B. M. Bryan, *Egypt's Dazzling Sun. Amenhotep III and his World* (Cleveland, 1992), p. 36. **p. 54** 'Living Horus, ... northern at Naharin.' 'Marriage scarab': after C. Blankenberg-van Delden, *The Large Commemorative Scarabs of Amenhotep III* (Leiden, 1969), p. 16. **pp. 55–56** 'For some moments ... a little open.' A. Weigall, quoted in J. Hankey, *KMT* 9/2 (summer, 1998), pp. 42–43. **pp. 57–58** 'The hereditary noble ... of Amun, Aanen.' Statue inscription of Aanen: after A. P. Kozloff & B. M. Bryan, *Egypt's Dazzling Sun. Amenhotep III and his World* (Cleveland, 1992), p. 250. **p. 58** 'Say to the king, ... my god, my Sun.' Amarna letter EA 187: after W. L. Moran, *The Amarna Letters* (Baltimore, 1992), p. 269. **p. 60** 'I have just ... concealing her passing ...?' Amarna letter EA 1: after W. L. Moran, *The Amarna Letters* (Baltimore, 1992), p. 1. **p. 61** 'To Milkilu, ... is no defect ...' Amarna letter EA 369: after W. L. Moran, *The Amarna Letters* (Baltimore, 1992), p. 366. **p. 61** 'the estate of ... king's son, Amenophis' W. C. Hayes, *Journal of Near Eastern Studies* 10 (1951), p. 172, fig. 27 (KK). **p. 63** 'westernmost academy of the cuneiform world' C. H. Gordon, in *Abstracts Book, An International Symposium to Commemorate the Centennial Anniversary of the Discovery of Tell El Amarna* (Chicago, 1–3 February 1987), p. 9. **p. 64** 'On the largest ... land of Egypt".' E. A. W. Budge, *By Nile and Tigris*, I (London, 1920), pp. 140–41. **p. 64** 'felt certain that ... great historical importance' ibid. **p. 64** 'Say to Nimmuarea ... taken to me ...' Amarna letter EA 6: after W. L. Moran, *The Amarna Letters* (Baltimore, 1992), p. 12. **p. 64** 'From time immemorial ... given to anyone' Amarna letter EA 4: after W. L. Moran, *The Amarna Letters* (Baltimore, 1992), p. 8. **p. 64** 'As to the gold ... me the gold ...' Amarna letter EA 4: after W. L. Moran, *The Amarna Letters* (Baltimore, 1992), p. 9. **p. 65** 'It is a ... nugget of gold!' Amarna letter EA 1: after W. L. Moran, *The Amarna Letters* (Baltimore, 1992), p. 2. **p. 65** 'In Egypt, gold ... plentiful than dirt' Amarna letter EA 20: after W. L. Moran, *The Amarna Letters* (Baltimore, 1992), p. 48. **p. 65** 'It pleased his ... the Two Lands' Mortuary temple stela of Amenophis III: after M. Lichtheim, *Ancient Egyptian Literature*, II (Berkeley, 1976), p. 44. **p. 65** 'grand, original, and integrated' A. P. Kozloff in A. P. Kozloff & B. M. Bryan, *Egypt's Dazzling Sun. Amenhotep III and his World* (Cleveland, 1992), p. 4. **p. 66** 'Their [the statues'] height ... shines at dawn.' Mortuary temple stela of Amenophis III: after M. Lichtheim, *Ancient Egyptian Literature*, II (Berkeley, 1976), p. 44. **pp. 66–67** '[It is] a monument ... Re rises in it.' ibid. **p. 72** 'in accordance with the ancient writings' Tomb of Kheruef: after L. M. Berman, in D. O'Connor & E. H. Cline, *Amenhotep III. Perspectives on his Reign* (Ann Arbor, 1998), p. 17. **p. 73** 'Re-Horakhty, mighty ... for all lands ...' Inscription on the quartzite statue of Amenophis III, Luxor cachette: after W. J. Murnane, *Texts from the Amarna Period in Egypt* (Atlanta, 1995), p. 20. **p. 75** 'astonishing complexity' J. D. S. Pendlebury, *Tell el-Amarna* (London, 1935), p. 13. **p. 77** '[Yea]r [...?]2, ... messenger [Tulubri] brought].' Amarna letter EA 27: after W. L. Moran, *The Amarna Letters* (Baltimore, 1992), p. 90. **p. 77** '[Yea]r [...?]2, ... messenger [Tulubri] brought]' ibid. **p. 78** 'The god ascended ... the people mourned.' Tale of Sinuhe: after M. Lichtheim, *Ancient Egyptian Literature*, I (Berkeley, 1973), pp. 223–24. **p. 83** 'of rather fragile constitution' F. Hussein and J. E. Harris, *Fifth International Congress of Egyptology. Abstracts of Papers* (Cairo, 1988), p. 140. **pp. 84–85** 'he [el-Hakim] is ... Al-Hakim's displeasure....' J. D. Ray, *Göttinger Miszellen* 86 (1985), p. 81. **p. 85** 'When my brother, ... it was before.'" Amarna letter EA 29: after W. L. Moran, *The Amarna Letters* (Baltimore, 1992), p. 94. **p. 86** 'You are the ... evidence of esteem' Amarna letter EA 26: after W. L. Moran, *The Amarna Letters* (Baltimore, 1992), p. 90. **p. 86** '... the affair of ... become a god' Amarna letter EA 29: after W. L. Moran, *The Amarna Letters* (Baltimore, 1992), p. 90. **p. 87** 'And now, ... peace in mind ...?' Amarna letter EA 42: after W. L. Moran, *The Amarna Letters* (Baltimore, 1992), p. 115. **p. 87** '... she who satisfies ... bearing the sistra' Inscription from the tomb of the god's father Ay: after W. J. Murnane, *Texts from the Amarna Period in Egypt* (Atlanta, 1995), p. 112. **p. 89** 'Gods had come ... of a fanatic.' J. D. S. Pendlebury, *Tell el-Amarna* (London, 1935), p. 8. **pp. 89–90** 'This king [Amenôphis], ... his own life ....' Manetho, fr. 54 , from Josephus, *Contra Apionem*, I.26–31, paras 227–87: after W. G. Waddell, *Manetho* (Cambridge, Ma., 1997), pp. 121–25. **p. 90** 'so long as ... certain prejudiced informants.' Manetho, fr. 54, from Josephus, *Contra Apionem*, I.26–31, paras 227–87: after W. G. Waddell, *Manetho* (Cambridge, Ma., 1997), p. 147. **p. 90** 'did not venture ... their years precisely' Manetho, fr. 54, from Josephus, *Contra Apionem*, I.26–31, paras. 227–87: after W. G. Waddell, *Manetho* (Cambridge, Ma., 1997), p. 121. **p. 98** 'Re-Horakhty who ... the sun disc (Aten)' After J. Baines & J. Málek, *Atlas of Ancient Egypt* (Oxford & New York, 1980), p. 45. **p. 103** 'Then said [Akhenaten]: ... and everlasting name ....'" Earlier proclamation, el-Amarna boundary stelae: after W. J. Murnane, *Texts from the Amarna Period in Egypt* (Atlanta, 1995), pp. 74–75. **p. 103** 'servant in the ... west of Akhetenaten [sic]' J. Cerny, *A Community of Workmen at Thebes in the Ramesside Period* (Cairo, 1973), p. 51. **p. 104** 'The rivalry between ... of all nations ...' L. A. White, *Journal of the American Oriental Society* 68 (1948), p. 107. **p. 106** '"It was after ... failing of the servants'" Teaching of Ammenemes I: after M. Lichtheim, *Ancient Egyptian Literature*, I (Berkeley, 1973), p. 137. **p.**

106 'his own eunuchs' Manetho, fr. 34, from Syncellus: after W. G. Waddell, *Manetho* (Cambridge, Ma., 1997), p. 67. **p. 106** '"Beware of subjects ... used it to plot ..."' Teaching of Ammenemes I: after M. Lichtheim, *Ancient Egyptian Literature*, I (Berkeley, 1973), p. 136. **p. 108** 'On this day ... they see him.' Earlier proclamation, el-Amarna boundary stelae: after W. J. Murnane, *Texts from the Amarna Period in Egypt* (Atlanta, 1995), p. 74. **p. 109** 'Then said his ... forever and eternity...'" Earlier proclamation, el-Amarna boundary stelae: after W. J. Murnane, *Texts from the Amarna Period in Egypt* (Atlanta, 1995), p. 75. **p. 109** 'Make Akhetaten as ... forever and eternity' ibid. **pp. 109–10** '"May his lordship ... he himself ordains ..."' Earlier proclamation, el-Amarna boundary stelae: after W. J. Murnane, *Texts from the Amarna Period in Egypt* (Atlanta, 1995), p. 76. **p. 110** '"Since he casts ... offer to him ..."' Earlier proclamation, el-Amarna boundary stelae: after W. J. Murnane, *Texts from the Amarna Period in Egypt* (Atlanta, 1995), pp. 76–77. **p. 110** '"As for the ... assumed the white crown!"' Earlier proclamation, el-Amarna boundary stelae: after W. J. Murnane, *Texts from the Amarna Period in Egypt* (Atlanta, 1995), p. 78. **p. 115** '"At Akhetaten in ... buried in it ..."' Earlier proclamation, el-Amarna boundary stelae: after W. J. Murnane, *Texts from the Amarna Period in Egypt* (Atlanta, 1995), pp. 77–78. **p. 116** 'Re, horizon ruler, ... the sun disc' After J. Baines & J. Málek, *Atlas of Ancient Egypt* (Oxford & New York, 1980), p. 45. **p. 119** 'Tell el-Amarna ... last for ever ...' J. D. S. Pendlebury, *Tell el-Amarna* (London, 1935), pp. 65–66. **p. 119** 'lived almost as ... as [they] could' B. J. Kemp, *Ancient Egypt. Anatomy of a Civilization* (London & New York, 1989), p. 294. **p. 119** 'the principal royal residence at Amarna' B. J. Kemp, in W. Helck, E. Otto & W. Westendorff (eds), *Lexikon der Ägyptologie*, VI (Wiesbaden 1986), col. 313. **p. 120** 'a kind of ... love of nature' J. D. S. Pendlebury, *Tell el-Amarna* (London, 1935), p. 98. **p. 121**

'Quite apart from ... city's economic substance.' B. J. Kemp, *Ancient Egypt. Anatomy of a Civilization* (London & New York, 1989), p. 309. **p. 121** 'an East wind ... servants and food.' J. D. S. Pendlebury, *Tell el-Amarna* (London, 1935), p. 111. **p. 122** 'A prince might ... cool is invariable.' J. D. S. Pendlebury, *Tell el-Amarna* (London, 1935), pp. 113–14. **p. 122** 'Why should messengers ... be a profit.' Amarna letter EA 16: W. L. Moran, *The Amarna Letters* (Baltimore, 1992), p. 39. **p. 126** 'It says much ... until so recently.' B. J. Kemp, *Ancient Egypt. Anatomy of a Civilization* (London & New York, 1989), p. 285. **p. 131** 'The interest of ... it goes down ...' J. D. S. Pendlebury, *Tell el-Amarna* (London, 1935), pp. 47–48. **p. 131** 'is to be ... of the people' J. D. S. Pendlebury, *Tell el-Amarna* (London, 1935), p. 59. **p. 133** 'skill of the sacred masons' Murray's *Handbook for Travellers in Lower and Upper Egypt* (8th ed., London, 1891), p. 419. **p. 133** 'In plan they ... the front Hall.' J. D. S. Pendlebury, *Tell el-Amarna* (London, 1935), pp. 46–47. **p. 137** 'One can say ... with religious associations' M. Mallinson, in B. J. Kemp (ed.), *Amarna Reports*, VI (London, 1995), p. 204. **p. 139** 'worship of the sun ... solstices and equinoxes' B. J. Kemp, *Ancient Egypt. Anatomy of a Civilization* (London & New York, 1989), p. 286. **p. 140** '... all that we ... by modern interpretations' E. Hornung, *Akhenaten and the Religion of Light* (Ithaca, 1999), p. 17. **p. 140** 'Look, I am ... by himself [Atum] ...' Royal speech of Amenophis IV, Karnak: after W. J. Murnane, *Texts from the Amarna Period in Egypt* (Atlanta, 1995), p. 31. **p. 140** 'Make holiday... comes back again!' M. Lichtheim, *Ancient Egyptian Literature*, I (Berkeley, 1975), pp. 196–97. **pp. 142–44** 'Beautifully you appear ... forever and eternity.' Great Hymn to the Aten, tomb of Ay, el-Amarna: after W. J. Murnane, *Texts from the Amarna Period in Egypt* (Atlanta, 1995), pp. 113–16. **p. 145** 'god as life' Jan Assman, quoted by J. P. Allen, in W. K. Simpson (ed.), *Religion and Philosophy in Ancient Egypt* (New Haven, 1989), p. 89. **p. 145** 'Thou makest darkness, ... of the earth.' Psalm 104, verses 20–24, 29–30, King James Authorized Version. **p. 145** 'has less to ... nature of reality' J. P. Allen, in W. K. Simpson (ed.), *Religion and Philosophy in Ancient Egypt* (New Haven, 1989), p. 91. **p. 146** 'The god of ... is Akhenaten himself.' J. P. Allen, in W. K. Simpson (ed.), *Religion and Philosophy in Ancient Egypt* (New Haven, 1989), p. 100. **p. 146** 'the new concept ... serve Akhenaten's purpose' D. B. Redford, *Akhenaten, the Heretic King* (Princeton, 1984), p. 178. **p. 148** 'The King was ... above spindle shanks.' C. Aldred, *Akhenaten and Nefertiti* (New York & London, 1973), p. 53. **p. 149** 'the disciple of his majesty' Statue of Bek: after W. J. Murnane, *Texts from the Amarna Period in Egypt* (Atlanta, 1995), pp. 129–30. **p. 149** 'sick ugliness and nervous decadence' W. Wolf, quoted by E. Hornung, *Akhenaten and the Religion of Light* (Ithaca, 1999), p. 43. **p. 150** 'The precise collection ... be mere co-incidence.' A. L. Burridge, *Journal of the Society for the Study of Egyptian Antiquities* 23 (1993), p. 66. **p. 151** 'Only two of ... confirm a diagnosis' A. L. Burridge, *Journal of the Society for the Study of Egyptian Antiquities* 23 (1993), p. 67. **p. 151** 'likely blind for ... his adult life' A. L. Burridge, *Journal of the Society for the Study of Egyptian Antiquities* 23 (1993), p. 70. **p. 152** 'When I was ... I carry it.' Amarna letter EA 296: after W. L. Moran, *The Amarna Letters* (Baltimore, 1992), p. 338. **p. 153** 'footstool for your feet' Amarna letter EA 84: after W. L. Moran, *The Amarna Letters* (Baltimore, 1992), p. 155. **p. 153** 'May the king, ... all my cities ...' Amarna letter EA 78: after W. L. Moran, *The Amarna Letters* (Baltimore, 1992), p. 148. **p. 153** 'you are going ... Everything is gone' Amarna letter EA 102: after W. L. Moran, *The Amarna Letters* (Baltimore, 1992), p. 175. **p. 153** 'writes to me ... the other mayors' Amarna letter EA 124: after W. L. Moran, *The Amarna Letters* (Baltimore, 1992), p. 203. **p. 153** 'Be informed, ... been taken away ...'

Amarna letter EA 284: after W. L. Moran, *The Amarna Letters* (Baltimore, 1992), p. 324. **p. 155** '... not only did ... men forth naked.' Manetho, fr. 54, from Josephus, *Contra Apionem*, I.26–31, paras. 227–87: after W. G. Waddell, *Manetho* (Cambridge, Ma., 1997), p. 131. **p. 155** 'At Akhetaten in ... Aten, my father.' Earlier proclamation, el-Amarna boundary stelae: after W. J. Murnane, *Texts from the Amarna Period in Egypt* (Atlanta, 1995), p. 77. **pp. 157–58** 'The only surviving ... noble lady *par excellence*"]' L. Manniche, *Göttinger Miszellen* 18 (1975), pp. 33–34. **p. 158** 'must have had ... wife of Akhenaten.' L. Manniche, *Göttinger Miszellen* 18 (1975), p. 33. **p. 162** 'There is an ... approached complete identity ...' A. H. Gardiner, *Egypt of the Pharaohs* (Oxford, 1961), p. 228. **pp. 163–64** 'Year 3, 3rd ... festival every day ...' Pawah graffito, Thebes: after A. H. Gardiner, *Journal of Egyptian Archaeology* 14 (1928), pp. 10–11, and W. J. Murnane, *Texts from the Amarna Period in Egypt* (Atlanta, 1995), p. 208. **pp. 169–70** '... the excavations at ... lived is unknown.' E. F. Campbell, *The Chronology of the Amarna Letters* (Baltimore, 1964), 57. **p. 171** 'the first and ... a subsequent modification' J. R. Harris, *Göttinger Miszellen* 4 (1973), p. 15. **p. 171** 'In the 13th ... merit objective assessment.' J. R. Harris, *Göttinger Miszellen* 4 (1973), p. 16. **p. 172** 'are here lifted ... the old king' E. F. Campbell, *The Chronology of the Amarna Letters* (Baltimore, 1964), p. 20. **p. 174** 'that death was ... refusing to recognize' J. D. S. Pendlebury, *Tell el-Amarna* (London, 1935), p. 158. **p. 175** 'My husband died. ... I am afraid!' Deeds of Suppiluliuma: after H. G. Güterbock, *Journal of Cuneiform Studies* 10 (1956), p. 96. **p. 175** 'Such a thing ... my entire life!' ibid. **p. 175** 'Why did you ... will be king!' Deeds of Suppiluliuma: after H. G. Güterbock, *Journal of Cuneiform Studies* 10 (1956), p. 97. **p. 176** 'beyond belief' J. R. Harris, public lecture, Copenhagen, 1993. **p. 182** '... the temples and ... come at all ...' Tutankhamun restoration inscription: after W. J. Murnane, *Texts*

from the Amarna Period in Egypt (Atlanta, 1995), p. 213. **p. 183** 'After some time ... come to pass ...' ibid. **p. 183** 'Nebkheprure [Tutankhamun], who ... of the gods ...' Tomb of Tutankhamun, large seal type C: N. Reeves, *The Complete Tutankhamun* (London & New York, 1990), p. 93. **pp. 184–85** 'Year 8, third ... Smanebbehdet (in the Delta) ...' Stela of Maya: after W. J. Murnane, *Texts from the Amarna Period in Egypt* (Atlanta, 1995), p. 215. **p. 185** 'one who approaches the god's flesh' Inscription from the tomb of Pentju, el-Amarna: after W. J. Murnane, *Texts from the Amarna Period in Egypt* (Atlanta, 1995), p. 180. **pp. 186–87** 'Slowly, desperately slowly ... "Yes, wonderful things".' H. Carter, in H. Carter & A. C. Mace, *The Tomb of Tut.ankh.Amen*, I (London, 1923), pp. 95–96. **p. 188** 'resembling a scab' D. E. Derry, in F. F. Leek, *The Human Remains from the Tomb of Tut'ankhamun* (Oxford, 1972), p. 14. **p. 188** 'chronic subdural hematoma' B. Brier, *The Murder of Tutankhamen* (New York & London, 1998), p. 172. **p. 191** 'to seal in ... the accursed spot' J. D. S. Pendlebury, *Tell el-Amarna* (London, 1935), p. 31. **p. 191** 'The beautiful child of the living Aten' Coffin of Kiya from tomb KV55: after W. J. Murnane, *Texts from the Amarna Period in Egypt* (Atlanta, 1995), p. 210. **p. 191** 'the enemy of Akhetaten' Inscription of Mose: after W. J. Murnane, *Texts from the Amarna Period in Egypt* (Atlanta, 1995), p. 241. **p. 191** 'of the rebellion' Ramessid tax record: after W. J. Murnane, *Texts from the Amarna Period in Egypt* (Atlanta, 1995), p. 241. **p. 193** 'For you, ... with his rays ...' Inscription from the tomb of Maya, el-Amarna: after W. J. Murnane, *Texts from the Amarna Period in Egypt* (Atlanta, 1995), p. 143.

ILLUSTRATION CREDITS

Antiquity 46 (1972), 46, no. 181, pl. 1 **188**
Archivio White Star, photo Araldo de Luca **43**, **125l**
Staatliche Museen zu Berlin – Ägyptisches Museum und Papyrussammlung. Photo © bpk **49a**, **52**, **59**, **77**, **90**, **100a**, **138**, **147**, **148a**, **149**, **156**, **158**, **161**, **167**, **169**, **177**, **189**, **192**; Hollander, 1914 **12** (detail), **23**; Margarete Büsing **24**
Museum of Fine Arts, Boston **124**
Brooklyn Museum of Art, New York **22**; Gift of the New Hermes Foundation **148b**
Betsy M. Bryan **76**
Egyptian Museum, Cairo frontispiece, **45**, **56l&r**, **58**, **81**, **88**, **105**, **116b**, **150**, **154**, **168b**, **182**
Fitzwilliam Museum, Cambridge **96**
John Carter **19a**
Peter Clayton **40**, **69**, **183**
Copyright CNRS/CFEETK. Fonds Chevrier **94**
Ny Carlsberg Glyptotek, Copenhagen **159**, **166**
The Daily Graphic, 23 March 1892 **19b**
N. de Garis Davies, *The Rock Tombs of el Amarna*, II (London, 1905), pl. 5 **100b**; pl. 41 **168a**; pl. 37 **173**; III (London, 1905), pl. 25 **16**; pl. 4 **131**; pl. 32A **109**; IV (London, 1906), pl. 20 **116a**; V (London, 1908) pl. 39 **102**, **111**; *The Tomb of the Vizier Ramose* (London, 1941), pl. 29 **98**; pl. 33 **99**
Description de l'Égypte (Paris, 1809–28), *Antiquités*, IV pl. 63 **15**
Courtesy of the Trustees of the National Museums of Scotland, Edinburgh **18**
Egypt Exploration Society **25**, **27**, **112**, **141**; Courtesy of Egypt Exploration Society, animated by Redvision. Designed by Michael Mallinson **117**, **120**; Ralph Lavers, Egypt Exploration Society **122**; Geoffrey Martin/Egypt Exploration Society **128–9**
Myers Museum, Eton College **54**
H. Frankfort & J. D. S. Pendlebury, *The City of Akhenaten*, II (London, 1933), pl. 12 **121**
Heidi Grassley, © Thames & Hudson Ltd **42**, **67**, **95**
Hirmer **28**, **66**
Abraham Guterman Collection of Ancient Egyptian Art, The Israel Museum, Jerusalem **74**, **101**, **193**

W. Raymond Johnson **72**
Collection of Jack A. Josephson, New York **87**;
Journal of Egyptian Archaeology 14 (1928), pls 5/6 **163**; 17 (1931), pl. iv. 5 **49b**;
C. R. Lepsius, *Denkmäler aus Aegypten und Aethiopien* (Berlin; 1849–59), III, pl. 34 **17**
Jürgen Liepe, Berlin **21**, **35b**, **39**, **190b**
Robert Hay, British Library, London **107**
British Museum, London **26**, **41a&b**, **63**, **86**, **171**; courtesy Richard Parkinson **106**
Petrie Museum of Egyptian Archaeology, University College London **20a**, **174**
The Metropolitan Museum of Art, New York. **57**; Egyptian Expedition **70**; Gift of Edward S. Harkness 1921 and Purchase Harris Brisbane Dick Fund, 1957 **125c&r**; Gift of Mr and Mrs V. Everit Macy, 1923 **191b**; Rogers Fund, 1929 **32**; Rogers Fund, 1950 **180b**
Paul T. Nicholson **10–11**, **14**, **136**
Gwil Owen **134**
Ashmolean Museum, Oxford **20b**
Griffith Institute, Ashmolean Museum, Oxford **34b**, **36–7**, **179**, **186**
Musée du Louvre, Paris **85**, **143**; © Maurice et Pierre Chuzeville **34a**
Nicholas Reeves **31**, **82**, **181a**
John G. Ross **36a**, **47**, **92**, **93**, **103**, **165**, **178**, **181b**, **184**, **190–1**
Alberto Siliotti/Geodia, Archivio Image Service **68**
G. E. Smith, *The Royal Mummies* (Cairo, 1912) pl. 36 **84**
Sotheby's **132**
Stockholm Nationalmuseum **155**
Nigel Strudwick **35a**
Copyright Egyptian Culture Centre, Waseda University, Tokyo **80**
Philip Winton **7**, **114**, **123**
Alain Zivie **180a**

INDEX